Tanya's Cat Food Data

US Cat Foods In Order Of Phosphorus Content For Cats With Chronic Kidney Disease

HELEN FITZSIMONS

DISCLAIMER

I AM NOT RECOMMENDING ANY OF THE FOODS MENTIONED IN THIS BOOK. IT SIMPLY CONTAINS LISTS OF MANY CAT FOODS AVAILABLE IN THE USA IN ORDER OF PHOSPHORUS CONTENT AND BRAND NAME.

THESE ANALYSES HAVE BEEN COMPILED IN GOOD FAITH FROM THE INFORMATION PROVIDED TO ME BY THE BRANDS CONCERNED. WHERE POSSIBLE, I HAVE OBTAINED THE DATA IN WRITING IN ORDER TO AVOID ANY MISUNDERSTANDINGS. EACH FOOD INCLUDED IN THIS BOOK HAS BEEN CROSS-CHECKED BY A THIRD PARTY. THE DATA MAY NOT NECESSARILY MATCH THE INFORMATION ON THE FOOD'S PACKAGING.

UNFORTUNATELY FOOD FORMULATIONS CAN CHANGE WITHOUT WARNING, AND THEREFORE I CANNOT GUARANTEE THAT THE DATA ARE STILL ACCURATE; NO RESPONSIBILITY CAN BE ACCEPTED.

SEVERAL OF THE BRANDS HAVE ASKED ME TO EMPHASISE THAT THEIR NON-THERAPEUTIC KIDNEY DIETS ARE NOT INTENDED FOR CKD CATS.

*****

TREATING YOUR CAT WITHOUT VETERINARY ADVICE CAN BE EXTREMELY DANGEROUS.

YOU MUST CONSULT A QUALIFIED VETERINARIAN AND OBTAIN PROFESSIONAL ADVICE ON THE CORRECT REGIMEN FOR YOUR CAT AND HIS OR HER PARTICULAR REQUIREMENTS; AND YOU SHOULD ONLY USE ANY FOODS LISTED HEREIN WITH THE FULL KNOWLEDGE AND APPROVAL OF YOUR VET.

NO RESPONSIBILITY CAN BE ACCEPTED.

CONTENTS

DISCLAIMER

INTRODUCTION

These food data tables are the book version of the food data tables contained in the website I run:

Tanya's Comprehensive Guide to Feline Chronic Kidney Disease

http://www.felinecrf.org

The food data tables quickly became one of the most popular parts of my website, and I know many people like to take the tables with them when they go cat food shopping, so I am making the food data tables available in standalone book form. As a bonus, the book includes the data in order of brand name as well as in order of phosphorus content, which should make things easier when you are standing in front of a particular brand in a pet food store.

Cats with chronic kidney disease, or CKD, have particular dietary requirements. The main considerations for a CKD cat are:

- phosphorus — this is the most important consideration
- protein
- sodium
- fat
- calories

You can read about why these matter on page 3.

The food data tables provide details of these components, plus carbohydrates, for over 1500 commercial cat foods available in the USA. Many of the foods are also available in Canada.

These data are calculated on the basis of **dry matter analysis** (DMA), which is what you need to use when choosing a food for a cat with chronic kidney disease. I created the tables because the values on cat food packaging do not provide the information in this form. I know many people are very confused about why the data in the tables differ so much from the percentages shown on the products themselves or on brand websites. Please see page 3 to understand why the food data tables are calculated in this way and page 13 to learn how best to use them.

Your vet will probably recommend that you feed your cat a therapeutic kidney diet. There are good reasons for feeding such a diet to cats with creatinine above 1.6 mg/dl (Stage 2 and beyond in the International Renal Interest Society's staging system). However, cats with earlier stage CKD may do better on ordinary foods, and any CKD cat may refuse to eat a therapeutic diet. Tips on persuading your cat to eat these foods can be found on my website:

http://www.felinecrf.org/which_foods.htm#therapeutic_diet_introduction

The most important thing is that your cat eats, and if you cannot persuade your cat to eat a therapeutic kidney diet, you need to find a food that your cat will eat, and ideally one with properties as similar as possible to such a diet. Hence my food data tables.

CONSIDERATIONS WHEN CHOOSING A FOOD FOR A CKD CAT

There are a number of issues to consider when choosing the best food for a CKD cat, which I discuss briefly below; there is a lot more information on my website.

Whichever food you opt for, always introduce a new food gradually (mix it with the food you have been using previously and gradually increase the percentage of the new food) so as to reduce the risk of tummy upsets.

Phosphorus

The single most important issue to consider when choosing a food for a CKD cat is the phosphorus content.

Phosphorus is a mineral essential for good health which is contained in many foods. The body is very good at regulating its phosphorus levels by removing excess phosphorus via the kidneys. However, the kidneys of a CKD cat can no longer efficiently excrete excess phosphorus, so the vast majority of CKD cats will develop levels of phosphorus in their blood which are too high (hyperphosphataemia), which:

- can make your cat feel ill

- may make the CKD progress faster. Survival in Cats with Naturally Occurring Chronic Kidney Disease (2000-2002) (2008) Boyd LM, Langston C, Thompson K, Zivin K & Imanishi M *Journal of Veterinary Internal Medicine* 22(5) pp1111-7, found that there was an 11.8% increase in the risk of death for every one mg/dl increase in phosphorus in the cat's blood. Another study, Survival of Cats with Naturally Occurring Chronic Renal Failure: Effect of Dietary Management (2000) Elliott J, Rawlings JM, Markwell PJ, Barber PJ *Journal of Small Animal Practice* 41(6) pp235-242, found that the cats who ate reduced phosphorus food or food with added phosphorus binders (see overleaf) lived more than twice as long as those who did not

- can cause a serious condition called secondary hyperparathyroidism

- may reduce response to anaemia treatment.

In order to reduce these risks, your goal is to have your cat's serum level of phosphorus (i.e. what your vet tests in bloodwork) no higher than 4.5 mg/dl if at all possible.

The easiest and most effective way to control blood phosphorus levels is by feeding foods low in phosphorus. This reduces the workload on the cat's damaged kidneys and reduces the risk of phosphorus levels in the cat's body rising too high.

According to Dr Scott Brown in Management of Feline Chronic Renal Failure (1998) *Waltham Focus* 8(3), ideally **you want to feed a food with a phosphorus level under 0.5% calculated on a dry matter analysis basis**.

3

Small Animal Clinical Nutrition - 5th Edition, Chapter 37 Chronic Kidney Disease (2010) Hand MS (Ed.) *Mark Morris Institute* has a slightly less ambitious goal of 0.3 to 0.6% for cats.

No complete adult cat food which meets AAFCO adult maintenance guidelines (see page 13) will meet Dr Scott's goal because the minimum DMA phosphorus level required by AAFCO is 0.5%. Some therapeutic kidney diets do meet this requirement but others have a phosphorus level of up to 0.7%.

Of course, you also need your cat to eat. Therefore you may have to have a less ambitious goal, at least to start with, of, say, feeding a food with less than 0.75% or less than 1% phosphorus. The first set of tables list foods in order of phosphorus content so you can clearly see which foods might be worth considering.

If your cat's phosphorus level (as shown in blood tests) is not too high, you have a bit more room for manoeuvre. But the ultimate aim is to feed your cat a food containing as little phosphorus as possible

If you are not feeding a therapeutic kidney food, you will probably have to give your cat a phosphorus binder. This is an oral supplement that binds with the excess phosphorus in the cat's body and helps to keep your cat's blood phosphorus levels low; however, phosphorus binders are not as effective as dietary phosphorus control. As your cat's CKD progresses, you may have to use phosphorus binders in addition to a therapeutic diet. Please read about binders on my website:

http://www.felinecrf.org/phosphorus_binders.htm

To summarise, your goal is to feed a food with a phosphorus level under 0.5% on a dry matter analysis basis, or as close to this as you can get.

Protein

There are a number of considerations when it comes to protein for CKD cats.

When to Restrict Protein Intake

As a species, cats need a relatively high protein intake. Therapeutic kidney diets used to be routinely recommended for all CKD cats. However, it is now usually not recommended to start them too soon, in order to avoid weight loss and muscle wasting in cats with early stage CKD who might not benefit massively from early dietary changes.

So when should you start such a diet? The International Renal Interest Society (2019) divides CKD into stages and suggests starting a therapeutic kidney diet in Stage 2, i.e. when the cat's creatinine is over 1.6 mg/dl. It also says that introducing a therapeutic diet may be easier at an early stage of diagnosis.

Another thing to consider when deciding when to introduce a therapeutic kidney diet is your cat's blood urea nitrogen (BUN) level. BUN is influenced by protein intake, so it does often help the cat feel better if you restrict protein intake as the CKD progresses. Generally speaking, once BUN levels are over 60 mg/dl, you are more likely to see symptoms such as vomiting and nausea and a therapeutic diet may help with this.

4

Degree of Protein Restriction

When people think of a therapeutic kidney diet, they often immediately think "low protein." It is true that therapeutic kidney foods are relatively low in protein. However, the key word there is "relatively": it does not mean these foods are too low in protein. On a dry matter analysis basis, most therapeutic kidney diets contain 28-35% protein, which is above the 26% minimum level of protein required by AAFCO (see page 13) for a food to be considered a complete adult food. As you can see from the food data tables, there are quite a lot of commercial non-therapeutic foods with a protein level as low as this, yet nobody refers to them as low protein foods.

Clinical Evaluation of Dietary Modification for Treatment of Spontaneous Chronic Kidney Disease in Cats (2006) Ross SJ, Osborne CA, Kirk CA, Lowry SR, Koehler LA, Polzin DJ *Journal of the American Veterinary Medical Association* 229(6) pp949-57 was a double-blinded randomised study in cats with a creatinine level between 2.1 and 4.5 mg/dl. In this two year study, 22% (five) of the cats eating a standard commercial food died, but none died in the group eating a therapeutic kidney diet. The therapeutic food used (Hill's k/d) contained 28% protein and 0.5% phosphorus on a DMA basis, while the non-therapeutic food contained 46% protein and 0.9-1.0% phosphorus on a DMA basis. The cats were deemed to be eating the therapeutic kidney diet if 85% of their food intake came from this source.

When choosing a commercial food from the lists, therefore, I would not only look at the phosphorus level but also consider the protein level. That is to say, if for example I have two foods to choose from with the same phosphorus level and my cat will eat both of them, but one food has 32% protein while the other has 50% protein, I would normally choose the lower protein food.

Protein Quality

What is important for CKD cats is that the protein is high quality protein. I hear from people quite regularly who think many therapeutic kidney diets contain poor quality ingredients, so how can the protein within them be considered high quality?

During the breakdown of dietary protein in the digestive process, waste substances are created which are filtered out of the blood by the kidneys and excreted via urination. This is sometimes referred to as the removal of nitrogenous wastes. Unfortunately damaged kidneys find it harder to do this, which is why BUN levels rise in CKD.

Therefore the goal is to feed a protein with the correct balance of amino acids to provide the cat with the ability to maintain and repair bodily tissues but in a form which needs as little breaking down as possible. That is what we mean in this context by "high quality protein." Proteins of this nature are sometimes referred to as having a "high biologic value." (The food with the highest biologic value is actually eggs, though egg yolks are too high in phosphorus for most CKD cats).

The therapeutic kidney diets may not have the type of protein that you would consider high quality for yourself (e.g. organic chicken breast) but the manufacturers do spend a lot of money trying to create foods that are relatively low in protein but which contain high quality protein from the CKD perspective, and studies do indicate that they tend to achieve this goal.

You can compare the phosphorus levels in commercial foods to those in therapeutic kidney diets quite easily because it is simply a matter of percentages; but it is harder to compare the protein levels because you cannot easily measure biologic value. Therapeutic kidney diets have a protein content of around 28-35% on a DMA basis, so when choosing a commercial food, I would advise at least trying to find one with protein around this level and with meat rather than grain proteins; but the fact remains that if you are feeding a non-therapeutic kidney diet, you are unlikely to be able to determine whether you are feeding high quality protein from a CKD perspective.

My goal would be to try to feed a food with a protein level of 35% on a dry matter analysis basis, or as close to this as you can get.

Sodium

Since CKD cats are prone to high blood pressure, it is generally advisable to try to feed a food low in sodium. Low sodium diets may also be recommended for cats with heart disease. Therapeutic kidney diets usually have a reduced sodium content.

Effects of Sodium Chloride on Selected Parameters in Cats (2006) Kirk CA, Jewell DE, Lowry SR *Veterinary Therapeutics: Research in Applied Veterinary Medicine* 7(4) pp333-346 found that there was actually no change in blood pressure in the CKD cats in this study, but levels of BUN, creatinine and phosphorus were higher in the cats eating a high sodium diet compared to those eating a low sodium diet.

The minimum level permitted by AAFCO (see page 13) is 0.2%. It is unlikely that you need to go much higher than this.

I would try to factor this into choosing a food. If for example I have two foods to choose from with the same phosphorus level and a similar protein level and my cat will eat both of them, and one food has 0.3% sodium while the other has 1% sodium, I would normally choose the lower sodium food.

Fat

As with protein, cats need relatively high levels of fat compared to a human or dog.

Fat does not result in a lot of waste products like protein, so processing it is not a strain on the kidneys. A diet relatively high in fat can also help an older cat to maintain his/her weight. In many therapeutic kidney foods, the fat content is increased to compensate for the reduced protein levels.

If you have a choice of two similar foods and you wish to maintain or even increase your cat's weight, it is probably better to choose the food with the higher fat content.

Carbohydrates

Carbohydrates are not normally a consideration for CKD cats. However, some people prefer to feed foods with lower carbohydrate levels, especially if their cats also have diabetes, so I have included the carbohydrate content of the foods where I can.

Calories

You also need to consider the calories in a food. Many CKD cats have poor appetites and it can be a struggle to get them to eat. Foods containing more calories per ounce can therefore be beneficial because the cat is still taking in a reasonable number of calories even if s/he is not eating much food.

Therapeutic kidney diets tend to have a relatively high calorie content, sometimes referred to as caloric density. When choosing a food for a CKD cat, all other things (particularly phosphorus and protein content) being equal, I would always choose the food with the most calories.

Essential Fatty Acids

Therapeutic kidney diets contain increased levels of essential fatty acids, which appear to be of increasing importance in the treatment of CKD, but it is not known exactly what is the optimum intake for CKD cats. Some people with a CKD cat do supplement these separately.

Potassium

Therapeutic kidney diets contain additional potassium, usually in the form of potassium citrate because this can help with metabolic acidosis. According to Prolonging Life and Kidney Function (2009) Chew DJ & DiBartola SP *CVC in Kansas City Proceedings*, dry CKD therapeutic foods have approximately twice as much potassium as standard dry cat foods.

B Vitamins

Therapeutic kidney diets contain higher levels of B vitamins, which can help with appetite and wellbeing. Many people feeding a non-therapeutic diets supplement B vitamins separately.

Fibre

Therapeutic kidney diet usually contain additional fibre which may be helpful to CKD cats, who tend to suffer from constipation.

Other Considerations

Many people who write to me do not like the idea of feeding a therapeutic kidney diet, and the most common reason for their reluctance is that they do not like the ingredients in these foods, often considering them to be poor quality compared to the foods they usually feed.

There are proven benefits to feeding therapeutic kidney diets, which I discuss on page 9. You can read more about nutritional and dietary concerns for CKD cats on my website:

http://www.felinecrf.org/nutritional_requirements.htm

http://www.felinecrf.org/which_foods.htm

If you want to check the actual ingredients in a food, you can find contact details for many cat food brands on my website or visit a pet food seller site online (such as Chewy) which tells you the ingredients of the foods it sells.

If you would like to discuss the various foods and ask what has worked for other cats, join Tanya's Feline CKD Support Group online:

https://tanyackd.groups.io/g/support

Remember, the most important thing is that your cat eats.

BENEFITS OF
THERAPEUTIC KIDNEY DIETS

When your cat is first diagnosed, your vet will probably recommend a therapeutic kidney diet. I often hear from people who have little enthusiasm for choosing foods from major cat food manufacturers, or who may not have been feeding their cat a commercial diet of any kind, and they are often surprised to hear that if I had a CKD cat, I would try to persuade him or her to eat a therapeutic kidney diet. It may be helpful to understand the reasoning behind this recommendation.

Therapeutic kidney diets are one of the few treatments with strong evidence that they are of benefit to CKD cats. Research indicates that therapeutic diets may:

- slow the progression of kidney disease

- reduce the incidence of crises, which usually include vomiting and appetite loss and which in the worst case may lead to the cat needing to be hospitalised

- even extend life.

In one early study, Survival of Cats with Naturally Occurring Chronic Renal Failure: Effect of Dietary Management (2000) Elliott J, Rawlings JM, Markwell PJ, Barber PJ *Journal of Small Animal Practice* 41 pp235-42, 29 cats were fed a reduced protein, low phosphorus therapeutic kidney diet, while a further 21 cats did not eat this diet. Some of the cats (presumably in both groups) were also given phosphorus binders. The cats fed the therapeutic kidney diet survived longer than the other cats, but it is not clear whether this was due to the reduction in phosphorus intake rather than the reduction in protein intake. The study concluded that feeding a therapeutic kidney diet, with additional phosphorus binders if necessary, increased survival time in cats whose CKD was stable.

Retrospective Study of the Survival of Cats with Acquired Chronic Renal Insufficiency Offered Different Commercial Diets (2005) Plantinga EA, Everts H Kastelein AM & Beynen AC *Veterinary Record* 157(7) pp185-187, looked at CKD cats who had been fed therapeutic kidney diets (seven different foods were fed during the study). The cats fed a therapeutic kidney diet survived for more than twice as long as the cats given non-therapeutic diets (16 months versus 7 months). The diet fed to the cat who survived the longest (23 months) contained a relatively high level of essential fatty acids (the food in question was apparently Specific Kidney Support, which is not available in the USA). In this non-randomised, non-double-blinded study, the cats could be fed a non-therapeutic diet for up to 25% of the time.

Clinical Evaluation of Dietary Modification for Treatment of Spontaneous Chronic Kidney Disease in Cats (2006) Ross SJ, Osborne CA, Kirk CA, Lowry SR, Koehler LA, Polzin DJ *Journal of the American Veterinary Medical Association* 229(6) pp949-57 was a double-blinded randomised study which found that feeding a therapeutic kidney diet helped to keep BUN (blood urea nitrogen) levels lower and appeared to help prevent metabolic acidosis in cats with more advanced CKD. The study concluded that the therapeutic kidney diet used in the study, Hill's k/d, was more effective than a standard adult maintenance food in reducing crises and kidney-related deaths in cats with creatinine between 2.1 and 4.5 mg/dL. In this two year study, 22% (five) of the cats eating a standard commercial food died, but none died in the group eating a therapeutic kidney diet. The therapeutic food used contained 28% protein and 0.5% phosphorus on a DMA basis, while the non-therapeutic food contained 46% protein and 0.9-1.0% phosphorus on a DMA basis. The cats were deemed to be eating the therapeutic kidney diet if 85% of their food intake came from this source.

A more recent study, Positive Impact of Nutritional Interventions on Serum Symmetric Dimethylarginine and Creatinine Concentrations in Client-Owned Geriatric Cats (2016) Hall JA, MacLeay J, Yerramilli M, Obare E , Yerramilli M, Schiefelbein H, Paetau-Robinson I & Jewell DE *PLoS One* 11(4) looked at feeding a therapeutic kidney diet to cats in IRIS stage 1 (which is earlier than the IRIS staging system recommends, see page 4). The study concluded that cats in early stage CKD who were fed a test food for six months were more likely to have stable kidney function compared to cats who received other foods chosen by their caregiver, whose kidney values were more likely to worsen. However, the food fed in this trial was specially formulated and is not commercially available. It is also difficult to compare the effect of the therapeutic kidney diet because not enough is known about the alternative foods that were fed.

You may well still be thinking "but I hate the quality of these foods." It is entirely up to you whether you use therapeutic kidney diets, and it may actually be too early for your cat to start one (see page 4), but please do read about what protein quality means from a CKD perspective on page 5 and keep an open mind. Some members of Tanya's CKD Support Group have also been reluctant to use therapeutic kidney diets, but quite a few of them have changed their minds, for the simple reason that their cats seem to feel better on these diets. They have also found that it saves them time and effort because they have been able to cut down on giving supplements to their cats, such as phosphorus binders or essential fatty acids, because the food meets their cats' requirements without additional supplementation.

Composition of Therapeutic Kidney Diets

Everybody seems to know that these foods have reduced protein levels, and some people are aware that they also have reduced phosphorus levels. People therefore sometimes think that if they feed a commercial food that is relatively low in protein and/or phosphorus, they have replicated a therapeutic kidney diet.

Unfortunately this is not the case, because there is a lot more to therapeutic CKD diets than reduced protein and/or low phosphorus levels. Staged Management of Chronic Kidney Disease in Dogs and Cats (2009) Polzin D, *Presentation to the World Small Animal Veterinary Association World Congress* says it is a common mistake to assume that therapeutic kidney diets are merely "low protein diets." He says that they have a number of different characteristics, to such a degree that the reduced protein content may not be the primary benefit. He adds that simply feeding a standard commercial diet which is lower in protein is not sufficient to replicate feeding a therapeutic kidney diet.

So how do therapeutic kidney diets differ to non-therapeutic kidney diets? Diagnostic Staging and Management of Dogs and Cats with Chronic Kidney Disease (2012) Ross SJ *Presentation to the Australian Veterinary Association NSW Annual Regional Conference* states that therapeutic kidney diets have lower protein, phosphorus, and sodium levels than adult maintenance diets, but have higher potassium and vitamin B levels, a higher essential fatty acid (omega-3:omega-6) ratio and increased caloric density. They are designed to have a neutral effect on acid-base balance. Please see page 6 onwards for more information about these various components.

Ongoing Use of Therapeutic Kidney Diets

If you purchase a therapeutic kidney cat food in the USA, you may note that the packaging says that you are not supposed to feed these diets for longer than six months, or that they are for supplementary or intermittent feeding only.

This statement is necessary because under AAFCO rules (see page 13) these diets are not a complete and balanced diet for a healthy adult cat — this is deliberate, otherwise they would not have their therapeutic qualities, such as low phosphorus levels. It is normally in order to feed these foods on an ongoing basis to CKD cats, although this may not be the case with a kitten or young cat under the age of two. Discuss this with your vet.

WHAT IS DRY MATTER ANALYSIS?

I created the food data tables because ideally you need to look at dry matter analysis figures when choosing a food for your CKD cat, but unfortunately these are not the figures supplied on cat food packaging in the USA.

The main reason I use dry matter analysis is because that is the format which leading vets use when making recommendations for target nutrient intake in CKD cats (see page 3).

Guaranteed Analysis (GA)

Virtually all US cat food brands provide their food data as Guaranteed Analysis (GA). This is to comply with AAFCO (Association of American Feed Control Officials) guidelines. AAFCO is responsible for overseeing pet food production in the USA, and its guidelines cover the production, labelling, and sale of pet foods. Guaranteed analysis is normally provided as "As Fed" data.

Unfortunately, guaranteed analysis is of only limited use when trying to compare foods for CKD cats. This is because guaranteed analysis only provides maximum and minimum values, and the only ones which are compulsory are protein and fat (minimums), and fibre and moisture (maximums). If phosphorus is shown (and it is not compulsory), it is usually given as a minimum. This makes it very hard to assess whether a food is suitable for a CKD cat, for whom you need to know the exact amount or at the very least the maximum amount of phosphorus in particular. The minimum is potentially very misleading. For example, I could tell you "I have a minimum income of US$25,000" when in fact my income was US$250,000. I would not have lied; on the other hand I would not have given you meaningful information either.

Here is an example of how this affects foods. Let's say we are looking at a food with the following GA figures:

> moisture: max 80%
> phosphorus: min 0.20%

If we assume these values are correct, this gives us a dry matter analysis figure of 1% for phosphorus.

Now let us say the actual figures are:

> moisture: 79.0%
> phosphorus: 0.25%

This gives us a DMA figure of 1.19% for phosphorus, some 20% higher, so very different from the figures we came up with using GA figures.

I have reluctantly included some foods where the brands have only been able to provide their data on a GA basis. These foods are marked with a * to indicate that the values for protein and fat and sometimes even phosphorus are minimums and could potentially be much higher.

13

Dry Matter Analysis (DMA)

Another problem with comparing cat foods is that they vary in how much moisture they contain, which makes it difficult to compare them to each other. It is very hard, for example, to compare a canned cat food to a dry cat food because the former naturally contains much more water; and this affects all the percentages of the different nutrients.

Dry matter analysis is a way of comparing foods by assuming all the moisture content has been removed: this makes it easier to compare different products.

Let's take an example. Let's say:

- you give your cat a food with 80% moisture, a typical level for many canned foods;

- according to the can, the food has a phosphorus content of 0.25%;

- your cat eats 100g of the food.

- It therefore appears that your cat is eating 0.25g of phosphorus (100g x 0.25%).

However, the food is 80% water. So of the 100g your cat has just eaten, 80g (80%) of it was simply water, and only 20% was actual food, or dry matter. So the amount of phosphorus is actually higher - in percentage terms - than it first appeared, i.e. your cat has eaten 0.25% divided by (100%-80%) or 1.25% phosphorus.

Another way of looking at it is to say that your cat food initially had 1.25% phosphorus. Then the manufacturers added 80% water. There is still the same total amount of phosphorus in the food, but at first the percentage appears lower because of the diluting effect of the water. So in order to understand exactly how much phosphorus your cat is eating, you need to discount the water in the food.

Metabolisable Energy (ME)

There are various other ways of calculating the values in cat foods, one of which is metabolisable energy (ME). ME is the amount of energy available from a food for your cat to use once your cat has digested the food. It focuses on protein, fat and carbohydrate.

Since phosphorus is the most important value for CKD cats, I do not look at ME values, but they may be of some use for people with diabetic cats, who often look to feed foods with an ME value for carbohydrates of 10-12% or lower.

HOW TO USE THE FOOD DATA TABLES

The tables are simply lists of cat foods available in the USA, showing the content for phosphorus, protein, sodium, fat, carbohydrates and calories, expressed as a percentage (%) on a dry matter analysis basis. They are divided into wet and dry food (with separate chapters for therapeutic kidney diets and raw foods), and you can view the data in two ways:

1. **In order of phosphorus content, from lowest to highest**
   You can see which foods have the lowest phosphorus content. This enables you to see how much phosphorus is in the food you are currently feeding, and can help you narrow down your choices if you wish to go shopping for other foods, particularly online.

2. **In order of brand name**
   This can be helpful if you can only access a limited number of brands, so you can focus on those brands rather than trying to spot the various flavours from that brand which may be widely spread throughout the table showing the foods in order of phosphorus content.

Although I do not recommend feeding raw foods to CKD cats (my reasons for this can be found at http://www.felinecrf.org/which_foods.htm#raw_food), data for some of these foods are included.

If you cannot see a brand or flavour, it is usually because the manufacturer has either not responded to my repeated requests for information or has declined to assist. My website has details about which brands fall into which category.

Your goals are to feed a food with:

- **a phosphorus level under 0.5%** on a dry matter analysis basis, or as close to this as you can get.

- **a protein level in the 28-35% range**, preferably at the higher end of the range.

In order to give you and your cat the best possible chance of success, please ensure all possible causes of inappetance are addressed, as discussed in detail on my website:

http://www.felinecrf.org/appetite_loss_nausea_vomiting.htm

http://www.felinecrf.org/persuading_cat_to_eat.htm

If your cat will not eat a food with a phosphorus content of 0.5%, try a few others in the 0.5-0.6% range. If your cat still will not eat, you will have to choose a food with a higher phosphorus content. The most important thing is that your cat eats. In 11 Guidelines for Conservatively Treating Chronic Kidney Disease (2007) Ve*terinary Medicine* December 2007, Dr D Polzin makes the shocking observation that in the majority of cats with CKD, death (including death through euthanasia) occurs because of starvation. Are you going to let your cat starve to death? I doubt it! So remember your new mantra: My cat must eat!

I have created these tables using information obtained from the brands in writing wherever possible, or from the brand's website. The values for each food included in this book have been cross-checked by a third party.

I am not recommending any food on these lists. I have not examined the ingredients or checked whether the foods are complete or appropriate for a CKD cat (foods labelled "urinary" are often not suitable for CKD cats, for example).

It is your responsibility to check a food's composition and to discuss your choices with your vet to ensure the food you choose is suitable for your cat.

WET THERAPEUTIC KIDNEY DIETS IN ORDER OF PHOSPHORUS CONTENT

Please see pages 3 and 15 for information on how to use these tables. All data are on a dry matter analysis basis, except calories, which are provided on an as fed per ounce basis.

"na" means the information was not available.

Brand and Variety	Phos	Prot	Sod	Fat	Carb	Cals	Obtained
My Perfect Pet Low Phosphorus Chicken Carnivore Grain-Free Blend	0.35	47.10	0.30	14.50	na	51.00	26-Jan-20
Purina Pro Plan Veterinary Diets NF Kidney Function Advanced Care	0.39	27.80	0.34	22.12	36.98	30.00	15-Jan-20
Dave's Pet Food Restricted Diet Protein-Phosphorus Chicken Lickin' Good For Cats [1]	0.39	45.15	0.14	22.07	19.59	30.55	07-Nov-19
Purina Pro Plan Veterinary Diets NF Kidney Function Early Care	0.43	39.49	0.39	19.10	31.49	29.45	15-Jan-20
Royal Canin Veterinary Diet Renal Support Diet	0.44	34.21	0.49	34.21	22.24	32.33	15-Jan-20
Hill's Prescription Diet k/d with Tuna	0.45	29.00	0.24	22.10	41.70	30.91	01-Feb-20
Royal Canin Veterinary Diet Renal Support E (Enticing) (pâté)	0.46	33.59	0.25	29.59	27.32	29.48	15-Jan-20
Royal Canin Veterinary Diet Renal LP Modified (pâté)	0.47	32.75	0.30	41.83	27.53	35.33	15-Jan-20
Hill's Prescription Diet k/d + Mobility Chicken & Vegetable Stew	0.48	29.60	0.24	24.90	37.90	23.45	01-Feb-20
Hill's Prescription Diet k/d Chicken & Vegetable Stew	0.49	30.00	0.23	24.60	38.00	24.14	01-Feb-20

[1] *Levels are minimums*

17

Brand and Variety	Phos	Prot	Sod	Fat	Carb	Cals	Obtained
Hill's Prescription Diet k/d with Chicken	0.49	30.00	0.24	23.00	38.90	32.18	01-Feb-20
Hill's Prescription Diet k/d Vegetable & Tuna Stew	0.49	30.00	0.24	24.80	37.40	26.55	01-Feb-20
Royal Canin Veterinary Diet Renal Support T (Tasty)	0.51	31.64	0.51	28.81	30.23	27.33	15-Jan-20
Blue Natural Veterinary Diet KM Kidney + Mobility Support	0.55	29.11	0.30	20.97	na	na	05-Feb-20
Rayne Clinical Nutrition Adult Health RSS	0.58	54.09	0.67	21.06	18.78	25.45	27-Nov-19
Hill's Prescription Diet k/d Early Support Chicken, Vegetable & Rice	0.59	34.10	0.27	24.10	34.50	27.24	01-Feb-20
Hi-Tor Veterinary Select Neo [2][3]	0.72	36.54	0.43	43.18	na	na	24-Jul-14
Forza10 Renal Sensitive + Active Grain-Free[2]	na	31.82	na	35.45	na	30.40	31-Jan-20
Darwins Intelligent Design Kidney Support Raw[2][3][4]	na	48.00	na	40.00	6.00	46.00	22-Jan-20

[2] Levels are minimums

[3] Hi-Tor and Darwins do not respond to my enquiries so the data are very old and/or limited

[4] I do not recommend raw food for CKD cats

DRY THERAPEUTIC KIDNEY DIETS IN ORDER OF PHOSPHORUS CONTENT

Please see pages 3 and 15 for information on how to use these tables. All data are on a dry matter analysis basis, except calories, which are provided per kg (2.2lbs) on an ME as fed basis.

"na" means the information was not available.

Brand and Variety	Phos	Prot	Sod	Fat	Carb	Cals	Obtained
Purina Pro Plan Veterinary Diets NF Kidney Function Advanced Care	0.39	30.40	0.31	18.21	41.94	4085	10-Jan-20
Purina Pro Plan Veterinary Diets NF Early Care	0.41	38.92	0.31	15.24	36.40	4041	10-Jan-20
Farmina VetLife Renal[5]	0.43	26.20	na	21.39	na	4070	31-Jan-20
Royal Canin Veterinary Diet Renal Support S (Savory)	0.44	25.78	0.44	22.60	41.36	4061	15-Jan-20
Royal Canin Veterinary Diet Renal Support A (Aromatic)	0.45	24.14	0.37	17.84	46.18	3790	15-Jan-20
Royal Canin Veterinary Diet Renal Support F (Flavorful)	0.46	27.13	0.41	17.73	43.41	3811	15-Jan-20
Hill's Prescription Diet k/d + Mobility	0.50	28.90	0.27	22.00	42.90	4155	01-Feb-20
Hill's Prescription Diet k/d with Ocean Fish	0.52	29.80	0.26	23.10	40.60	4235	01-Feb-20
Hill's Prescription Diet k/d	0.52	30.00	0.26	23.00	40.80	4239	01-Feb-20
Hill's Prescription Diet k/d Early Support Chicken	0.56	34.00	0.25	21.00	38.40	4203	01-Feb-20
Royal Canin Veterinary Diet Multifunction Renal Support + Hydrolyzed Protein (for cats with both CKD and food allergies)	0.70	29.35	na	19.57	na	3958	15-Jan-20
Forza 10 Renal Active[1]	0.87	28.26	0.26	20.11	na	3837	31-Jan-20
Rayne Clinical Nutrition Adult Health RSS	0.94	35.54	0.72	14.49	40.33	3887	27-Nov-19

---

[5] *levels are minimums*

WET FOODS IN ORDER OF PHOSPHORUS CONTENT

Please see pages 3 and 15 for information on how to use these tables. All data are on a dry matter analysis basis, except calories, which are provided on an as fed per ounce basis.

Foods marked * show minimum values for protein and fat and in some cases phosphorus — the actual values could be much higher. Page 13 explains more about this.

"na" means the information was not available.

Brand and Variety	Phos	Prot	Sod	Fat	Carb	Cals	Obtained
My Perfect Pet Bengal's Beef Carnivore Grain-Free Blend	0.50	69.30	0.20	17.60	na	61.50	26-Jan-20
Hill's Science Diet Adult Tender Tuna Dinner	0.52	41.30	0.48	17.50	32.60	29.45	1-Feb-20
Hill's Science Diet Adult 7+ Tender Tuna Dinner	0.54	41.80	0.47	18.90	30.00	27.64	1-Feb-20
Wellness Healthy Indulgence Morsels Chicken & Chicken Liver Pouch	0.55	37.87	1.54	30.91	23.01	20.67	1-Feb-20
Wellness Healthy Indulgence Morsels Chicken & Salmon Pouch	0.56	39.86	1.53	27.18	21.04	20.67	1-Feb-20
Hill's Science Diet Adult 11+ Healthy Cuisine Seared Tuna & Carrot Medley	0.57	37.60	0.38	19.90	35.50	23.57	1-Feb-20
Truluxe Steak Frites	0.57	61.90	0.22	27.80	7.50	20.67	26-Jan-20
Nature's Logic Beef Feast	0.58	47.20	0.62	36.89	3.30	40.91	20-Feb-20
Hill's Science Diet Adult Healthy Cuisine Roasted Chicken & Rice Medley	0.59	36.50	0.54	21.10	33.50	23.57	1-Feb-20
Soulistic Harvest Sunrise Chicken & Pumpkin in Gravy	0.59	56.47	0.16	12.30	27.81	21.27	27-Jan-20
Hill's Science Diet Adult Tender Chicken Dinner	0.60	37.50	0.40	21.60	33.60	29.09	1-Feb-20
Wellness Healthy Indulgence Morsels Salmon & Tuna Pouch	0.60	42.70	1.61	25.32	20.23	20.67	1-Feb-20
Wysong Epigen Turkey	0.60	45.10	0.50	35.70	7.80	39.15	16-Oct-19
Wysong Epigen Duck	0.60	45.50	0.50	36.20	6.90	37.67	16-Oct-19

Brand and Variety	Phos	Prot	Sod	Fat	Carb	Cals	Obtained
Wellness Healthy Indulgence Morsels Chicken & Turkey Pouch	0.61	37.12	1.43	31.95	18.22	20.67	1-Feb-20
Wellness Healthy Indulgence Morsels Tuna Pouch	0.61	39.87	1.35	28.41	22.73	20.67	1-Feb-20
Wellness Healthy Indulgence Morsels Turkey & Duck Pouch	0.62	38.35	1.19	30.15	23.25	20.67	1-Feb-20
Koha Poké Bowl Tuna & Duck Entrée in Gravy*	0.62	56.19	1.90	15.71	17.67	25.09	27-Nov-19
Hill's Science Diet Adult 7+ Healthy Cuisine Roasted Chicken & Rice Medley	0.63	38.00	0.37	19.10	34.30	22.86	1-Feb-20
Hill's Science Diet Youthful Vitality 7+ Tuna & Vegetable Stew	0.63	38.80	0.44	17.60	35.50	23.79	1-Feb-20
JustFoodForCats Fish & Chicken Recipe	0.63	52.00	0.83	22.00	17.50	35.00	8-Nov-19
Hill's Science Diet Adult 7+ Savory Turkey Entrée	0.64	33.70	0.29	24.00	31.40	33.64	1-Feb-20
Organix Organic Turkey & Organic Spinach	0.64	36.36	0.49	31.05	23.01	36.00	29-Oct-19
Hill's Science Diet Adult 7+ Savory Chicken Entrée	0.64	38.70	0.33	24.30	27.20	31.09	1-Feb-20
Fussie Cat Super Premium Chicken with Sweet Potato*	0.64	49.57	0.23	7.68	na	22.94	5-Dec-19
Hill's Science Diet Adult Indoor Cat Savory Chicken Entrée	0.65	33.60	0.50	23.80	25.30	30.91	1-Feb-20
Hill's Science Diet Youthful Vitality Adult 7+ Chicken & Vegetable Entrée	0.65	34.60	0.43	17.90	39.30	33.45	1-Feb-20
Hill's Science Diet Adult Savory Chicken Entrée	0.65	40.10	0.37	26.60	22.40	32.91	1-Feb-20
Organix Organic Turkey, Brown Rice & Chicken	0.66	34.61	0.40	28.47	21.30	35.45	29-Oct-19
Hill's Science Diet Adult Indoor Cat Ocean Fish Entrée	0.67	38.30	0.46	21.00	26.20	31.64	1-Feb-20
Hill's Science Diet Adult Ocean Fish Entrée	0.67	38.30	0.46	21.20	29.50	33.27	1-Feb-20
Cats in the Kitchen Chick Magnet Pouch	0.67	59.00	0.40	18.10	19.30	23.00	26-Jan-20

Brand and Variety	Phos	Prot	Sod	Fat	Carb	Cals	Obtained
Hill's Science Diet Youthful Vitality 7+ Salmon & Vegetable Stew	0.68	39.40	0.31	18.00	34.10	25.52	1-Feb-20
Hill's Science Diet Adult 7+ Tender Chicken Dinner	0.68	46.10	0.36	21.60	25.90	30.00	1-Feb-20
Fussie Cat Super Premium Chicken with Vegetables*	0.68	66.38	0.23	7.89	na	23.02	5-Dec-19
RAWZ Shredded Chicken Breast & Egg Pouch	0.68	68.40	0.35	12.81	7.87	23.58	3-Dec-19
Hill's Science Diet Adult 7+ Savory Beef Entrée	0.69	39.50	0.38	22.70	27.60	28.91	1-Feb-20
Hill's Science Diet Adult Tender Ocean Fish Dinner	0.69	40.70	0.41	18.40	32.80	27.82	1-Feb-20
Hill's Science Diet Sensitive Stomach & Skin Chicken & Vegetable Entrée	0.70	35.20	0.40	23.90	34.60	30.00	1-Feb-20
Halo Grain-Free Turkey and Chickpea Senior	0.70	39.30	0.30	35.00	na	32.73	30-Jan-20
Halo Holistic Gluten-Free Turkey and Quail Indoor	0.70	41.20	0.50	43.50	5.31	33.64	30-Jan-20
Wysong Uretic with Organic Chicken	0.70	41.60	0.60	24.30	11.10	31.64	16-Oct-19
Wysong Epigen Salmon	0.70	44.30	0.50	31.40	8.80	36.43	16-Oct-19
Wysong Epigen Chicken	0.70	45.50	0.50	35.70	7.20	37.98	16-Oct-19
Wysong Epigen Rabbit	0.70	46.00	0.50	38.70	4.00	43.57	16-Oct-19
Koha Poké Bowl Tuna & Beef Entrée in Gravy*	0.70	61.50	2.10	18.25	10.95	25.45	27-Nov-19
Evanger's Beef it Up	0.71	37.94	0.35	22.34	8.60	44.17	25-Jan-17
Weruva What a Crock Pouch	0.71	42.70	0.55	40.80	12.40	33.67	26-Jan-20
Best Feline Friend OMG Live N' Love Chicken & Lamb Ground in Gravy	0.71	42.90	0.56	40.80	11.50	36.07	27-Jan-20
Weruva Goody Stew Shoes	0.71	43.20	0.59	39.80	13.00	31.27	26-Jan-20
Weruva Simmer Down Pouch	0.71	44.00	0.59	38.00	13.90	32.33	26-Jan-20
Weruva Stew's Clues	0.71	44.60	0.59	37.30	14.10	31.82	26-Jan-20
Dave's Naturally Healthy Grain-Free Chicken and Herring Dinner*	0.71	44.60	0.71	34.70	12.67	38.36	7-Nov-19

Brand and Variety	Phos	Prot	Sod	Fat	Carb	Cals	Obtained
Best Feline Friend PLAY Cherish Chicken Pâté Pouch	0.71	47.10	0.60	40.70	7.60	31.33	27-Jan-20
Best Feline Friend PLAY Tiptoe Chicken & Turkey Pâté Pouch	0.71	47.50	0.60	40.10	7.70	31.00	27-Jan-20
Best Feline Friend PLAY Checkmate Chicken Pâté	0.71	47.70	0.61	40.00	7.70	30.73	27-Jan-20
Soulistic Chicken Dinner Pâté	0.71	47.70	0.61	40.00	7.70	30.91	27-Jan-20
Best Feline Friend PLAY Topsy Turvy Chicken & Turkey Pâté	0.71	48.10	0.61	39.40	7.80	30.55	27-Jan-20
Soulistic Chicken & Turkey Dinner Pâté	0.71	48.10	0.61	39.40	7.80	30.73	27-Jan-20
Hill's Healthy Advantage Adult Chicken Entrée	0.72	40.40	0.40	18.00	35.20	29.27	1-Feb-20
Best Feline Friend OMG Shine Bright Chicken & Salmon in Gravy Pouch	0.72	42.10	0.55	42.40	11.20	37.14	27-Jan-20
Best Feline Friend OMG Stir It Up Chicken & Salmon Ground in Gravy	0.72	42.60	0.56	41.80	11.30	36.55	27-Jan-20
Hill's Science Diet Sensitive Stomach & Skin Tuna & Vegetable Entrée	0.72	44.70	0.46	21.50	26.40	29.66	1-Feb-20
Best Feline Friend OMG Devour Me Tuna & Duck Pouch	0.72	62.60	0.64	16.10	14.60	21.00	27-Jan-20
Soulistic Moist & Tender Tuna & Duck in Gravy Pouch	0.72	62.61	0.64	16.11	14.61	20.73	27-Jan-20
Fussie Cat Super Premium Chicken in Gravy*	0.72	68.56	0.26	8.87	na	23.79	5-Dec-19
Hill's Science Diet Adult Hairball Control Ocean Fish Entrée	0.73	37.70	0.44	22.70	23.70	32.73	1-Feb-20
Performatrin Senior Chicken & Turkey	0.73	40.70	0.40	31.50	18.20	31.45	28-Nov-19
Best Feline Friend OMG Text Me Chicken & Turkey in Gravy Pouch	0.73	42.20	0.55	42.20	11.20	37.50	27-Jan-20
Redbarn Naturals Beef Pâté for Urinary Support	0.73	42.92	0.39	30.55	20.40	31.64	31-Oct-19
Best Feline Friend OMG Charge Me Up Chicken in Gravy Pouch	0.73	43.80	0.56	40.90	10.90	36.79	27-Jan-20

Brand and Variety	Phos	Prot	Sod	Fat	Carb	Cals	Obtained
Best Feline Friend OMG Cloud 9 Chicken Ground in Gravy	0.73	44.30	0.57	40.30	11.00	35.82	27-Jan-20
Soulistic Good Karma Chicken in Gravy Pouch	0.73	69.17	0.13	11.65	15.87	23.09	27-Jan-20
Hill's Science Diet Youthful Vitality Adult 7+ Chicken & Vegetable Stew	0.74	35.70	0.42	17.90	38.30	23.45	1-Feb-20
Hill's Science Diet Adult Healthy Cuisine Seared Tuna & Carrot Medley	0.74	39.10	0.53	20.80	30.40	25.36	1-Feb-20
Performatrin Ultra Grain-Free Senior Chicken Pâté	0.74	48.00	0.48	28.00	13.50	28.55	21-Jan-20
Koha Poké Bowl Tuna & Pumpkin Entrée in Gravy*	0.74	60.32	2.59	15.71	13.23	24.55	27-Nov-19
Koha Poké Bowl Tuna & Salmon Entrée in Gravy*	0.74	61.27	2.35	14.17	12.40	24.91	27-Nov-19
Fussie Cat Super Premium Chicken with Egg*	0.74	67.38	0.26	10.90	na	25.23	5-Dec-19
Truluxe On The Cat Wok	0.74	69.10	0.12	22.80	4.90	16.50	26-Jan-20
PetGuard Organic Chicken & Vegetable	0.75	36.36	0.29	31.80	7.30	36.50	18-Dec-19
Evanger's Chicken Lickin'	0.75	37.97	0.38	22.56	7.60	38.00	25-Jan-17
Identity 95% Free-Range Canadian Duck	0.75	39.19	0.29	35.28	5.27	31.45	20-Jan-20
Koha Grain-Free Limited Ingredient Beef Pâté*	0.75	49.88	0.42	40.65	3.57	36.00	13-Aug-19
Best Feline Friend OMG Tell Me Tuna & Turkey Minced in Gravy	0.75	61.10	0.66	18.50	13.30	20.73	27-Jan-20
Best Feline Friend OMG Start Me Up Tuna & Salmon Minced in Gravy	0.75	61.40	0.65	18.60	13.00	20.73	27-Jan-20
Best Feline Friend OMG Chase Me Tuna & Chicken Minced in Gravy	0.75	61.50	0.64	18.60	12.90	20.73	27-Jan-20
Fussie Cat Super Premium Chicken with Duck*	0.75	65.21	0.27	12.95	na	25.57	5-Dec-19
Hill's Science Diet Adult Savory Turkey Entrée	0.76	33.90	0.30	26.10	29.30	33.64	1-Feb-20

Brand and Variety	Phos	Prot	Sod	Fat	Carb	Cals	Obtained
Hill's Science Diet Adult Urinary Hairball Control Savory Chicken Entrée	0.76	36.30	0.34	21.10	26.30	28.91	1-Feb-20
Hill's Science Diet Adult Healthy Cuisine Poached Salmon & Spinach Medley	0.76	36.90	0.36	25.20	28.50	28.21	1-Feb-20
Hill's Science Diet Adult Perfect Weight Liver & Chicken Entrée	0.76	38.40	0.36	13.00	31.30	24.83	1-Feb-20
Identity 95% Free Range Quail & Turkey	0.77	41.92	0.32	26.63	8.03	26.55	20-Jan-20
Best Feline Friend OMG Be Happy Chicken & Beef Ground in Gravy	0.77	42.30	0.58	42.60	10.50	36.55	27-Jan-20
Best Feline Friend OMG Dream Team Chicken & Duck Ground in Gravy	0.77	42.60	0.57	41.80	11.20	36.55	27-Jan-20
Identity 95% Free-Range Heritage Turkey	0.77	46.46	0.35	24.42	10.01	27.45	20-Jan-20
Weruva Grandma's Chicken Soup	0.77	61.10	0.55	12.30	23.70	19.27	26-Jan-20
Cats in the Kitchen La Isla Bonita	0.77	66.50	0.56	24.90	4.50	18.17	26-Jan-20
Cats in the Kitchen Pumpkin Lickin' Chicken Pouch	0.77	70.60	0.23	11.50	13.90	20.00	26-Jan-20
Truluxe Meow Me A River	0.77	82.60	0.35	10.70	1.30	18.00	26-Jan-20
Hill's Science Diet Adult Turkey & Liver Entrée	0.78	35.30	0.33	29.50	24.10	34.00	1-Feb-20
Identity 95% Sustainable Atlantic Salmon & Herring	0.78	41.12	0.35	32.57	10.51	29.09	20-Jan-20
Hill's Science Diet Kitten Tender Chicken Dinner	0.78	45.50	0.33	25.30	19.20	28.18	1-Feb-20
Best Feline Friend OMG Lights Out Tuna & Lamb Minced in Gravy	0.78	60.70	0.66	18.50	13.40	20.73	27-Jan-20
Soulistic Golden Fortune Chicken & Tuna in Pumpkin Soup	0.78	62.78	0.32	12.22	19.44	20.00	27-Jan-20
Best Feline Friend OMG Baby Cakes Tuna & Beef in Gravy Pouch	0.78	62.90	0.64	13.40	17.00	20.00	27-Jan-20
Soulistic Moist & Tender Tuna & Beef Dinner in Gravy Pouch	0.78	62.91	0.64	13.41	16.98	20.00	27-Jan-20

Brand and Variety	Phos	Prot	Sod	Fat	Carb	Cals	Obtained
Koha Poké Bowl Tuna & Chicken Entrée in Gravy*	0.78	65.69	2.60	17.75	7.06	25.64	27-Nov-19
Hill's Science Diet Adult Hairball Control Savory Chicken Entrée	0.79	33.70	0.46	24.20	24.90	30.36	1-Feb-20
Hill's Science Diet Adult Savory Salmon Entrée	0.79	36.60	0.34	25.90	27.40	33.64	1-Feb-20
Hill's Science Diet Perfect Weight Roasted Vegetables & Chicken Medley	0.79	38.80	0.45	11.90	33.30	21.38	1-Feb-20
Hill's Science Diet Adult Liver & Chicken Entrée	0.79	41.40	0.31	20.20	27.00	28.36	1-Feb-20
Soulistic Sweet Salutations Chicken & Tuna Dinner in Gravy	0.79	59.63	0.22	13.68	22.68	21.82	27-Jan-20
Koha Poké Bowl Tuna & Lamb Entrée in Gravy*	0.79	61.40	2.60	14.70	12.33	25.82	27-Nov-19
Soulistic Moist & Tender Tuna & Turkey Dinner in Gravy Pouch	0.79	62.68	0.61	15.26	15.74	21.82	27-Jan-20
Best Feline Friend OMG Tickles Tuna & Turkey in Gravy Pouch	0.79	62.70	0.61	15.30	15.70	23.67	27-Jan-20
Best Feline Friend OMG Charm Me Tuna & Chicken in Gravy Pouch	0.79	67.80	0.65	15.20	10.80	17.67	27-Jan-20
Soulistic Moist & Tender Tuna & Chicken Dinner in Gravy Pouch	0.79	67.81	0.65	15.17	10.84	20.36	27-Jan-20
Soulistic Seaside Serenity Salmon & Tuna Dinner in Gravy	0.79	68.02	0.48	13.37	14.55	23.09	27-Jan-20
Truluxe Peking Ducken	0.79	72.30	0.23	13.90	10.60	18.67	26-Jan-20
Merrick Limited Ingredient Grain-Free Duck	0.80	30.40	0.30	52.40	5.54	26.20	26-Jun-19
Hill's Science Diet Adult Light Liver & Chicken Entrée	0.80	36.70	0.45	15.00	34.60	26.73	1-Feb-20
Whole Earth Farms Grain-Free Real Salmon Morsels in Gravy	0.80	43.80	0.99	28.50	14.53	24.00	25-Oct-19
Wysong Epigen Beef	0.80	46.00	0.50	38.30	4.50	41.94	16-Oct-19
Halo Holistic Sensitive Stomach Grain-Free Chicken, Egg & Garden Greens Pâté	0.80	46.20	0.40	40.40	7.30	33.09	30-Jan-20
My Perfect Pet Toby's Turkey Carnivore Grain-Free Blend	0.80	58.10	1.30	15.30	na	50.75	26-Jan-20

Brand and Variety	Phos	Prot	Sod	Fat	Carb	Cals	Obtained
Cats in the Kitchen 1 if By Land, 2 if by Sea Pouch	0.80	62.70	0.68	13.80	18.90	20.00	26-Jan-20
Koha Poké Bowl Tuna & Shrimp Entrée in Gravy*	0.80	65.83	2.46	15.18	8.59	24.73	27-Nov-19
Wellness Healthy Indulgence Shreds with Chicken & Turkey Pouch	0.81	32.26	0.76	31.09	25.50	19.00	1-Feb-20
Best Feline Friend PLAY Take a Chance Chicken, Duck & Turkey Pâté	0.81	48.50	0.62	39.20	7.90	30.36	27-Jan-20
Cats in the Kitchen Chicken Frick 'A Zee	0.81	67.40	0.21	25.80	2.70	23.83	26-Jan-20
Weruva Mideast Feast	0.81	69.80	0.44	15.10	8.00	21.45	26-Jan-20
Best Feline Friend PLAY Laugh Out Loud Chicken & Lamb Pâté	0.82	47.60	0.62	40.20	7.70	31.09	27-Jan-20
Soulistic Moist & Tender Chicken Dinner in Gravy Canned	0.82	50.72	0.58	30.43	10.77	27.82	27-Jan-20
Weruva Press Your Lunch! Chicken Pâté	0.82	58.80	0.31	27.30	7.90	18.73	26-Jan-20
Weruva Funky Chunky	0.82	60.30	0.31	13.90	22.80	17.45	26-Jan-20
Soulistic Triple Harmony Chicken, Salmon & Tuna Dinner in Gravy Pouch	0.82	60.93	0.39	9.84	24.86	20.00	27-Jan-20
Cats in the Kitchen Love Me Tender Pouch	0.82	63.90	0.22	12.50	19.50	21.33	26-Jan-20
Soulistic Pure Bliss Tuna Whole Meat Dinner in Gravy	0.82	64.23	0.23	10.20	21.58	21.45	27-Jan-20
Weruva Paw Lickin' Chicken & Beef	0.82	77.00	0.24	15.70	3.90	19.09	26-Jan-20
Soulistic Autumn Bounty Chicken Dinner in Pumpkin Soup Pouch	0.82	78.32	0.13	7.61	9.73	19.45	27-Jan-20
Soulistic Aromatic Chicken Dinner in Gelée	0.82	79.81	0.11	13.29	1.08	17.82	27-Jan-20
Stella and Chewy's Marvelous Morsels Grain-Free Cage-Free Chicken*	0.83	42.90	1.05	14.30	2.57	27.09	3-Dec-19
Best Feline Friend OMG Luv Ya Tuna & Lamb in Gravy Pouch	0.83	62.80	0.60	14.00	17.50	19.00	27-Jan-20

Brand and Variety	Phos	Prot	Sod	Fat	Carb	Cals	Obtained
Soulistic Moist & Tender Tuna & Lamb Dinner in Gravy Pouch	0.83	62.85	0.60	13.99	17.46	21.82	27-Jan-20
Soulistic Nautical Nirvana Tuna & Skipjack Dinner in Gravy	0.83	64.86	0.37	14.68	16.33	25.27	27-Jan-20
Best Feline Friend OMG Crazy 4 U! Chicken & Salmon Minced in Gravy	0.84	59.70	0.47	25.00	9.70	20.18	27-Jan-20
Weruva Nine Liver	0.84	70.50	0.22	16.10	10.30	19.82	26-Jan-20
VeRUS Grain-Free Beef Pâté	0.85	43.00	0.58	28.10	0.00	33.82	27-Jan-20
Caru Classics Natural Chicken Stew	0.85	46.08	0.23	22.31	12.79	25.50	28-Oct-19
Cats in the Kitchen Meowisss Bueller Pâté Pouch	0.85	53.90	0.44	31.30	9.70	23.00	26-Jan-20
Soulistic Chicken & Lamb Pâté Pouch	0.85	53.90	0.44	31.30	9.70	23.00	27-Jan-20
Soulistic Moist & Tender Turkey Dinner in Gravy Canned	0.85	54.73	0.50	30.35	7.56	27.09	27-Jan-20
Cats in the Kitchen Mack, Jack & Sam Pouch	0.85	61.00	0.40	13.60	21.00	21.00	26-Jan-20
Soulistic Good Karma Chicken Dinner in Gravy Canned	0.85	65.60	0.42	12.00	18.75	22.55	27-Jan-20
Identity 95% Grass-Fed Angus Beef	0.86	40.14	0.35	37.31	3.99	29.09	20-Jan-20
Best Feline Friend OMG Seeya Sooner! Chicken & Tuna in Gravy Pouch	0.86	59.30	0.38	28.40	7.10	21.07	27-Jan-20
Best Feline Friend OMG Ciao Baby! Chicken & Shrimp in Gravy Pouch	0.86	60.70	0.49	24.80	9.00	20.00	27-Jan-20
Hill's Science Diet Kitten Healthy Cuisine Roasted Chicken & Rice Medley	0.87	38.00	0.55	24.10	28.90	25.36	1-Feb-20
Best Feline Friend PLAY Destiny Chicken & Duck Pâté Pouch	0.87	47.80	0.62	39.90	7.70	30.67	27-Jan-20
Soulistic Aqua Grill Tilapia & Tuna Dinner in Gravy	0.87	59.60	0.51	12.72	23.06	19.45	27-Jan-20
Dave's Naturally Healthy Grain-Free Turkey & Salmon Dinner*	0.88	42.29	0.33	28.50	3.50	33.82	7-Nov-19

Brand and Variety	Phos	Prot	Sod	Fat	Carb	Cals	Obtained
Wellness Core Tiny Tasters Tuna Pouch	0.88	48.75	1.17	34.63	7.56	36.00	1-Feb-20
Best Feline Friend OMG QT Patootie! Chicken & Turkey Minced in Gravy	0.88	60.30	0.48	21.90	12.30	19.45	27-Jan-20
Newman's Own Beef & Vegetable Grain-Free Stew	0.88	61.00	0.11	13.00	3.80	33.64	14-Nov-19
Newman's Own Beef Liver & Vegetable Grain-Free Stew	0.88	61.00	0.11	13.00	3.80	34.55	14-Nov-19
Newman's Own Lamb, Liver & Vegetable Stew	0.88	61.00	0.11	13.00	3.80	42.55	14-Nov-19
Caru Classics Natural Wild Salmon & Turkey Stew	0.88	65.40	0.53	12.20	14.38	22.33	28-Oct-19
Lotus Grain-Free Just Juicy Turkey Stew	0.88	68.01	0.84	13.61	12.65	26.98	28-Jan-20
Truluxe Mediterranean Harvest	0.88	69.20	0.74	9.20	14.20	20.50	26-Jan-20
Identity 95% Free-Range Cobb Chicken	0.89	40.13	0.41	27.02	10.71	27.64	20-Jan-20
Stella and Chewy's Marvelous Morsels Chicken & Salmon*	0.89	41.20	1.08	13.70	2.97	27.27	3-Dec-19
Cats in the Kitchen Fowl Ball	0.89	57.10	0.28	32.20	5.80	22.33	26-Jan-20
Nutrisca Truly Shredded Chicken & Chicken Liver Entrée In Savory Broth*	0.89	58.90	0.35	24.40	8.90	27.41	21-Jan-20
Best Feline Friend OMG Love Munchkin! Chicken & Pumpkin Minced in Gravy	0.89	59.10	0.45	25.20	10.00	19.45	27-Jan-20
Best Feline Friend OMG Belly Rubs Tuna & Beef Minced in Gravy	0.89	61.10	0.69	18.50	12.10	20.71	27-Jan-20
Best Feline Friend OMG Dilly Dally Tuna & Duck Minced in Gravy	0.89	61.70	0.67	18.60	13.10	20.73	27-Jan-20
Halo Grain-Free Chicken and Chickpeas Senior	0.90	40.50	0.40	29.60	18.20	33.09	30-Jan-20
GO! Solutions Sensitivities Limited Ingredient Grain-Free Pollock Pâté	0.90	42.00	0.36	18.00	33.00	23.94	31-Oct-19

Brand and Variety	Phos	Prot	Sod	Fat	Carb	Cals	Obtained
Open Farm Herring & Mackerel Rustic Blend	0.90	44.99	0.64	26.31	15.38	22.73	17-Jan-20
Weruva Stir the Pot Pouch	0.90	45.20	0.61	32.10	15.30	28.67	26-Jan-20
Open Farm Wild-Caught Salmon Rustic Blend	0.90	47.18	0.64	26.31	13.19	24.55	17-Jan-20
Halo Holistic Sensitive Stomach Grain-Free Guinea Fowl & Garden Greens Pâté	0.90	48.30	0.40	35.00	9.30	33.64	30-Jan-20
FirstMate Wild Pacific Salmon & Rice	0.90	50.00	0.80	14.00	16.00	22.00	25-Nov-19
FirstMate Limited Ingredient Wild Salmon	0.90	50.00	0.80	14.00	26.00	22.00	25-Nov-19
FirstMate Wild Salmon & Wild Tuna 50/50	0.90	50.00	0.80	18.00	19.00	27.00	25-Nov-19
Kasiks Grub Formula	0.90	55.00	0.90	18.00	18.00	24.00	1-Dec-19
Wellness Core Signature Selects Flaked Skipjack Tuna with Wild Salmon in Broth	0.90	55.96	0.61	22.02	15.75	25.09	1-Feb-20
Dave's Naturally Healthy Grain-Free Tuna and Salmon Dinner in Aspic*	0.90	58.50	0.62	26.10	5.70	27.09	7-Nov-19
Aujus by RAWZ Aku Tuna & Mackerel in a Silky Broth Pouch	0.90	65.62	0.60	13.20	13.82	23.17	3-Dec-19
Tiki Cat Grain-Free After Dark Chicken*	0.90	75.00	na	18.75	0.00	20.36	30-Jan-20
Best Feline Friend Originals 4EVA Tuna & Chicken Minced in Gravy	0.90	75.50	0.58	13.10	2.50	23.27	27-Jan-20
RAWZ Shredded Chicken & Pumpkin	0.90	80.33	0.30	9.00	1.86	23.45	3-Dec-19
Aujus by RAWZ Chicken Breast & Pumpkin in a Silky Broth Pouch	0.90	80.33	0.30	9.00	1.86	24.39	3-Dec-19
RAWZ Shredded Chicken Breast & Cheese Pouch	0.90	80.33	0.30	9.00	11.80	23.98	3-Dec-19
Truluxe Pretty In Pink	0.90	80.60	0.69	13.40	0.00	17.67	26-Jan-20
Dave's 95% Premium Meat Beef & Beef Liver Pâté*	0.91	33.73	0.32	31.21	6.36	31.09	7-Nov-19
Dave's Cat's Meow Chicken with Lamb*	0.91	42.56	1.73	26.65	16.91	32.00	7-Nov-19

Brand and Variety	Phos	Prot	Sod	Fat	Carb	Cals	Obtained
Caru Classics Natural Chicken & Crab Stew	0.91	43.06	0.25	20.53	20.32	25.00	28-Oct-19
Wellness Core Tiny Tasters Chicken Pouch	0.91	46.08	0.91	42.60	2.05	40.00	1-Feb-20
Chicken Soup for the Soul Classic Weight & Mature Care Ocean Fish, Chicken & Turkey Pâté	0.91	46.97	0.39	19.29	23.08	27.27	28-Oct-19
Best Feline Friend PLAY Best Buds Chicken & Beef Pâté	0.91	49.30	0.66	37.80	7.90	30.00	27-Jan-20
Soulistic Midnight Delight Mackerel & Tuna Dinner in Gravy Pouch	0.91	59.95	0.22	13.71	21.73	22.55	27-Jan-20
Koha Poké Bowl Tuna & Turkey Entrée in Gravy*	0.91	61.54	2.12	18.46	9.13	25.64	27-Nov-19
Performatrin Ultra Grain-Free Tuna Bisque	0.91	63.00	1.03	14.00	9.10	26.36	21-Jan-20
RAWZ Shredded Tuna & Chicken	0.91	66.80	0.61	15.50	8.08	23.45	3-Dec-19
RAWZ Shredded Tuna & Salmon	0.91	66.80	0.61	15.50	8.08	24.00	3-Dec-19
Aujus by RAWZ Aku Tuna & Salmon in a Silky Broth Pouch	0.91	66.82	0.61	15.51	10.57	24.39	3-Dec-19
RAWZ Shredded Chicken & Chicken Liver	0.91	81.40	0.30	9.00	1.05	24.36	3-Dec-19
Aujus by RAWZ Chicken Breast & Chicken Liver in a Silky Broth Pouch	0.91	81.40	0.30	9.00	1.05	24.80	3-Dec-19
Nature's Harvest Adult Grain-Free Ocean Fish Pâté*	0.92	38.05	0.32	30.36	18.21	29.09	2-Dec-19
VeRUS Grain-Free Turkey Pâté	0.92	40.20	0.77	29.70	14.27	34.55	27-Jan-20
Wellness Core Tiny Tasters Chicken & Beef Pouch	0.92	43.64	0.87	38.77	8.74	37.14	1-Feb-20
Dave's Cat's Meow Beef with Lamb*	0.92	44.21	1.55	25.31	18.51	33.64	7-Nov-19
Weruva Stewy Lewis	0.92	45.80	0.62	31.30	15.50	28.18	26-Jan-20
Nature's Logic Rabbit Feast	0.92	52.11	0.63	30.17	4.80	38.55	20-Feb-20
RAWZ Shredded Chicken Breast, Pumpkin & New Zealand Green Mussels Pouch	0.92	66.44	0.35	12.54	10.33	23.17	3-Dec-19

Brand and Variety	Phos	Prot	Sod	Fat	Carb	Cals	Obtained
Soulistic Double Happiness Tuna & Crab Surimi Dinner in Gelée	0.92	69.64	0.62	22.05	2.15	24.18	27-Jan-20
RAWZ Shredded Chicken & Duck	0.92	80.06	0.33	9.04	1.01	24.55	3-Dec-19
Aujus by RAWZ Chicken Breast & Duck in a Silky Broth Pouch	0.92	83.84	0.33	9.00	0.57	24.39	3-Dec-19
Wellness Healthy Indulgence Gravies Chicken & Turkey Pouch	0.93	34.21	0.78	29.50	24.33	19.00	1-Feb-20
Dave's 95% Premium Meat Turkey & Turkey Liver Pâté*	0.93	34.94	0.32	31.24	4.60	30.73	7-Nov-19
AvoDerm Grain-Free Chicken & Duck Entrée in Gravy	0.93	42.72	0.22	23.27	13.90	27.33	15-Oct-19
Organix Grain-Free Organic Shredded Chicken	0.93	44.20	0.74	29.70	14.42	31.64	29-Oct-19
Wellness Core Signature Selects Shredded Chicken & Chicken Liver in Gravy	0.93	44.53	0.48	15.95	32.89	23.77	1-Feb-20
Truluxe Glam 'N Punk	0.93	54.00	0.49	38.40	1.00	34.67	26-Jan-20
Wellness Core Signature Selects Flaked Skipjack Tuna with Shrimp Entrée in Broth	0.93	56.54	0.67	20.09	17.01	24.53	1-Feb-20
Best Feline Friend OMG Purr-fect Plannin'! Chicken, Turkey & Salmon in Gravy Pouch	0.93	59.10	0.46	27.80	7.50	20.36	27-Jan-20
Cats in the Kitchen Cattyshack Pâté Pouch	0.93	59.50	0.30	22.90	11.00	20.67	26-Jan-20
Natural Balance Delectable Delights O'Fishally Scampi Stew	0.93	60.69	0.55	19.74	10.79	24.00	9-Jan-17
Soulistic Island Illusion Salmon & Tuna Dinner in Pumpkin Soup Pouch	0.93	65.06	0.55	14.20	15.62	18.55	27-Jan-20
AvoDerm Indoor Weight Control	0.94	35.81	0.29	20.61	22.00	27.45	15-Oct-19
Organix Grain-Free Organic Chicken Pâté	0.94	45.10	0.85	39.20	5.90	35.27	29-Oct-19
Rayne Clinical Nutrition Kangaroo-MAINT	0.94	51.66	0.42	19.39	22.99	29.64	27-Nov-19
Best Feline Friend OMG Sweet Cheeks Tuna & Salmon in Gravy Pouch	0.94	66.10	0.67	10.50	14.00	17.33	27-Jan-20

Brand and Variety	Phos	Prot	Sod	Fat	Carb	Cals	Obtained
Soulistic Moist & Tender Tuna & Salmon Dinner in Gravy Pouch	0.94	66.14	0.67	10.53	13.98	18.00	27-Jan-20
Soulistic Polynesian Picnic Chicken & Tilapia Dinner in Gelée	0.94	74.44	0.55	11.88	6.81	17.45	27-Jan-20
Nature's Logic Duck & Salmon Feast	0.95	43.64	0.62	37.82	4.02	41.82	20-Feb-20
Merrick Backcountry Real Duck Cuts	0.95	49.21	1.40	26.27	15.55	28.33	26-Nov-19
Rayne Clinical Nutrition Rabbit-MAINT	0.95	49.81	0.33	20.30	24.44	30.18	27-Nov-19
Earthborn Holistic Grain-Free Chicken Fricatssee	0.95	52.55	0.26	14.48	29.41	29.40	15-Jan-20
Earthborn Holistic Grain-Free Chicken Catcciatori	0.95	60.54	0.26	12.45	22.22	25.80	15-Jan-20
Lotus Grain-Free Rabbit Pâté	0.96	37.23	0.64	33.36	20.61	34.88	28-Jan-20
Wellness Core Signature Selects Chunky Chicken & Turkey in Sauce	0.96	39.37	0.53	18.96	34.09	25.28	1-Feb-20
Wellness Core Signature Selects Shredded Chicken & Turkey in Gravy	0.96	43.94	0.48	16.36	32.82	24.15	1-Feb-20
Dave's Naturally Healthy Grain-Free Beef & Chicken Pâté*	0.96	46.15	0.38	41.08	1.50	35.36	11-Nov-19
Fromm Beef & Venison Pâté	0.96	49.74	0.96	25.83	na	28.18	31-Jan-20
Merrick Backcountry Real Turkey Cuts	0.96	50.30	1.42	26.45	14.53	28.00	26-Nov-19
AvoDerm Grain-Free Chicken Chunks Entrée in Gravy	0.96	62.12	1.65	18.85	22.20	22.00	15-Oct-19
Cats in the Kitchen Pumpkin Jack Splash Pouch	0.96	72.00	0.31	8.40	14.40	19.00	26-Jan-20
Natural Balance L.I.D. Limited Ingredient Chicken & Pumpkin in Broth	0.96	76.29	0.69	13.49	3.01	24.36	9-Jan-17
Best Feline Friend Originals Soulmates Tuna & Salmon Minced in Geleé	0.96	77.00	0.61	15.10	2.70	23.27	27-Jan-20
Best Feline Friend Originals Be Mine Tuna & Bonito Minced in Geleé	0.96	77.50	0.61	14.20	2.70	23.82	27-Jan-20

Brand and Variety	Phos	Prot	Sod	Fat	Carb	Cals	Obtained
Wellness Core Tiny Tasters Chicken & Turkey Pouch	0.97	44.85	0.89	39.68	5.91	38.29	1-Feb-20
AvoDerm Grain-Free Salmon & Chicken Entrée in Gravy	0.97	46.04	0.22	21.62	13.90	25.00	15-Oct-19
Weruva Jeopurrdy Licious Chicken Breast Pâté Pouch	0.97	50.50	0.27	37.70	6.10	31.27	26-Jan-20
President's Choice Extra Meaty Poached Trout	0.97	54.58	0.93	33.39	3.39	na	12-Dec-19
AvoDerm Grain-Free Sardine, Shrimp & Crab Entrée in Gravy	0.97	58.89	0.37	11.87	5.60	22.66	15-Oct-19
Weruva Family Food Chicken Breast Pâté with Tuna Pouch	0.97	59.50	0.40	36.40	0.00	23.82	26-Jan-20
RAWZ Shredded Salmon, Aku Tuna & Tuna Oil Pouch	0.97	61.36	0.74	22.41	7.54	26.02	3-Dec-19
RAWZ Shredded Chicken Breast & Coconut Oil Pouch	0.97	61.36	0.74	22.41	7.82	26.83	3-Dec-19
Dave's Naturally Healthy Grain-Free Tuna Entrée in Gravy*	0.97	62.00	0.46	17.70	11.20	26.36	7-Nov-19
Caru Classics Natural Turkey Stew	0.97	64.30	0.31	22.30	13.78	29.33	28-Oct-19
Wellness Core Tiny Tasters Tuna & Salmon Pouch	0.97	66.21	1.54	17.47	6.05	29.71	1-Feb-20
Weruva Green Eggs & Chicken	0.97	67.50	0.27	17.50	11.00	21.27	26-Jan-20
Soulistic Shrimply Divine Tuna & Shrimp Dinner in Gelée	0.97	73.81	0.44	19.89	0.00	21.27	27-Jan-20
Best Feline Friend Originals Sweethearts Tuna & Shrimp Minced in Gravy	0.97	75.30	0.62	16.10	2.70	22.91	27-Jan-20
Best Feline Friend Originals Too Cool Tuna Minced in Geleé	0.97	76.90	0.62	13.10	2.70	23.09	27-Jan-20
Soulistic Luna Tuna Runa Dinner in Pumpkin Soup Pouch	0.97	79.09	0.28	10.29	5.37	19.09	27-Jan-20
Best Feline Friend Originals Chuckles Tuna & Chicken Minced in Geleé	0.97	80.10	0.62	14.00	2.70	23.45	27-Jan-20
RAWZ Shredded Chicken	0.97	81.80	0.30	9.00	0.61	23.64	3-Dec-19
Stella and Chewy's Marvelous Morsels Grain-Free Cage-Free Turkey*	0.98	39.10	0.42	17.40	3.72	27.45	3-Dec-19

Brand and Variety	Phos	Prot	Sod	Fat	Carb	Cals	Obtained
Nature's Harvest Adult Grain-Free Duck Pâté*	0.98	41.30	0.37	27.50	17.53	24.55	2-Dec-19
Redbarn Naturals Grain-Free Beef Stew	0.98	45.37	1.42	23.30	20.80	24.67	31-Oct-19
Lotus Grain-Free Just Juicy Chicken Stew	0.98	66.24	0.68	15.96	12.88	27.36	28-Jan-20
Best Feline Friend Originals Twosome Tuna & Tilapia Minced in Geleé	0.98	79.30	0.63	14.10	2.70	23.09	27-Jan-20
Wellness Core Signature Selects Shredded Chicken & Beef in Gravy	0.99	45.53	0.48	15.58	31.79	23.96	1-Feb-20
Lovibles One Cool Chick	0.99	45.90	2.49	29.60	12.00	25.68	21-Jan-20
Weruva Jolly Good Fares Chicken & Salmon Pâté	0.99	61.10	0.29	22.90	9.50	21.27	26-Jan-20
Cats in the Kitchen Cat to the Future Pâté Pouch	0.99	61.10	0.29	22.90	9.50	21.33	26-Jan-20
Soulistic Chicken & Salmon Pâté Pouch	0.99	61.10	0.29	22.90	9.50	21.33	27-Jan-20
Truluxe Kawa Booty	0.99	69.60	1.06	15.80	6.40	18.67	26-Jan-20
Cats in the Kitchen Funk in the Trunk	0.99	72.00	0.38	13.50	8.90	17.83	26-Jan-20
Catered Bowl Antibiotic-Free Turkey & Brown Rice*	1.00	30.00	0.36	18.40	39.00	33.64	11-Nov-19
Tender & True Antibiotic-Free Turkey & Brown Rice*	1.00	30.00	0.36	18.40	39.00	33.64	11-Nov-19
GO! Solutions Sensitivities Limited Ingredient Grain-Free Duck Pâté	1.00	36.00	0.64	26.00	31.00	28.66	31-Oct-19
PetGuard Weight Management Chicken & Stew Dinner	1.00	37.50	0.32	16.60	33.10	27.00	18-Dec-19
PetGuard Weight Management Turkey & Barley Dinner	1.00	38.60	0.30	15.90	28.60	28.30	18-Dec-19
NOW! Fresh Pork Pâté	1.00	39.00	0.32	19.00	35.00	31.59	31-Oct-19
Nature's Harvest Kitten Grain-Free Chicken Pâté*	1.00	40.64	0.38	34.10	12.73	31.27	2-Dec-19
Halo Gluten-Free Chicken and Trout Indoor	1.00	44.50	0.60	38.20	9.04	33.64	30-Jan-20
PetGuard Premium Feast Dinner	1.00	45.40	0.37	22.70	17.70	31.00	18-Dec-19

Brand and Variety	Phos	Prot	Sod	Fat	Carb	Cals	Obtained
Rayne Clinical Nutrition Growth/Sensitive-GI	1.00	52.01	0.45	23.65	18.67	33.82	27-Nov-19
Kasiks Wild Caught Coho Salmon	1.00	59.00	0.80	16.00	26.00	24.00	25-Nov-19
Best Feline Friend PLAY Tubular Chicken & Tuna Pâté Pouch	1.00	59.40	0.76	29.40	4.50	27.67	27-Jan-20
Natural Balance Delectable Delights Sea Brûlée Stew	1.00	59.41	0.67	20.10	12.42	28.00	9-Jan-17
Dave's Naturally Healthy Grain-Free Tuna & Mackerel Dinner In Gravy*	1.00	62.40	0.44	17.50	11.20	17.64	7-Nov-19
Weruva Meows n' Holler PurrAmid Chicken & Shrimp Pâté	1.00	62.60	0.46	20.80	9.10	20.73	26-Jan-20
Soulistic Tri-Fusion Tuna with Grilled Salmon, Beef & Duck Dinner in Gravy	1.00	63.83	0.48	12.44	19.45	22.73	27-Jan-20
Koha L.I.D. Shredded Chicken Entrée in Gravy*	1.00	68.98	1.12	21.34	1.12	23.82	27-Nov-19
AvoDerm Grain-Free Tuna & Chicken Entrée with Vegetables	1.00	69.80	0.50	19.33	16.70	27.00	15-Oct-19
Tiki Cat Grain-Free Succulent Chicken with Egg in Chicken Consommé (Koolina Luau)*	1.00	72.73	na	18.18	0.00	25.00	30-Jan-20
Best Feline Friend Originals Valentine Tuna & Pumpkin Minced in Gravy	1.00	75.00	0.64	15.20	5.60	23.64	27-Jan-20
Tiki Cat Grain-Free Ahi Tuna with Crab in Tuna Consommé (Hana Grill)*	1.00	75.00	na	16.67	0.00	26.79	30-Jan-20
Solid Gold Flavorful Feast Grain-Free Pâté with Salmon & Beef*	1.01	35.00	0.52	24.00	34.20	29.33	22-Jan-20
Wellness Core Signature Selects Chunky Beef & Chicken in Sauce	1.01	40.63	0.53	14.57	36.74	23.58	1-Feb-20
Organix Grain-Free Organic Shredded Chicken and Chicken Liver	1.01	41.80	0.70	33.80	12.94	31.82	29-Oct-19
Performatrin Adult Grain-Free Beef	1.01	47.90	0.69	35.80	6.70	35.00	28-Nov-19
Performatrin Ultra Grain-Free Trout Bisque	1.01	53.00	1.17	24.00	10.30	29.64	21-Jan-20

Brand and Variety	Phos	Prot	Sod	Fat	Carb	Cals	Obtained
Tiki Cat Grain-Free Velvet Mousse Chicken with Egg*	1.01	54.55	na	36.36	na	28.21	30-Jan-20
Cats in the Kitchen The Breakfast Cat Pâté Pouch	1.01	59.10	0.30	21.40	11.90	19.33	26-Jan-20
Soulistic Chicken & Pumpkin Pâté Pouch	1.01	59.10	0.30	21.40	11.90	19.33	27-Jan-20
Weruva Who Wants to be a Meowionaire? Chicken & Pumpkin Pâté	1.01	59.10	0.30	21.40	11.90	19.33	26-Jan-20
AvoDerm Grain-Free Tuna & Crab Entrée in Gravy	1.01	59.77	0.90	13.26	8.30	23.33	15-Oct-19
Best Feline Friend PLAY 'Til Then Chicken & Tuna Pâté	1.01	60.50	0.80	28.10	4.60	26.18	27-Jan-20
Soulistic Chicken & Tuna Pâté	1.01	60.50	0.80	28.10	4.60	26.36	27-Jan-20
Best Feline Friend PLAY Totes! Tuna & Turkey Pâté Pouch	1.01	66.70	0.60	24.00	2.90	27.33	27-Jan-20
Soulistic Upstream Dream Salmon & Tuna Dinner in Gelée	1.01	72.81	0.76	15.73	5.28	20.55	27-Jan-20
Cats in the Kitchen Goldie Lox	1.01	75.40	0.39	14.10	4.60	18.50	26-Jan-20
Lotus Grain-Free Turkey Pâté	1.02	35.64	0.73	28.14	25.54	27.12	28-Jan-20
Nature's Harvest Mature Grain-Free Chicken Pâté*	1.02	38.24	0.38	32.05	16.24	29.09	2-Dec-19
Wellness Core Grain-Free 95% Beef & Chicken	1.02	49.41	0.39	39.80	1.38	37.64	1-Feb-20
Fromm Turkey & Duck Pâté	1.02	49.76	0.97	25.92	na	30.36	31-Jan-20
Fromm Beef Pâté	1.02	53.30	1.08	21.09	na	25.27	31-Jan-20
Natural Balance Delectable Delights Catatouille Stew	1.02	63.52	0.55	19.27	9.33	24.00	9-Jan-17
Best Feline Friend PLAY Chill Out Tuna & Chicken Pâté Pouch	1.02	65.80	0.60	25.30	2.60	27.67	27-Jan-20
Best Feline Friend PLAY TTYL Tuna & Turkey Pâté	1.02	67.20	0.60	22.60	3.80	26.73	27-Jan-20
Weruva Tic Tac Whoa! Tuna & Salmon Pâté	1.02	75.20	0.56	7.90	9.00	14.18	26-Jan-20
Truluxe Quick 'N Quirky	1.02	78.60	0.36	13.80	0.50	17.17	26-Jan-20
Dave's Cat's Meow Chicken with Duck*	1.03	38.24	1.78	26.85	21.10	32.36	7-Nov-19

Brand and Variety	Phos	Prot	Sod	Fat	Carb	Cals	Obtained
Organix Grain-Free Organic Turkey Pâté	1.03	41.60	0.76	42.40	7.86	34.91	29-Oct-19
Best Feline Friend OMG Shazaam! Lamb & Tuna in Gravy Pouch	1.03	48.00	0.40	34.20	12.70	26.43	27-Jan-20
Performatrin Ultra Grain-Free Beef Stew	1.03	49.40	0.91	23.70	13.70	32.00	28-Nov-19
Performatrin Adult Grain-Free Beef & Liver	1.03	49.60	0.51	33.50	7.30	33.00	28-Nov-19
Soulistic Moist & Tender Salmon Dinner in Gravy Canned	1.03	50.48	0.67	32.45	8.41	28.36	27-Jan-20
Dave's Naturally Healthy Grain-Free Tuna & Shrimp Dinner In Gravy*	1.03	63.70	0.51	18.00	10.00	24.91	7-Nov-19
Best Feline Friend PLAY Check Please! Tuna & Chicken Pâté	1.03	66.30	0.60	23.90	3.50	26.91	27-Jan-20
Earthborn Holistic Grain-Free Monterey Medley	1.03	70.82	0.48	10.25	11.11	24.20	15-Jan-20
Truluxe Honor Roll	1.03	71.30	0.33	18.30	3.40	18.33	26-Jan-20
Performatrin Healthy Weight Turkey	1.04	42.20	0.43	19.70	23.10	26.91	28-Nov-19
Hound & Gatos Grain-Free 98% Salmon, Mackerel & Sardine	1.04	52.95	0.48	47.26	na	39.82	8-Nov-19
Weruva Meow Luau	1.04	74.90	0.29	15.90	3.60	20.91	26-Jan-20
Tiki Cat Grain-Free Ahi Tuna & Mackerel in Tuna Consommé (Papeekeo Luau)*	1.04	79.17	na	16.67	0.00	25.71	30-Jan-20
Tiki Cat Grain-Free Ahi Tuna & Chicken in Chicken Consommé (Hookena Luau)*	1.04	83.33	na	12.50	0.00	29.64	30-Jan-20
Wellness Core Signature Selects Chunky Chicken & Wild Salmon in Sauce	1.05	34.53	0.53	25.80	32.04	24.72	1-Feb-20
Only Natural Pet Chicken & Chicken Liver Dinner*	1.05	40.91	0.73	22.73	29.09	31.89	29-Jan-20
Only Natural Pet Chicken & Egg Dinner*	1.05	40.91	0.73	22.73	29.14	30.94	29-Jan-20
Identity 95% Free-Range Prairie Pork	1.05	44.22	0.42	10.86	10.41	23.64	20-Jan-20

Brand and Variety	Phos	Prot	Sod	Fat	Carb	Cals	Obtained
Whole Earth Farms Grain-Free Real Salmon Pâté	1.05	45.20	0.32	30.80	11.77	33.20	25-Oct-19
Whole Earth Farms Grain-Free Real Turkey Pâté	1.05	46.80	0.36	28.50	14.15	37.20	25-Oct-19
Organix Grain-Free Organic Chicken and Chicken Liver Pâté	1.05	47.50	0.84	36.60	5.31	33.27	29-Oct-19
Azmira Beef & Chicken*	1.05	57.18	0.64	22.55	na	34.55	5-Dec-16
Cats in the Kitchen Lamb Burger-ini	1.05	57.70	0.55	24.70	9.70	25.67	26-Jan-20
Best Feline Friend PLAY Shhh… Tuna & Salmon Pâté Pouch	1.05	62.60	0.59	27.90	3.60	30.00	27-Jan-20
Dave's Naturally Healthy Grain-Free Tuna and Chicken Dinner in Gravy*	1.05	66.10	0.50	13.70	11.70	23.09	7-Nov-19
Weruva Marbella Paella	1.05	73.40	0.42	18.00	1.00	20.55	26-Jan-20
Tiki Cat Grain-Free Aloha Friends Tuna & Pumpkin*	1.05	75.00	na	18.75	0.00	17.33	30-Jan-20
Nature's Harvest Adult Grain-Free Chicken Pâté*	1.06	40.16	0.65	34.72	12.16	26.36	2-Dec-19
Grandma Mae's Country Naturals Grain-Free Beef & Chicken Chunks in Gravy*	1.06	44.44	0.72	13.89	na	24.29	23-Nov-19
Earthborn Holistic Grain-Free Chicken Jumble with Liver	1.06	48.33	0.29	20.83	29.41	25.00	15-Jan-20
Merrick Backcountry Grain-Free Real Beef Cuts	1.06	51.06	1.38	25.11	14.17	26.67	26-Nov-19
RAWZ 96% Turkey & Salmon Pâté	1.06	55.68	0.46	29.47	4.10	30.73	3-Dec-19
Tiki Cat Grain-Free Velvet Mousse Chicken*	1.06	59.09	na	36.36	na	28.21	30-Jan-20
Weruva Meal of Fortune Chicken Breast Pâté with Chicken Liver Pouch	1.06	59.90	0.34	24.10	9.70	20.00	26-Jan-20
Nature's Harvest Adult Grain-Free Turkey Pâté*	1.07	38.29	0.43	35.18	14.23	26.36	2-Dec-19
Wellness Complete Health Chicken Pâté	1.07	42.07	0.30	21.14	26.96	33.82	1-Feb-20
Trader Joe Chicken/Turkey & Rice	1.07	44.11	0.57	33.38	17.80	33.09	28-Nov-16
Nutrisca Truly Flaked Tuna & Crab Entrée In Savory Broth*	1.07	64.20	1.23	16.00	8.80	20.74	21-Jan-20

Brand and Variety	Phos	Prot	Sod	Fat	Carb	Cals	Obtained
Natural Balance L.I.D. Limited Ingredient Tuna & Pumpkin in Broth	1.07	74.10	1.64	14.71	1.36	23.27	9-Jan-17
Tiki Cat Grain-Free Succulent Chicken in Chicken Consommé (Puka Puka Luau)*	1.07	81.82	na	13.64	0.00	24.64	30-Jan-20
Dave's 95% Premium Meat Chicken & Chicken Liver Pâté*	1.08	35.20	0.60	29.12	10.70	37.09	7-Nov-19
Dave's Cat's Meow Beef with Duck*	1.08	44.86	1.60	25.22	18.02	33.27	7-Nov-19
AvoDerm Chicken Formula	1.08	47.80	0.85	38.30	13.50	33.82	15-Oct-19
Best Feline Friend OMG Selfie Cam! Chicken & Lamb Minced in Gravy	1.08	48.40	0.38	32.80	12.00	24.18	27-Jan-20
Merrick Backcountry Grain-Free Real Whitefish Cuts	1.08	50.96	1.51	22.07	17.13	25.67	26-Nov-19
Dr Elsey's Clean Protein Turkey Pâté	1.08	51.88	0.42	38.33	1.25	36.73	22-Sep-19
Best Feline Friend OMG Booya! Beef & Chicken in Gravy Pouch	1.08	60.70	0.46	23.40	9.70	18.57	27-Jan-20
Solid Gold Five Oceans Shreds with Shrimp & Tuna in Gravy*	1.08	68.00	0.32	15.00	9.00	19.83	22-Jan-20
Merrick Limited Ingredient Grain-Free Salmon	1.09	39.90	0.30	39.40	5.84	26.20	26-Jun-19
Only Natural Pet Seafood Dinner*	1.09	40.91	0.55	22.73	33.41	28.11	29-Jan-20
Performatrin Indoor Chicken	1.09	43.20	0.46	24.00	15.80	29.27	28-Nov-19
Fromm Turkey Pâté	1.09	43.28	0.97	29.67	na	29.64	31-Jan-20
Azmira Ocean Fish*	1.09	50.18	0.50	45.82	na	30.72	5-Dec-16
Merrick Backcountry Real Rabbit Cuts	1.09	52.35	1.41	22.98	14.91	26.67	26-Nov-19
Dave's Cat's Meow 95% Turkey & Turkey Liver*	1.09	58.68	0.47	27.95	9.22	35.82	7-Nov-19
Weruva Name 'Dat Tuna Tuna Pâté Pouch	1.09	71.70	0.18	14.60	7.30	15.64	26-Jan-20
Dave's Naturally Healthy Grain-Free Poultry Platter Dinner*	1.10	38.09	0.52	29.39	6.16	36.73	7-Nov-19
NOW Fresh Chicken Pâté	1.10	39.00	0.42	27.00	27.00	33.02	31-Oct-19
NOW Fresh Wild Salmon Stew	1.10	40.00	0.30	23.00	39.00	30.72	31-Oct-19

Brand and Variety	Phos	Prot	Sod	Fat	Carb	Cals	Obtained
NOW Fresh Wild Salmon Pâté	1.10	40.00	0.35	23.00	29.00	30.04	31-Oct-19
NOW Fresh Turkey Stew	1.10	40.00	0.40	24.00	26.00	30.21	31-Oct-19
Identity 95% Free-Range NZ Lamb	1.10	42.03	0.45	36.01	9.41	31.45	20-Jan-20
PetGuard Beef & Barley Dinner	1.10	43.00	0.27	22.70	19.50	31.00	18-Dec-19
Halo Holistic Grain-Free Turkey Adult	1.10	43.20	0.20	40.70	6.80	35.45	30-Jan-20
AvoDerm Grain-Free Chicken & Duck Recipe in Gravy Pouch	1.10	44.00	0.45	16.00	13.90	19.13	15-Oct-19
PetGuard Fish, Chicken & Liver Dinner	1.10	45.40	0.44	20.00	20.90	29.30	18-Dec-19
PetGuard Chicken & Beef Dinner	1.10	45.50	0.32	29.50	11.30	34.10	18-Dec-19
Nulo FreeStyle Shredded Turkey & Halibut in Gravy	1.10	56.07	1.20	24.00	9.99	26.00	26-Nov-19
Nulo MedalSeries Shredded Turkey & Halibut in Gravy	1.10	56.07	1.20	24.00	9.99	26.00	26-Nov-19
Cats in the Kitchen The Double Dip	1.10	61.00	0.28	23.30	9.70	16.67	26-Jan-20
Tiki Cat Grain-Free Velvet Mousse Chicken and Wild Salmon*	1.10	61.90	na	33.33	na	28.93	30-Jan-20
Soulistic Tuna & Salmon Pâté	1.10	63.20	0.59	26.40	4.30	0.00	27-Jan-20
Best Feline Friend PLAY Oh Snap Tuna & Salmon Pâté	1.10	63.20	0.59	26.40	4.30	29.82	27-Jan-20
Earthborn Holistic Grain-Free Harbor Harvest	1.10	64.24	0.33	12.79	16.67	25.60	15-Jan-20
Petite Cuisine Sister Rose's Tuna, Pumpkin & Ocean Fish	1.10	74.70	1.68	19.50	na	23.21	29-Oct-19
Against the Grain Shrimp Daddy with Tuna & Salmon	1.10	76.20	0.80	14.20	1.94	25.00	30-Oct-19
Petite Cuisine Baby Bluebell's Chicken & Pumpkin	1.10	80.30	0.32	11.20	na	22.86	29-Oct-19
Fussie Cat Premium Tuna with Smoked Tuna*	1.10	80.82	0.18	9.72	na	21.55	5-Dec-19
Tiki Cat Grain-Free Velvet Mousse Tuna & Chicken*	1.11	68.18	na	27.27	na	26.79	30-Jan-20
Fancy Feast Purely Natural White Meat Chicken and Flaked Tuna Entrée in a Delicate Broth*	1.11	72.22	1.11	8.33	0.00	20.50	9-May-18

Brand and Variety	Phos	Prot	Sod	Fat	Carb	Cals	Obtained
Fancy Feast Purely Natural Wild Alaskan Salmon & White Meat Chicken in a Delicate Broth*	1.11	75.00	0.28	8.33	0.00	23.50	9-May-18
Fussie Cat Super Premium Chicken & Beef in Pumpkin Soup*	1.11	76.25	0.17	13.18	na	20.10	5-Dec-19
Fussie Cat Premium Tuna with Threadfin Bream*	1.11	76.50	0.18	9.15	na	21.18	5-Dec-19
Fancy Feast Purely Natural White Meat Chicken Entrée in a Delicate Broth*	1.11	80.56	0.28	8.33	0.00	22.50	9-May-18
Hill's Healthy Advantage Kitten Chicken Entrée	1.12	43.40	0.39	22.90	25.60	31.45	1-Feb-20
Hound & Gatos Grain-Free 98% Pork	1.12	54.08	0.39	35.42	na	35.64	8-Nov-19
Nutrisca Truly Flaked Salmon Entrée In Savory Broth*	1.12	54.10	0.51	24.80	12.70	22.96	21-Jan-20
Tiki Cat Grain-Free Wild Salmon in Salmon Consommé (Hanalei Luau)*	1.12	65.22	na	21.74	0.00	19.64	30-Jan-20
NutriSource Grain-Free High Plains Select	1.13	40.83	0.33	27.08	na	31.82	28-Jan-20
Whole Earth Farms Grain-Free Real Chicken Pâté	1.13	47.20	0.30	25.90	12.29	33.60	25-Oct-19
Merrick Backcountry Grain-Free Real Kitten Cuts	1.13	50.70	1.24	26.74	na	27.33	26-Nov-19
RAWZ 96% Beef & Beef Liver Pâté	1.13	51.64	0.65	24.76	11.38	32.00	3-Dec-19
Lotus Grain-Free Just Juicy Pork Stew	1.13	68.28	1.17	16.43	7.45	24.55	28-Jan-20
Artemis OSOPure Grain-Free Tuna & Pumpkin	1.13	70.71	0.65	12.05	1.62	21.33	23-Nov-16
Artemis OSOPure Grain-Free Tuna	1.13	71.70	0.56	12.43	1.42	21.67	23-Nov-16
Artemis OSOPure Grain-Free Tuna & Shrimp	1.13	71.94	0.67	12.03	1.40	22.00	23-Nov-16
Tiki Cat Grain-Free Aloha Friends Tuna, Tilapia & Pumpkin*	1.13	77.78	na	16.67	0.00	18.67	30-Jan-20
PureVita Grain-Free Beef Entrée	1.14	52.45	0.41	29.00	na	31.47	28-Jan-20
Nutrisca Truly Flaked Tuna & Salmon Entrée In Savory Broth*	1.14	60.60	0.47	14.40	16.30	22.22	21-Jan-20

43

Brand and Variety	Phos	Prot	Sod	Fat	Carb	Cals	Obtained
Tiki Cat Grain-Free Ahi Tuna with Prawns in Tuna Consommé (Manana Grill)*	1.14	76.00	na	16.00	0.00	25.36	30-Jan-20
Earthborn Holistic Grain-Free Catalina Catch	1.14	78.65	0.29	13.29	0.55	30.00	15-Jan-20
Newman's Own Organic Grain-Free Liver	1.15	40.00	0.47	35.00	16.00	30.91	14-Nov-19
Newman's Own Premium Chicken & Brown Rice	1.15	40.00	0.47	35.00	16.00	32.00	14-Nov-19
Newman's Own Organic Grain-Free Beef & Liver	1.15	40.00	0.47	35.00	16.00	32.55	14-Nov-19
Newman's Own Premium Turkey	1.15	40.00	0.47	35.00	16.00	32.55	14-Nov-19
Newman's Own Premium Turkey & Vegetable	1.15	40.00	0.47	35.00	16.00	34.00	14-Nov-19
Newman's Own Premium Chicken & Salmon	1.15	40.00	0.47	35.00	16.00	37.27	14-Nov-19
Newman's Own Organic Grain-Free Beef	1.15	40.00	0.47	35.00	16.00	38.18	14-Nov-19
Koha Grain-Free Limited Ingredient Guineafowl Pâté*	1.15	45.20	0.63	41.50	4.28	37.09	13-Aug-19
Merrick Backcountry Real Chicken Cuts	1.15	50.48	1.44	25.55	14.75	26.33	26-Nov-19
President's Choice Extra Meaty Sliced Duck & Wild Rice	1.15	51.05	1.29	22.01	16.75	na	12-Dec-19
Natural Balance Delectable Delights Purrrfect Paella Stew	1.15	59.74	0.71	19.18	10.31	24.00	9-Jan-17
Tiki Cat Grain-Free After Dark Chicken & Beef*	1.15	66.67	na	16.67	0.00	24.29	30-Jan-20
Artemis OSOPure Grain-Free Tuna & Salmon	1.15	70.24	0.52	13.59	1.50	21.67	23-Nov-16
Artemis OSOPure Grain-Free Tuna & Chicken	1.15	71.60	0.52	12.57	1.42	21.67	23-Nov-16
Petite Cuisine Sweet Ivy's Chicken & Sweet Potato Entrée in Broth	1.15	73.80	0.47	11.30	na	22.50	29-Oct-19
Wellness Healthy Indulgence Shreds with Skipjack Tuna & Shrimp Pouch	1.16	40.09	0.68	30.40	18.81	19.00	1-Feb-20
Trader Joe Turkey & Giblets	1.16	44.50	0.58	34.20	13.30	32.73	28-Nov-16

Brand and Variety	Phos	Prot	Sod	Fat	Carb	Cals	Obtained
Trader Joe Ocean Fish, Salmon & Rice	1.16	45.82	0.72	31.99	14.66	32.00	28-Nov-16
Dave's Naturally Healthy Grain-Free Beef & Chicken Dinner*	1.16	48.19	0.46	41.50	1.83	35.45	7-Nov-19
VeRUS Chicken and Liver	1.16	49.40	0.76	38.00	0.20	30.91	27-Jan-20
Holistic Select Grain-Free Turkey Pâté Recipe	1.16	52.71	0.43	35.09	2.92	36.62	1-Feb-20
Solid Gold Flavorful Feast Grain-Free Kitten Classic Pâté with Chicken*	1.16	56.00	0.26	17.00	18.00	35.67	22-Jan-20
Performatrin Grain-Free Ultra Chicken Stew	1.16	57.10	0.81	20.10	9.10	26.36	28-Nov-19
Solid Gold Five Oceans Shreds with Sardine & Tuna in Gravy*	1.16	61.11	0.34	11.11	8.00	22.50	8-Nov-19
AvoDerm Grain-Free Ocean Fish Recipe in Gravy Pouch	1.16	62.00	0.94	12.50	12.50	17.70	15-Oct-19
Best Feline Friend PLAY Twinkles Turkey & Tuna Pâté Pouch	1.16	62.30	0.44	29.30	0.00	27.67	27-Jan-20
Dave's Naturally Healthy Grain-Free Ahi Tuna & Chicken Dinner*	1.16	72.30	0.46	13.50	3.00	25.45	11-Nov-19
Tiki Cat Grain-Free Wild Salmon & Chicken in Chicken Consommé (Napili Luau)*	1.16	73.91	na	17.39	0.00	25.36	30-Jan-20
Fussie Cat Premium Tuna with Mussels*	1.16	79.45	0.20	12.19	na	20.78	5-Dec-19
Catered Bowl Ocean Whitefish & Potato*	1.17	30.00	0.41	18.60	38.00	28.18	11-Nov-19
Tender & True Ocean Whitefish & Potato*	1.17	30.00	0.41	18.60	38.00	28.18	11-Nov-19
Fromm Lamb Pâté	1.17	42.88	1.04	29.50	na	27.82	31-Jan-20
Grandma Mae's Country Naturals Grain-Free Chicken Chunks in Gravy*	1.17	44.44	0.61	16.67	na	25.71	23-Nov-19
President's Choice Extra Meaty Chicken	1.17	48.47	0.95	38.07	5.01	na	12-Dec-19
Performatrin Adult Grain-Free Turkey	1.17	49.40	0.50	37.10	3.60	34.00	28-Nov-19
Life's Abundance Instinctive Choice All Life Stage	1.17	50.00	0.45	33.33	na	36.00	27-Nov-19

45

Brand and Variety	Phos	Prot	Sod	Fat	Carb	Cals	Obtained
Dr Elsey's Clean Protein Beef Pâté	1.17	50.00	0.50	28.79	15.71	32.73	22-Sep-19
NutriSource Grain-Free Ocean Select	1.17	57.17	0.54	28.88	na	31.82	28-Jan-20
Nulo FreeStyle Shredded Beef & Rainbow Trout in Gravy	1.17	58.56	1.17	19.96	10.37	24.67	26-Nov-19
Nulo MedalSeries Shredded Beef & Rainbow Trout in Gravy	1.17	58.56	1.17	19.96	10.37	24.67	26-Nov-19
Fancy Feast Purely Natural Flaked Skipjack Tuna in a Delicate Broth*	1.17	77.78	0.56	8.33	0.22	21.00	9-May-18
Fussie Cat Premium Tuna with Clams*	1.17	79.49	0.21	12.31	na	20.55	5-Dec-19
Fussie Cat Premium Tuna with Chicken*	1.17	81.73	0.20	11.22	na	21.26	5-Dec-19
Fancy Feast Purely Natural Tender Tongol Tuna Entrée in a Delicate Broth*	1.17	83.33	0.44	8.33	0.00	22.50	9-May-18
Only Natural Pet Turkey & Liver Dinner*	1.18	40.91	0.86	22.73	31.91	34.15	29-Jan-20
Lotus Grain-Free Chicken Pâté	1.18	41.51	0.85	23.39	22.70	29.84	28-Jan-20
Lotus Grain-Free Pork Pâté	1.18	41.87	0.86	24.31	23.29	31.44	28-Jan-20
Diamond Naturals Indoor Cat Hairball Control Adult Dinner	1.18	42.58	0.43	26.98	15.74	29.64	11-Nov-19
Hound & Gatos Grain-Free 98% Paleolithic	1.18	42.92	0.37	31.92	na	33.27	8-Nov-19
Hill's Science Diet Kitten Savory Turkey Entrée	1.18	44.20	0.50	29.60	15.10	36.91	1-Feb-20
Koha Grain-Free Turkey Stew*	1.18	45.60	1.23	34.20	11.14	26.55	13-Aug-19
AvoDerm Salmon Formula	1.18	47.68	0.49	31.63	13.55	36.00	15-Oct-19
President's Choice Extra Meaty Chicken & Liver	1.18	50.77	0.92	31.99	7.53	na	12-Dec-19
Solid Gold Five Oceans Shreds with Mackerel & Tuna in Gravy*	1.18	61.11	0.39	11.11	9.00	22.17	8-Nov-19
Lotus Grain-Free Just Juicy Venison Stew	1.18	61.91	0.82	21.36	7.79	32.26	28-Jan-20
Tiki Cat Grain-Free Aloha Friends Tuna, Whitefish & Pumpkin*	1.18	70.00	na	15.00	0.00	18.67	30-Jan-20
Tiki Cat Grain-Free Ahi Tuna (Hawaiian Grill)*	1.18	73.91	na	17.39	0.00	26.43	30-Jan-20

Brand and Variety	Phos	Prot	Sod	Fat	Carb	Cals	Obtained
Fussie Cat Super Premium Chicken with Chicken Liver in Pumpkin Soup*	1.18	76.27	0.12	12.13	na	18.71	5-Dec-19
AvoDerm Wild by Nature Grain-Free Tuna with Prawns in Consommé	1.18	78.77	1.04	15.32	5.60	23.67	15-Oct-19
Fussie Cat Premium Tuna with Anchovies*	1.18	79.16	1.53	11.08	na	22.28	5-Dec-19
Fussie Cat Premium Tuna with Shrimp*	1.18	80.42	0.44	11.61	na	21.09	5-Dec-19
Natural Balance Platefulls Chicken & Pumpkin in Gravy Pouch	1.19	42.15	0.90	27.15	20.83	26.67	9-Jan-17
Wellness Core Tiny Tasters Duck Pouch	1.19	46.63	0.86	39.12	3.82	36.57	1-Feb-20
Holistic Select Grain-Free Ocean Fish & Tuna Pâté Recipe	1.19	55.49	0.68	30.89	4.21	35.31	1-Feb-20
Best Feline Friend PLAY Tweet Me! Turkey & Tuna Pâté	1.19	58.40	0.45	28.10	5.00	26.36	27-Jan-20
Fussie Cat Premium Tuna with Ocean Fish*	1.19	77.14	0.41	11.40	na	20.87	5-Dec-19
Fussie Cat Premium Tuna with Salmon*	1.19	80.87	0.23	12.07	na	21.26	5-Dec-19
Catered Bowl Organic Turkey & Liver*	1.20	30.00	0.32	19.50	33.00	33.64	11-Nov-19
Tender & True Organic Turkey & Liver*	1.20	30.00	0.32	19.50	33.00	33.64	11-Nov-19
FirstMate Cage-Free Turkey & Rice	1.20	31.00	0.70	31.00	29.00	31.00	25-Nov-19
FirstMate Limited Ingredient Free Run Turkey	1.20	31.00	0.80	31.00	29.00	31.00	25-Nov-19
Kasiks Cage-Free Turkey	1.20	31.00	0.80	31.00	30.00	29.00	25-Nov-19
Redbarn Naturals Lamb Pâté for Skin & Coat Health	1.20	43.31	0.28	41.20	7.70	37.27	31-Oct-19
Hound & Gatos Grain-Free 98% Turkey & Liver	1.20	44.38	0.62	38.09	na	34.73	8-Nov-19
Tiki Cat Grain-Free After Dark Chicken & Lamb*	1.20	44.44	na	22.22	0.00	23.21	30-Jan-20

Brand and Variety	Phos	Prot	Sod	Fat	Carb	Cals	Obtained
Halo Holistic Grain-Free Chicken Kitten	1.20	44.90	0.40	37.70	8.60	35.33	30-Jan-20
Halo Holistic Grain-Free Chicken Adult	1.20	46.60	0.30	35.10	7.80	29.09	30-Jan-20
Halo Holistic Sensitive Stomach Grain-Free Quail and Garden Greens Recipe Pâté	1.20	46.90	0.40	32.00	10.10	33.64	30-Jan-20
Halo Holistic Grain-Free Chicken and Beef Adult	1.20	47.70	0.30	38.50	4.80	34.36	30-Jan-20
Taste of the Wild Rocky Mountain with Salmon and Roasted Venison in Gravy	1.20	48.30	1.20	22.90	17.80	27.50	23-Sep-19
Taste of the Wild Canyon River with Trout and Salmon in Gravy	1.20	48.30	1.20	30.00	10.70	26.93	23-Sep-19
PetGuard Chicken & Wheat Germ Dinner	1.20	50.00	0.30	22.70	11.80	32.50	18-Dec-19
PetGuard Savory Seafood Dinner	1.20	50.00	0.54	20.40	12.20	32.70	18-Dec-19
Nulo MedalSeries Minced Turkey & Duck in Gravy	1.20	55.91	1.15	23.10	10.76	25.67	26-Nov-19
Nulo FreeStyle Minced Turkey & Duck in Gravy	1.20	55.91	1.15	23.10	10.76	25.67	26-Nov-19
Solid Gold Flavorful Feast Grain-Free Pâté Indoor Recipe with Chicken*	1.20	56.00	0.23	17.00	18.00	34.00	22-Jan-20
Against the Grain Aloha Tuna with Seaweed & Crab	1.20	75.30	0.63	16.90	0.00	23.93	30-Oct-19
Fussie Cat Premium Tuna with Prawns*	1.20	80.20	0.37	11.86	na	20.84	5-Dec-19
Performatrin Ultra Grain-Free Turkey, Salmon & Duck Pâté	1.21	44.90	0.42	40.30	4.20	39.45	28-Nov-19
NutriSource Grain-Free Lamb & Lamb Liver Select	1.21	45.00	0.38	33.50	na	33.64	28-Jan-20
Performatrin Adult Grain-Free Chicken	1.21	45.40	0.58	41.10	3.70	38.00	28-Nov-19
Lotus Grain-Free Sardine Pâté	1.21	50.36	1.17	16.17	20.09	27.36	28-Jan-20
Hound & Gatos Grain-Free 98% Lamb & Liver	1.21	53.56	0.38	35.42	na	34.00	8-Nov-19
Nulo MedalSeries Minced Beef & Mackerel in Gravy	1.21	57.99	1.16	19.53	11.24	24.67	26-Nov-19

48

Brand and Variety	Phos	Prot	Sod	Fat	Carb	Cals	Obtained
Nulo FreeStyle Minced Beef & Mackerel in Gravy	1.21	57.99	1.16	19.53	11.24	24.67	26-Nov-19
Tiki Cat Grain-Free Velvet Mousse Wild Salmon*	1.21	66.67	na	23.81	na	28.57	30-Jan-20
Tiki Cat Grain-Free Aloha Friends Tuna, Calamari & Pumpkin*	1.21	72.22	na	16.67	0.00	17.67	30-Jan-20
Wellness Core Hearty Cuts Shredded Whitefish & Salmon	1.22	50.89	1.45	18.73	18.68	23.64	1-Feb-20
Lovibles Put a Wing on It	1.22	51.60	0.45	33.10	4.10	32.14	21-Jan-20
Instinct Original Grain-Free 95% Real Beef Pâté	1.22	52.96	0.42	34.49	1.39	40.36	8-Nov-19
Best Feline Friend PLAY Lovers' Lane Tuna & Lamb Pâté	1.22	65.30	0.61	24.30	3.60	27.86	27-Jan-20
Weruva Asian Fusion	1.22	73.40	1.00	18.00	1.00	21.82	26-Jan-20
Fussie Cat Premium Tuna with Chicken Liver*	1.22	76.05	0.18	11.33	na	17.83	5-Dec-19
Tiki Cat Grain-Free Ahi Tuna in Crab Surimi Consommé (Lanai Grill)*	1.22	77.27	na	18.18	0.00	26.79	30-Jan-20
Fancy Feast Purely Natural Seabass and Shrimp in a Delicate Broth*	1.22	77.78	0.67	11.11	0.00	22.50	9-May-18
Against the Grain Bimini Brunch with Krill & Egg	1.22	79.10	0.41	12.60	0.00	25.00	30-Oct-19
Only Natural Pet Turkey & Chicken Dinner*	1.23	40.91	0.86	22.73	30.55	34.34	29-Jan-20
Lotus Grain-Free Duck Pâté	1.23	44.70	0.90	19.75	23.15	28.16	28-Jan-20
Hill's Science Diet Kitten Liver & Chicken Entrée	1.23	45.50	0.50	29.20	14.80	37.82	1-Feb-20
Redbarn Naturals Grain-Free Salmon Stew	1.23	50.12	1.50	31.18	6.87	27.67	31-Oct-19
Merrick Purrfect Bistro Grain-Free Beef Wellington	1.23	54.50	1.71	21.33	9.81	25.10	26-Jun-19
Best Feline Friend PLAY Tuck Me In Salmon & Tuna Pâté	1.23	54.90	0.53	33.50	4.70	31.27	27-Jan-20
Fussie Cat Premium Tuna in Aspic*	1.23	81.35	2.08	9.51	na	19.99	5-Dec-19

Brand and Variety	Phos	Prot	Sod	Fat	Carb	Cals	Obtained
Natural Balance Platefulls Indoor Chicken & Chicken Liver in Gravy Pouch	1.24	42.29	0.85	23.50	24.36	24.33	9-Jan-17
Redbarn Naturals Grain-Free Chicken Stew	1.24	42.93	1.44	33.94	12.20	26.00	31-Oct-19
Performatrin Grain-Free Ultra Turkey Pâté	1.24	44.90	0.40	40.40	4.00	39.64	28-Nov-19
Natural Balance Platefulls Tuna & Beef in Gravy Pouch	1.24	45.64	1.04	24.59	18.14	26.67	9-Jan-17
Natural Balance Ultra Premium Tuna with Shrimp	1.24	50.51	0.88	22.96	16.93	31.45	9-Jan-17
Nulo MedalSeries Limited Ingredient Diet 95% Turkey & Turkey Liver in Broth	1.24	52.70	0.44	32.98	7.01	37.27	26-Nov-19
Performatrin Ultra Grain-Free Turkey Stew	1.24	53.70	0.81	20.10	11.30	27.09	28-Nov-19
Weruva Love Connection Chicken & Salmon Pâté Pouch	1.24	55.40	0.23	32.10	5.30	27.09	26-Jan-20
Natural Balance Original Ultra Whole Body Health Reduced Calorie Chicken, Salmon & Duck	1.25	40.73	0.61	37.67	12.24	33.33	9-Jan-17
Wellness Core Grain-Free 95% Turkey	1.25	46.85	0.40	42.00	0.32	39.45	1-Feb-20
NutriSource Grain-Free Pork & Pork Liver Select	1.25	49.92	0.67	25.00	na	30.91	28-Jan-20
Solid Gold Flavorful Feast Grain-Free Sardine & Tuna Classic Paté in Gravy*	1.25	50.00	0.25	20.00	16.00	30.67	22-Jan-20
Dr Elsey's Clean Protein Chicken Pâté	1.25	50.00	0.38	39.75	2.08	35.82	22-Sep-19
PureVita Grain-Free Whitefish Entrée	1.25	54.21	0.42	36.92	na	34.36	28-Jan-20
Lovibles Seashore Love	1.25	55.90	0.78	23.00	7.60	27.27	21-Jan-20
Against the Grain Tuna Mango Tango with Duck	1.25	65.20	0.28	15.00	0.00	20.29	30-Oct-19
Against the Grain Tuna Aubergine with Snapper & Eggplant Dinner	1.25	73.70	0.23	14.70	0.00	24.29	30-Oct-19
Against the Grain Big Kahuna with Crab & Tilapia	1.25	78.80	0.72	11.20	2.61	23.93	30-Oct-19

50

Brand and Variety	Phos	Prot	Sod	Fat	Carb	Cals	Obtained
Hound & Gatos Grain-Free 98% Chicken & Liver	1.26	45.00	0.40	43.48	na	36.55	8-Nov-19
Hound & Gatos Grain-Free 98% Beef	1.26	45.00	0.63	36.85	na	35.64	8-Nov-19
Fromm Chicken & Duck Pâté	1.26	46.75	0.95	38.96	na	30.73	31-Jan-20
Soulistic Moist & Tender Lamb Dinner in Gravy Canned	1.26	56.68	0.59	25.67	7.11	23.45	27-Jan-20
Solid Gold Five Oceans Shreds with Sea Bream & Tuna in Gravy*	1.26	61.11	0.47	11.11	11.00	21.33	8-Nov-19
Instinct Grain-Free Minced Tuna in Savory Gravy Cup	1.26	62.60	1.21	13.00	12.09	23.14	8-Nov-19
Tiki Cat Grain-Free Seabass in Seabass Consommé (Oahu Luau)*	1.26	63.16	na	21.05	0.00	26.07	30-Jan-20
Tiki Cat Grain-Free Velvet Mousse Tuna & Mackerel*	1.26	68.18	na	22.73	na	29.29	30-Jan-20
Petite Cuisine L'il Violet's Tuna, Pumpkin & Tilapia	1.26	70.70	1.15	15.90	na	22.86	29-Oct-19
Weruva Mack & Jack	1.26	83.50	0.61	9.40	0.10	22.00	26-Jan-20
Catered Bowl Organic Chicken & Liver*	1.27	30.00	0.25	19.50	33.00	30.91	11-Nov-19
Tender & True Organic Chicken & Liver*	1.27	30.00	0.25	19.50	33.00	30.91	11-Nov-19
Natural Balance Platefulls Indoor Turkey & Duck in Gravy Pouch	1.27	42.37	0.84	23.85	22.42	27.00	9-Jan-17
Natural Balance Platefulls Indoor Salmon, Tuna, Chicken & Shrimp in Gravy Pouch	1.27	43.54	0.89	21.80	23.85	23.33	9-Jan-17
Wellness Core Hearty Cuts Shredded Chicken & Turkey	1.27	46.92	1.19	25.18	16.78	28.00	1-Feb-20
Dr Elsey's Clean Protein Rabbit & Turkey Pâté	1.27	50.19	0.38	33.24	3.04	32.36	22-Sep-19
Redbarn Naturals Ocean Fish Pâté for Weight Control	1.27	51.82	0.38	25.00	12.80	30.18	31-Oct-19
Whole Earth Farms Grain-Free Real Tuna & Whitefish Pate	1.27	52.40	0.39	21.10	13.10	33.00	25-Oct-19
PureVita Grain-Free Chicken Entrée	1.27	53.64	0.45	43.36	na	35.24	28-Jan-20

Brand and Variety	Phos	Prot	Sod	Fat	Carb	Cals	Obtained
PureVita Grain-Free Salmon Entrée	1.27	55.91	0.41	41.95	na	34.81	28-Jan-20
Weruva Too Hot to Handle Pouch	1.28	42.80	0.61	38.40	12.90	32.67	26-Jan-20
Merrick Purrfect Bistro Grain-Free Grammy's Pot Pie	1.28	43.16	1.75	38.29	8.46	30.91	26-Jun-19
Merrick Purrfect Bistro Grain-Free Thanksgiving Day Dinner	1.28	43.16	1.75	38.29	8.46	30.91	26-Jun-19
Wellness Core Hearty Cuts Shredded Indoor Chicken & Turkey	1.28	44.37	1.14	21.90	19.04	26.18	1-Feb-20
Natural Balance Platefulls Salmon, Tuna & Crab in Gravy Pouch	1.28	45.20	1.12	23.58	20.00	26.67	9-Jan-17
Chicken Soup for the Soul Classic Adult Chicken & Turkey Pâté	1.28	46.00	0.62	34.54	9.67	36.00	28-Oct-19
Instinct Original Grain-Free 95% Real Lamb Pâté	1.28	48.06	0.58	39.53	0.78	37.45	8-Nov-19
Instinct Original Grain-Free 95% Real Duck Pâté	1.28	49.81	0.54	35.41	2.72	35.45	8-Nov-19
Merrick Purrfect Bistro Grain-Free Cowboy Cookout	1.28	50.64	2.20	16.83	20.60	28.18	26-Jun-19
Merrick Backcountry Grain-Free Real Chicken + Trout Cuts Pouch	1.28	52.55	1.31	28.52	na	25.67	26-Nov-19
Lovibles Love of my Life	1.28	53.60	0.91	31.60	5.30	31.67	21-Jan-20
Lovibles Poetry in Motion	1.28	53.60	0.98	30.40	6.00	29.33	21-Jan-20
Lotus Grain-Free Just Juicy Salmon & Pollock Stew	1.28	54.92	0.92	25.13	9.03	24.15	28-Jan-20
Nature's Logic Sardine Feast	1.28	59.63	0.56	16.90	3.40	31.09	20-Feb-20
Fancy Feast Purely Natural White Meat Chicken and Shredded Beef Entrée in a Delicate Broth*	1.28	77.78	0.56	13.89	0.00	22.50	9-May-18
Natural Balance Ultra Premium Indoor	1.29	40.67	0.58	30.29	19.36	35.83	9-Jan-17
Natural Balance Platefulls Indoor Duck, Chicken & Pumpkin in Gravy Pouch	1.29	43.11	0.83	25.06	20.10	27.33	9-Jan-17
NutriSource Chicken, Turkey & Lamb	1.29	45.75	0.46	39.58	na	22.73	28-Jan-20

Brand and Variety	Phos	Prot	Sod	Fat	Carb	Cals	Obtained
NutriSource Grain-Free Chicken, Turkey & Lamb Select	1.29	45.75	0.46	39.58	na	35.64	28-Jan-20
President's Choice Extra Meaty Beef	1.29	50.86	0.86	34.46	5.88	na	12-Dec-19
Life's Abundance Grain-Free Limited Ingredient Pork & Duck	1.29	54.55	1.31	22.73	3.06	32.67	30-Jan-20
NutriSource Grain-Free Great Northwest Select[6]	1.29	55.83	0.46	44.04	na	37.27	28-Jan-20
Tiki Cat Grain-Free After Dark Chicken & Pork*	1.29	60.00	na	26.67	0.00	23.57	30-Jan-20
Catered Bowl Antibiotic-Free Chicken & Brown Rice*	1.30	30.00	0.29	18.40	39.00	33.64	11-Nov-19
Tender & True Antibiotic-Free Chicken & Brown Rice*	1.30	30.00	0.29	18.40	39.00	33.64	11-Nov-19
Chicken Soup for the Soul Classic Indoor Chicken & Salmon Pâté	1.30	42.39	0.50	30.49	11.26	36.73	28-Oct-19
Weruva Stewbacca	1.30	43.20	0.65	37.20	13.50	30.91	26-Jan-20
Fromm Chicken Pâté	1.30	47.66	1.06	25.03	na	29.27	31-Jan-20
Halo Holistic Grain-Free Whitefish Kitten	1.30	47.80	0.50	38.50	1.50	35.00	30-Jan-20
NOW Fresh Minced Chicken	1.30	49.00	0.79	29.00	13.00	27.57	31-Oct-19
Halo Holistic Sensitive Stomach Grain-Free Rabbit & Garden Greens Pâté	1.30	49.40	0.50	36.10	6.00	32.73	30-Jan-20
Wellness Core Grain-Free Turkey & Duck Pâté	1.30	49.87	0.41	35.34	6.12	39.09	1-Feb-20
Solid Gold Triple Layer Grain-Free with Salmon & Pumpkin*	1.30	50.00	0.54	18.00	22.00	32.00	22-Jan-20
Halo Holistic Grain-Free Lamb Adult	1.30	50.00	0.60	34.60	4.10	27.64	30-Jan-20
Solid Gold Purrfect Pairings Grain-Free Savory Mousse with Chicken Liver & Goat Milk*	1.30	50.00	2.50	18.18	na	27.64	8-Nov-19
Tiki Cat Grain-Free After Dark Chicken & Duck*	1.30	50.00	na	31.25	0.00	22.86	30-Jan-20

---

[6] *This food contains over 100%, so something is incorrect. I have asked NutriSource to clarify but had not received a response at the time of this book's publication.*

Brand and Variety	Phos	Prot	Sod	Fat	Carb	Cals	Obtained
Instinct Grain-Free Limited Ingredient Diet Real Turkey Pâté	1.30	50.19	0.50	33.33	4.60	35.82	8-Nov-19
President's Choice Extra Meaty Turkey & Giblets	1.30	56.59	0.80	30.81	2.77	na	12-Dec-19
Cats in the Kitchen Splash Dance	1.30	63.70	0.43	24.00	5.60	25.67	26-Jan-20
AvoDerm Grain-Free Tuna Recipe in Gravy Pouch	1.30	72.00	0.93	11.00	11.00	17.70	15-Oct-19
Tiki Cat Grain-Free Tilapia in Tilapia Consommé (Kapi'olani Luau)*	1.30	72.22	na	22.22	0.00	26.79	30-Jan-20
Wellness Healthy Indulgence Gravies Tuna & Mackerel Pouch	1.32	41.72	1.05	30.38	18.38	19.00	1-Feb-20
AvoDerm Grain-Free Salmon Recipe in Gravy Pouch	1.32	44.00	0.57	11.00	11.00	17.70	15-Oct-19
Hill's Science Diet Kitten Savory Salmon Entrée	1.32	44.20	0.56	28.40	16.30	37.45	1-Feb-20
Natural Balance Platefulls Indoor Mackerel & Sardine in Gravy Pouch	1.32	46.76	0.96	20.87	20.32	23.33	9-Jan-17
Dave's Naturally Healthy Grain-Free Turkey & Giblets Dinner*	1.32	48.42	0.53	39.02	3.73	35.36	7-Nov-19
Redbarn Naturals Chicken Pâté for Indoor Cats	1.32	51.44	0.39	27.08	11.60	30.90	31-Oct-19
Canidae Under The Sun Witty Kitty Ruffle My Feathers with Turkey & Turkey Liver in Broth	1.32	54.70	1.12	23.21	na	29.67	14-Dec-16
Catered Bowl Salmon & Sweet Potato*	1.33	28.33	na	11.67	na	34.00	11-Nov-19
Tender & True Salmon & Sweet Potato*	1.33	28.33	na	11.67	na	34.00	11-Nov-19
Hound & Gatos Grain-Free 98% Lamb, Chicken & Salmon	1.33	45.01	0.55	39.60	na	36.18	8-Nov-19
Natural Balance Ultra Premium Turkey & Giblets	1.33	45.83	0.60	31.67	11.93	30.00	9-Jan-17
AvoDerm Ocean Fish Formula	1.33	47.68	0.42	33.12	10.53	33.09	15-Oct-19
Dave's Naturally Healthy Grain-Free Shredded Salmon in Gravy*	1.33	48.72	1.54	27.79	11.42	26.36	11-Nov-19
Wellness Core Hearty Cuts Shredded Chicken & Tuna	1.33	49.76	1.19	22.18	16.97	26.91	1-Feb-20

Brand and Variety	Phos	Prot	Sod	Fat	Carb	Cals	Obtained
Redbarn Naturals Grain-Free Tuna Pâté	1.33	52.51	0.43	36.00	2.50	35.45	31-Oct-19
Weruva Kettle Call Pouch	1.34	40.70	0.71	42.50	9.30	17.27	26-Jan-20
Dr Tim's Nimble Chicken & Vegetable Pâté	1.34	41.50	0.93	27.30	20.20	31.19	29-Oct-19
Natural Balance Platefulls Chicken & Giblets in Gravy Pouch	1.34	42.69	0.83	25.93	21.31	23.33	9-Jan-17
Dave's Cat's Meow Beef with Turkey*	1.34	43.46	1.56	24.54	18.54	33.64	7-Nov-19
Solid Gold Tropical Blendz Grain-Free Pâté with Chicken & Coconut Oil*	1.34	46.00	0.35	18.00	28.00	37.00	22-Jan-20
Solid Gold Tropical Blendz Grain-Free Pâté with Turkey & Coconut Oil*	1.34	46.00	0.36	18.00	28.00	37.33	22-Jan-20
ZiwiPeak New Zealand Rabbit & Lamb	1.34	54.00	0.39	21.00	15.00	31.11	1-Feb-20
Solid Gold Purrfect Pairings Grain-Free Savory Mousse with Tuna & Goat Milk*	1.34	54.55	2.80	18.18	na	29.09	8-Nov-19
Wellness Core Grain-Free Beef, Venison & Lamb Pâté	1.34	55.24	0.65	30.19	4.02	33.64	1-Feb-20
Best Feline Friend PLAY Blast Off! Tuna & Beef Pâté Pouch	1.34	68.10	0.64	21.30	2.80	26.00	27-Jan-20
Weruva Taco Stewsday	1.35	41.20	0.72	41.80	9.40	31.09	26-Jan-20
Fromm Chicken, Duck & Salmon Pâté	1.35	45.06	0.98	38.37	na	30.55	31-Jan-20
ZiwiPeak New Zealand Venison	1.35	54.00	0.39	23.00	13.00	34.02	1-Feb-20
Grandma Mae's Country Naturals Grain-Free Dog & Cat Salmon Soft Stew*	1.35	55.56	0.41	30.41	na	35.23	23-Nov-19
Lovibles Key to My Heart	1.35	59.00	1.01	25.80	5.90	29.00	21-Jan-20
Best Feline Friend PLAY Double Dare Tuna & Duck Pâté	1.35	67.20	0.63	21.70	3.70	26.00	27-Jan-20
NutriSource Chicken & Rice	1.36	44.55	0.45	37.73	na	35.09	28-Jan-20
NutriSource Chicken, Turkey, Lamb & Fish	1.36	46.82	0.45	37.73	na	na	28-Jan-20

Brand and Variety	Phos	Prot	Sod	Fat	Carb	Cals	Obtained
Natural Balance Ultra Premium Ocean Fish	1.36	52.70	0.84	25.69	10.77	33.33	9-Jan-17
Nulo MedalSeries Salmon & Turkey in Gravy	1.36	55.62	1.41	22.29	10.71	25.00	26-Nov-19
Nulo FreeStyle Minced Salmon & Turkey in Gravy	1.36	55.62	1.41	22.29	10.71	25.00	26-Nov-19
Tiki Cat Grain-Free Aloha Friends Tuna, Shrimp & Pumpkin*	1.36	70.59	na	17.65	0.00	18.00	30-Jan-20
Merrick Limited Ingredient Grain-Free Turkey	1.37	44.80	0.42	36.70	5.77	27.80	26-Jun-19
Fromm Turkey & Pumpkin Pâté	1.37	46.70	0.62	24.10	na	27.27	31-Jan-20
Lovibles A-moo-zing Love	1.37	47.90	0.58	36.60	7.70	34.18	21-Jan-20
Instinct Grain-Free Limited Ingredient Diet Rabbit	1.37	51.56	0.51	16.02	19.53	28.36	8-Nov-19
Natural Planet Organic Turkey Dinner	1.38	45.00	0.42	45.79	na	34.18	28-Jan-20
Performatrin Kitten Grain-Free Chicken	1.38	45.80	0.49	39.60	4.50	39.82	28-Nov-19
Solid Gold Tropical Blendz Grain-Free Pâté with Chicken Liver & Coconut Oil*	1.38	46.00	0.32	18.00	28.00	34.33	22-Jan-20
Koha Grain-Free Chicken Stew*	1.38	46.60	1.19	34.70	8.57	24.36	13-Aug-19
Grandma Mae's Country Naturals Grain-Free Dog & Cat Beef Soft Stew*	1.38	47.62	0.29	24.29	na	31.06	23-Nov-19
Grandma Mae's Country Naturals Grain-Free Whitefish Pâté Entrée*	1.38	50.00	1.25	12.50	na	19.29	23-Nov-19
Dave's Cat's Meow 95% Beef & Beef Liver*	1.38	52.37	0.92	31.89	9.19	38.00	7-Nov-19
Grandma Mae's Country Naturals Grain-Free Tuna & Chicken Pâté Entrée*	1.38	56.25	0.69	12.50	na	20.36	23-Nov-19
Koha L.I.D. Shredded Lamb Entrée in Gravy*	1.39	39.36	1.14	35.84	10.79	22.00	27-Nov-19
Natural Balance Platefulls Chicken & Salmon in Gravy Pouch	1.39	42.60	0.82	25.39	21.27	23.33	9-Jan-17

Brand and Variety	Phos	Prot	Sod	Fat	Carb	Cals	Obtained
Under The Sun Witty Kitty Wingin' It with Chicken & Turkey Recipe in Broth	1.39	50.00	1.14	26.40	na	25.00	14-Dec-16
Dr Elsey's Clean Protein Single Source Pork Pâté	1.39	60.40	0.35	18.46	16.54	29.27	22-Sep-19
Cats in the Kitchen Cat Times at Fridgemont Pâté Pouch	1.39	64.80	0.54	19.60	7.70	18.33	26-Jan-20
Soulistic Duck & Tuna Pâté Pouch	1.39	64.80	0.54	19.60	7.70	18.33	27-Jan-20
Soulistic Tuna and Beef Pâté	1.39	68.60	0.64	19.80	3.50	0.00	29-Jan-20
Best Feline Friend PLAY Bodacious Tuna & Beef Pâté	1.39	68.60	0.64	19.80	3.50	25.82	27-Jan-20
Against the Grain Chicken & Polyhauai'l Berry Dinner	1.39	82.10	0.26	8.94	0.00	16.00	30-Oct-19
FirstMate Limited Ingredient Free Run Chicken	1.40	41.00	0.80	23.00	24.00	26.00	25-Nov-19
FirstMate Cage-Free Chicken & Wild Tuna 50/50	1.40	41.00	0.90	23.00	23.00	26.00	25-Nov-19
FirstMate Cage-Free Chicken & Rice	1.40	41.00	0.90	23.00	24.00	26.00	25-Nov-19
Kasiks Cage-Free Chicken	1.40	41.00	0.90	23.00	25.00	27.00	25-Nov-19
FirstMate Cage-Free Turkey & Wild Tuna 50/50	1.40	41.00	0.90	32.00	14.00	26.00	25-Nov-19
NOW Fresh Cod Pâté	1.40	43.00	0.50	24.00	25.00	31.94	31-Oct-19
GO! Solutions 98% Carnivore Grain-Free Salmon & Cod Pâté	1.40	43.00	0.77	30.00	18.00	24.47	31-Oct-19
Grandma Mae's Country Naturals Grain-Free Chicken Pâté Entrée*	1.40	45.00	0.45	25.00	na	30.36	23-Nov-19
Nature's Logic Chicken Feast	1.40	45.44	0.60	35.60	4.00	41.82	20-Feb-20
RAWZ 96% Turkey & Turkey Liver Pâté	1.40	48.00	0.48	40.80	2.28	36.18	3-Dec-19
Instinct Grain-Free 95% Real Chicken Pâté	1.40	49.80	0.60	35.60	2.40	35.09	8-Nov-19
Solid Gold Triple Layer Grain-Free with Turkey & Pumpkin*	1.40	50.00	0.54	23.00	14.00	30.18	22-Jan-20
FirstMate Limited Ingredient Wild Tuna	1.40	50.00	0.70	23.00	12.00	27.00	25-Nov-19

Brand and Variety	Phos	Prot	Sod	Fat	Carb	Cals	Obtained
Solid Gold Purrfect Pairings Grain-Free Savory Mousse with Chicken & Goat Milk*	1.40	50.00	2.50	22.73	na	31.27	8-Nov-19
Dave's Naturally Healthy Grain-Free Shredded Chicken in Gravy*	1.40	50.38	1.65	24.96	11.73	25.64	7-Nov-19
VeRUS Ocean Fish	1.40	51.80	0.93	33.20	0.10	30.00	27-Jan-20
Solid Gold Holistic Delights Grain-Free Creamy Bisque with Chicken Liver & Coconut Milk Pouch*	1.40	56.00	0.20	19.00	10.00	23.33	22-Jan-20
Against the Grain Tuna Toscano with Salmon & Tomato Dinner	1.40	65.00	0.32	15.70	0.00	22.14	30-Oct-19
Solid Gold Five Oceans Shreds with Blended Tuna in Gravy*	1.40	68.00	0.30	10.00	10.00	26.67	22-Jan-20
Only Natural Pet Rabbit & Pork Dinner*	1.41	40.91	0.45	22.73	20.86	34.72	29-Jan-20
Only Natural Pet Duck & Beef Dinner*	1.41	40.91	0.68	22.73	21.59	34.53	29-Jan-20
Performatrin Adult Grain-Free Chicken & Lamb	1.41	44.80	0.50	40.20	4.40	38.33	28-Nov-19
Nature's Logic Turkey Feast	1.41	45.50	0.59	35.49	4.69	39.82	20-Feb-20
Solid Gold Tropical Blendz Grain-Free Pâté with Salmon & Coconut Oil*	1.41	46.00	0.34	18.00	28.00	35.33	22-Jan-20
I and Love and You Beef, Right Meow! Pâté	1.41	46.77	0.51	38.66	na	30.67	11-Nov-19
Fromm Salmon & Tuna Pâté	1.41	47.53	1.00	35.38	na	30.18	31-Jan-20
Nulo FreeStyle Grain-Free Beef & Lamb	1.41	47.57	0.44	40.08	3.37	33.82	26-Nov-19
Nulo MedalSeries Grain-Free Beef & Lamb	1.41	47.57	0.44	40.08	3.37	33.82	26-Nov-19
Solid Gold Holistic Delights Grain-Free Creamy Bisque with Tuna & Coconut Milk Pouch*	1.41	55.56	1.06	18.00	na	25.67	8-Nov-19
Nulo FreeStyle Shredded Chicken & Duck in Gravy	1.41	55.61	1.17	22.63	10.78	25.33	26-Nov-19
Nulo MedalSeries Shredded Chicken & Duck in Gravy	1.41	55.61	1.17	22.63	10.78	25.33	26-Nov-19
Performatrin Indoor Salmon	1.42	42.20	0.64	22.40	10.70	27.82	28-Nov-19

Brand and Variety	Phos	Prot	Sod	Fat	Carb	Cals	Obtained
Natural Balance L.I.D. Limited Ingredient Salmon & Green Pea	1.42	46.44	0.64	26.54	14.83	37.00	9-Jan-17
Victor Grain-Free Shredded Chicken Dinner in Gravy	1.42	48.16	1.58	27.15	13.13	25.64	23-Nov-19
Fromm Duck À La Veg Pâté	1.42	49.30	0.80	32.40	na	30.18	31-Jan-20
Instinct Grain-Free Ultimate Protein Real Chicken Pâté	1.42	49.80	0.55	35.57	2.37	35.09	8-Nov-19
Tiki Cat Grain-Free Aloha Friends Chicken, Egg & Pumpkin Pouch*	1.42	50.00	na	33.33	0.00	24.40	30-Jan-20
Dr Elsey's Clean Protein Duck & Turkey Pâté	1.42	50.46	0.40	36.66	3.29	35.82	22-Sep-19
Lovibles Tender Lovin'	1.42	53.20	0.92	32.30	3.40	33.27	21-Jan-20
Holistic Select Grain-Free Salmon & Shrimp Pâté	1.42	54.39	0.63	32.02	4.47	37.31	1-Feb-20
Natural Balance Delectable Delights Land 'n Sea Cats-serole Pâté	1.42	58.13	0.71	20.16	11.63	30.00	9-Jan-17
RAWZ 96% Salmon Pâté	1.43	44.57	0.47	40.31	2.33	36.00	3-Dec-19
ZiwiPeak New Zealand Beef	1.43	45.00	0.38	29.00	16.00	35.40	1-Feb-20
Chicken Soup for the Soul Grain-Free Beef, Red Potato & Carrots Minced in Gravy	1.43	48.64	1.49	21.91	17.36	26.00	28-Oct-19
Hound & Gatos Grain-Free 98% Gamebird Poultry	1.43	49.80	0.68	39.52	na	34.73	8-Nov-19
Holistic Select Grain-Free Chicken Pâté	1.43	52.02	0.43	33.68	4.60	36.54	1-Feb-20
ZiwiPeak New Zealand Mackerel & Lamb	1.43	55.00	0.38	22.00	16.00	34.02	1-Feb-20
Solid Gold Holistic Delights Grain-Free Creamy Bisque with Chicken & Coconut Milk Pouch*	1.43	55.56	1.75	22.22	na	27.33	8-Nov-19
Best Feline Friend PLAY Told Ya' Lamb & Tuna Pâté	1.43	58.60	0.80	28.70	4.80	27.86	27-Jan-20
Cats in the Kitchen Two Tu Tango	1.43	67.80	0.52	18.80	5.60	19.83	26-Jan-20
Koha Grain-Free Limited Ingredient Turkey Pâté*	1.44	47.80	0.42	40.44	2.05	38.67	13-Aug-19
Grandma Mae's Country Naturals Grain-Free Tuna Pâté Entrée*	1.44	56.25	0.69	12.50	na	20.36	23-Nov-19

Brand and Variety	Phos	Prot	Sod	Fat	Carb	Cals	Obtained
Natural Balance Original Ultra Whole Body Health Chicken, Salmon & Duck	1.45	41.38	0.53	38.36	11.28	36.67	9-Jan-17
Fromm Chicken & Salmon Pâté	1.45	43.37	1.00	38.88	na	27.45	31-Jan-20
Nulo FreeStyle Grain-Free Trout & Salmon	1.45	49.62	0.46	39.69	1.15	36.55	26-Nov-19
Nulo MedalSeries Grain-Free Trout & Salmon	1.45	49.62	0.46	39.69	1.15	36.55	26-Nov-19
Grandma Mae's Country Naturals Grain-Free Chicken Pâté in Gravy*	1.45	52.27	0.41	31.82	na	32.55	23-Nov-19
Grandma Mae's Country Naturals Grain-Free Ocean Fish & Chicken Pâté*	1.45	52.27	0.41	31.82	na	32.55	23-Nov-19
Grandma Mae's Country Naturals Grain-Free Chicken & Liver Pâté*	1.45	52.27	0.41	31.82	na	32.55	23-Nov-19
Grandma Mae's Country Naturals Grain-Free Mackerel & Sardine Pâté*	1.45	52.27	0.41	31.82	na	32.55	23-Nov-19
Grandma Mae's Country Naturals Grain-Free Sardine & Ocean Fish Pâté*	1.45	52.27	0.41	31.82	na	32.55	23-Nov-19
Grandma Mae's Country Naturals Grain-Free Pork Liver & Chicken Pâté*	1.45	52.27	0.41	31.82	na	32.55	23-Nov-19
Lovibles Sizzling Summer Love	1.45	53.30	0.34	32.70	3.80	31.67	21-Jan-20
Instinct Original Kitten Grain-Free Real Chicken Pâté	1.45	53.91	0.63	33.20	1.17	34.55	8-Nov-19
Victor Turkey & Salmon Pâté	1.46	42.98	0.37	36.11	9.76	33.45	23-Nov-19
ZiwiPeak New Zealand Free Range Chicken	1.46	46.00	0.31	31.00	13.00	37.54	1-Feb-20
President's Choice Extra Meaty Salmon	1.46	48.43	0.75	38.50	2.24	na	12-Dec-19
Dave's Naturally Healthy Grain-Free Chicken & Whitefish Dinner*	1.46	50.40	0.71	36.08	3.28	35.82	7-Nov-19
Lovibles My One and Only	1.46	55.40	0.80	27.60	5.40	30.00	21-Jan-20

Brand and Variety	Phos	Prot	Sod	Fat	Carb	Cals	Obtained
Solid Gold Holistic Delights Grain-Free Creamy Bisque with Turkey & Coconut Milk Pouch*	1.46	56.00	0.36	19.00	13.00	25.67	22-Jan-20
President's Choice Extra Meaty Flaked Tuna	1.46	61.38	1.46	20.06	6.48	na	12-Dec-19
Natural Balance Platefulls Indoor Turkey, Salmon & Chicken in Gravy Pouch	1.47	42.72	0.91	24.08	20.89	23.33	9-Jan-17
Chicken Soup for the Soul Grain-Free Salmon & Chicken Cuts in Gravy	1.47	49.73	1.58	20.96	17.51	25.67	28-Oct-19
Dave's Naturally Healthy Grain-Free Gobbleicious*	1.47	51.10	0.69	22.80	15.45	36.73	7-Nov-19
Instinct Grain-Free Minced Salmon in Savory Gravy Cup	1.47	52.90	1.52	22.00	13.59	25.14	8-Nov-19
Under The Sun Witty Kitty The Big Catch with Tuna & Sardine Recipe in Broth	1.47	59.42	1.33	20.53	na	26.67	14-Dec-16
Tiki Cat Grain-Free After Dark Chicken & Quail Egg*	1.47	61.54	na	30.77	0.00	22.14	30-Jan-20
Against the Grain Chicken Mayflower with Turnip	1.47	78.70	0.52	9.26	0.00	13.71	30-Oct-19
Natural Balance L.I.D. Limited Ingredient Chicken & Green Pea	1.48	45.06	0.56	30.67	12.65	33.33	9-Jan-17
Earthborn Holistic Grain-Free Ranch House Stew	1.48	45.71	0.87	24.09	23.53	27.60	15-Jan-20
RAWZ 96% Chicken & Chicken Liver Pâté	1.48	50.00	0.49	36.89	4.00	35.27	3-Dec-19
ZiwiPeak New Zealand Lamb	1.49	43.00	0.37	31.00	16.00	37.54	1-Feb-20
Diamond Naturals Chicken Dinner Cat and Kitten	1.49	43.04	0.54	33.25	13.69	38.00	11-Nov-19
Best Feline Friend OMG Best Day Eva! Beef & Salmon Minced in Gravy	1.49	64.90	0.60	16.20	11.20	16.18	27-Jan-20
GO! Solutions Skin & Coat Care Salmon Pâté	1.50	38.00	0.77	29.00	25.00	29.13	31-Oct-19
Natural Balance Original Ultra Whole Body Health Chicken, Salmon & Duck Kitten	1.50	41.57	0.54	36.54	10.48	36.67	9-Jan-17

Brand and Variety	Phos	Prot	Sod	Fat	Carb	Cals	Obtained
Grandma Mae's Country Naturals Grain-Free Lamb Chunks in Gravy*	1.50	44.44	0.67	16.67	na	29.64	23-Nov-19
Lotus Grain-Free Just Juicy Pollock Stew	1.50	45.33	1.50	26.17	10.72	21.32	28-Jan-20
Halo Holistic Grain-Free Salmon Adult	1.50	45.80	0.30	37.40	6.80	34.18	30-Jan-20
GO! Solutions 96% Carnivore Chicken, Turkey & Duck Pâté	1.50	47.00	0.77	27.00	17.00	28.35	31-Oct-19
Dave's Naturally Healthy Grain-Free Fisherman's Stew in Gravy*	1.50	50.27	1.61	24.38	12.67	25.09	7-Nov-19
Wellness Complete Health Gravies Turkey Dinner	1.50	51.06	1.61	23.72	13.36	23.64	1-Feb-20
Halo Holistic Grain-Free Chicken, Shrimp & Crab Adult	1.50	51.20	0.40	33.30	4.90	30.00	30-Jan-20
Dr Elsey's Clean Protein Ocean Whitefish Pâté	1.50	57.75	0.63	35.25	0.00	34.55	22-Sep-19
Balanced Blends Species Balanced Steamed Turkey	1.50	62.37	0.53	30.37	na	38.70	01-Dec-19
Solid Gold Purrfect Pairings Grain-Free Savory Mousse with Salmon & Goat Milk*	1.50	63.64	2.40	9.09	na	28.36	8-Nov-19
Solid Gold Triple Layer Grain-Free with Beef & Pumpkin*	1.50	64.00	0.53	9.00	17.00	31.64	22-Jan-20
Chicken Soup for the Soul Grain-Free Chicken, Sweet Potato & Spinach Minced	1.51	49.00	1.48	23.10	16.32	25.67	28-Oct-19
AvoDerm Wild by Nature Grain-Free Chopped Sardines in Consommé	1.51	69.49	0.21	17.78	11.10	22.67	15-Oct-19
Performatrin Healthy Weight Ocean Whitefish	1.52	41.50	0.57	14.80	25.50	24.18	28-Nov-19
Natural Balance Platefulls Cod, Chicken, Sole & Shrimp in Gravy Pouch	1.52	44.42	0.91	20.64	23.39	23.33	9-Jan-17
Dr Elsey's Clean Protein Single Source Salmon Pâté	1.52	48.13	0.59	30.67	12.71	38.36	29-Oct-19
Feline Natural New Zealand Lamb & Salmon Feast*	1.53	44.74	na	39.47	na	30.00	1-Feb-20

Brand and Variety	Phos	Prot	Sod	Fat	Carb	Cals	Obtained
Open Farm Harvest Chicken Rustic Blend	1.53	44.99	0.50	38.98	7.11	28.36	17-Jan-20
Open Farm Grass-Fed Beef Rustic Blend	1.53	44.99	0.53	34.39	4.19	30.73	17-Jan-20
Open Farm Homestead Turkey Rustic Blend	1.53	44.99	0.53	34.39	4.19	36.36	17-Jan-20
Open Farm Chicken & Salmon Rustic Blend	1.53	47.18	0.53	34.39	2.01	27.45	17-Jan-20
I and Love and You Purrky Turkey Pâté	1.53	47.42	0.54	33.05	14.30	33.33	11-Nov-19
Instinct Grain-Free Minced Chicken in Savory Gravy Cup	1.53	50.50	1.25	24.00	13.76	27.71	8-Nov-19
Holistic Select Grain-Free Chicken Liver & Lamb Pâté	1.53	53.31	0.47	33.01	3.70	38.15	1-Feb-20
Performatrin Ultra Grain-Free Salmon Bisque	1.54	41.50	0.92	36.90	8.30	37.27	28-Nov-19
Hound & Gatos Grain-Free 98% Salmon	1.54	44.95	1.26	47.27	na	39.27	8-Nov-19
Nulo FreeStyle Grain-Free Salmon & Mackerel	1.54	51.22	0.67	31.97	6.69	34.18	26-Nov-19
Nulo MedalSeries Grain-Free Salmon & Mackerel	1.54	51.22	0.67	31.97	6.69	34.18	26-Nov-19
Feline Natural New Zealand Chicken & Lamb Feast*	1.54	54.86	na	28.57	na	25.33	1-Feb-20
Solid Gold Holistic Delights Grain-Free Creamy Bisque with Salmon & Coconut Milk Pouch*	1.54	55.56	0.93	22.22	na	29.33	8-Nov-19
Redbarn Naturals Grain-Free Turkey Pâté	1.54	56.61	0.44	36.88	0.00	34.91	31-Oct-19
I and Love and You Tuna Fintastic Canned Chunks in Gravy	1.54	58.26	1.58	17.03	28.50	24.00	11-Nov-19
Against the Grain Caribbean Club with Chicken & Cheese	1.54	84.00	0.21	10.50	0.00	26.43	30-Oct-19
RAWZ 96% Duck & Duck Liver Pâté	1.55	49.58	0.48	32.80	6.05	32.91	3-Dec-19
I and Love and You Salmon Chanted Evening Canned Chunks in Gravy	1.55	49.90	1.37	26.07	30.49	25.00	11-Nov-19

Brand and Variety	Phos	Prot	Sod	Fat	Carb	Cals	Obtained
Nulo FreeStyle Grain-Free Duck & Tuna	1.55	51.13	0.47	32.56	6.18	34.73	26-Nov-19
Nulo MedalSeries Grain-Free Duck & Tuna	1.55	51.13	0.47	32.56	6.18	34.73	26-Nov-19
Lovibles Feast of My Dreams	1.56	49.10	1.56	36.30	8.70	36.36	21-Jan-20
Chicken Soup for the Soul Classic Kitten Chicken & Turkey Pâté	1.57	45.81	0.62	34.11	8.91	38.18	28-Oct-19
VeRUS Turkey, Chicken & Ocean Fish	1.57	46.10	0.87	37.30	0.40	32.18	27-Jan-20
Dave's Naturally Healthy Grain-Free Turkey*	1.57	48.23	0.39	36.50	4.58	32.80	7-Nov-19
Balanced Blends Species Balanced Steamed Chicken	1.57	62.16	0.54	29.89	na	37.90	01-Dec-19
Weruva Polynesian BBQ	1.57	81.30	0.51	15.70	7.40	20.91	26-Jan-20
Natural Balance Ultra Premium Salmon	1.58	45.41	0.76	30.29	13.28	33.33	9-Jan-17
Nulo FreeStyle Grain-Free Chicken & Herring	1.58	49.43	0.49	35.55	4.79	36.73	26-Nov-19
Nulo MedalSeries Grain-Free Chicken & Herring	1.58	49.43	0.49	35.55	4.79	36.73	26-Nov-19
Performatrin Adult Grain-Free Salmon	1.58	50.10	0.93	34.50	3.80	32.67	28-Nov-19
NutriSource Grain-Free Country Select	1.58	55.42	0.38	31.83	na	35.27	28-Jan-20
Cats in the Kitchen The Karate Kitty Pâté Pouch	1.58	68.80	0.71	9.90	10.00	15.33	26-Jan-20
Health Extension Grain-Free Real Beef Entrée for Kittens & Cats	1.59	45.00	0.77	45.00	1.00	45.00	7-Dec-16
Koha Grain-Free Limited Ingredient Chicken Pâté*	1.59	49.36	0.43	39.41	1.32	37.00	13-Aug-19
Fancy Feast Classic Salmon & Shrimp Pâté Feast*	1.59	54.30	0.53	31.00	3.30	30.67	26-Nov-19
Weruva Let's Make a Meal Lamb & Mackerel Pâté Pouch	1.59	54.80	0.29	30.80	5.30	27.82	26-Jan-20
Dave's 95% Premium Meat Tuna & Chicken Pâté*	1.60	39.11	0.32	29.46	4.58	36.36	7-Nov-19
GO! Solutions 99% Carnivore Grain-Free Minced Lamb & Wild Boar	1.60	44.00	1.00	35.00	12.00	23.93	31-Oct-19

Brand and Variety	Phos	Prot	Sod	Fat	Carb	Cals	Obtained
GO! Solutions Skin + Coat Care Minced Chicken	1.60	45.00	0.90	26.00	20.00	26.25	31-Oct-19
Feline Natural New Zealand Chicken & Venison Feast*	1.60	51.43	na	28.57	na	24.33	1-Feb-20
VeRUS Grain-Free Tuna Pâté	1.60	60.80	0.76	26.10	0.20	26.73	27-Jan-20
Newman's Own Organic 95% Turkey Grain-Free Dinner	1.61	44.00	0.64	43.00	3.95	35.64	14-Nov-19
Newman's Own Organic 95% Turkey & Liver Grain-Free Dinner	1.61	44.00	0.64	43.00	3.95	35.64	14-Nov-19
Newman's Own Organic 95% Chicken Grain-Free Dinner	1.61	44.00	0.64	43.00	3.95	36.36	14-Nov-19
Newman's Own Organic 95% Chicken & Liver Grain-Free Dinner	1.61	44.00	0.64	43.00	3.95	36.55	14-Nov-19
Feline Natural New Zealand Lamb Feast*	1.61	44.44	0.56	44.44	na	34.33	1-Feb-20
Grandma Mae's Country Naturals Grain-Free Salmon Slices in Gravy*	1.61	44.44	2.11	25.00	na	26.18	23-Nov-19
Sheba Perfect Portions Premium Cuts in Gravy Roasted Chicken*	1.61	45.74	1.30	26.74	13.30	na	7-Dec-16
Sheba Perfect Portions Premium Cuts in Gravy Tender Turkey*	1.61	45.74	1.30	26.74	13.30	na	7-Dec-16
Sheba Perfect Portions Premium Cuts in Gravy Savory Salmon and Chicken*	1.61	45.74	1.30	26.74	13.30	na	7-Dec-16
Sheba Perfect Portions Premium Cuts in Gravy Tender Trout*	1.61	45.74	1.30	26.74	13.30	na	7-Dec-16
Sheba Perfect Portions Premium Cuts in Gravy Savory Mixed Grill*	1.61	45.74	1.30	26.74	13.30	na	7-Dec-16
Sheba Perfect Portions Premium Cuts in Gravy Delicate Whitefish and Tuna*	1.61	45.74	1.30	26.74	13.30	na	7-Dec-16
Wellness Core Grain-Free 95% Chicken	1.61	46.14	0.40	36.87	6.14	35.82	1-Feb-20
Merrick Purrfect Bistro Grain-Free Chicken Divan	1.61	49.55	2.32	21.29	15.04	25.27	26-Jun-19

Brand and Variety	Phos	Prot	Sod	Fat	Carb	Cals	Obtained
Whole Earth Farms Grain-Free Chicken & Turkey Morsels in Gravy	1.61	49.60	2.32	21.30	15.04	28.73	25-Oct-19
Dr Elsey's Clean Protein Single Source Duck Pâté	1.61	49.98	0.38	35.30	6.92	34.91	22-Sep-19
I and Love and You Chicken Dalish Canned Chunks in Gravy	1.61	50.34	1.41	26.31	na	26.00	11-Nov-19
Solid Gold Holistic Delights Grain-Free Creamy Bisque with Beef & Coconut Milk Pouch*	1.61	55.56	1.05	22.22	na	26.33	22-Jan-20
I and Love and You Savory Salmon Pâté	1.62	49.73	0.64	32.81	na	29.67	11-Nov-19
Cats in the Kitchen Kitty Gone Wild	1.62	67.70	0.66	16.20	5.30	18.17	26-Jan-20
Stella and Chewy's Purrfect Pâté Grain-Free Cage-Free Chicken*	1.63	39.00	0.86	19.50	5.77	32.55	3-Dec-19
Natural Balance Ultra Premium Chicken & Liver Pâté	1.63	43.16	0.85	37.14	8.22	35.33	9-Jan-17
Wellness Core Grain-Free 95% Chicken & Salmon	1.63	49.31	0.64	39.31	0.30	36.00	1-Feb-20
Performatrin Ultra Grain-Free Chicken Pâté	1.64	45.70	0.46	36.30	5.10	34.00	28-Nov-19
Balanced Blends Species Balanced Steamed Beef Heart & Offal	1.64	59.90	0.53	30.59	na	33.40	01-Dec-19
Whole Earth Farms Grain-Free Real Duck Pâté	1.66	40.80	0.30	41.30	5.27	35.20	25-Oct-19
Dave's Naturally Healthy Grain-Free Chicken*	1.66	49.87	0.39	34.54	4.33	33.95	7-Nov-19
RAWZ 96% Chicken & Herring Pâté	1.66	52.95	0.46	29.17	7.31	33.27	3-Dec-19
Performatrin Adult Grain-Free Whitefish	1.66	54.30	0.73	28.90	3.30	30.55	28-Nov-19
Natural Balance L.I.D. Limited Ingredient Venison & Green Pea	1.67	42.90	0.76	26.77	15.35	31.67	9-Jan-17
Grandma Mae's Country Naturals Grain-Free Duck Soft Stew*	1.67	44.44	0.33	25.00	na	31.82	23-Nov-19

Brand and Variety	Phos	Prot	Sod	Fat	Carb	Cals	Obtained
Grandma Mae's Country Naturals Grain-Free Chicken Slices in Gravy*	1.67	44.44	1.94	25.00	na	25.82	23-Nov-19
Whole Earth Farms Grain-Free Real Chicken & Turkey Pâté	1.67	44.84	0.73	27.55	16.54	31.80	25-Oct-19
NutriSource Grain-Free Meadow & Stream Select	1.67	50.67	0.71	31.08	na	32.00	28-Jan-20
Natural Balance Delectable Delights Life's a Beach Pâté	1.67	60.24	0.55	18.51	9.65	28.00	9-Jan-17
Natural Balance Platefulls Turkey, Chicken & Duck in Gravy Pouch	1.68	41.01	0.83	23.85	22.56	23.33	9-Jan-17
Stella and Chewy's Purrfect Pâté Grain-Free Chicken & Salmon*	1.68	41.70	0.96	20.80	5.68	32.73	3-Dec-19
Wellness Core Grain-Free Salmon, Whitefish & Herring Pâté	1.68	50.51	0.86	22.47	12.53	28.55	1-Feb-20
Wellness Complete Health Gravies Salmon Dinner	1.68	51.10	1.73	21.72	13.90	22.91	1-Feb-20
Solid Gold Wholesome Selects Grain-Free Turkey & Pumpkin Chunks in Gravy*	1.68	53.00	0.67	22.92	20.68	29.00	22-Jan-20
Instinct Grain-Free Minced Rabbit in Savory Gravy Cup	1.68	55.00	1.29	15.00	14.85	21.14	8-Nov-19
Fancy Feast Classic Pâté Turkey & Giblets Feast*	1.69	53.30	0.49	32.70	3.90	32.00	26-Nov-19
Instinct Grain-Free Limited Ingredient Diet Duck	1.70	45.29	0.47	33.33	7.25	36.36	8-Nov-19
Lovibles Beggin' for Love	1.70	48.20	0.59	39.50	4.00	39.09	21-Jan-20
Wellness Complete Health Morsels Turkey Dinner	1.70	48.62	1.60	27.44	11.15	27.27	1-Feb-20
Grandma Mae's Country Naturals Grain-Free Chicken Soft Stew*	1.70	56.14	0.35	28.07	na	33.33	23-Nov-19
Best Feline Friend PLAY Tap Dance Duck & Tuna Pâté Pouch	1.70	61.30	0.82	24.60	5.00	25.33	27-Jan-20
Best Feline Friend PLAY Ta Da! Beef & Tuna Pâté Pouch	1.70	64.30	0.87	20.80	4.90	24.00	27-Jan-20
NutriSource Grain-Free Turkey & Turkey Liver Select	1.71	45.00	0.46	40.58	na	35.82	28-Jan-20
Merrick Purrfect Bistro Grain-Free Beef Pâté	1.71	54.50	2.07	27.07	5.68	30.55	26-Jun-19

Brand and Variety	Phos	Prot	Sod	Fat	Carb	Cals	Obtained
Whole Earth Farms Grain-Free Real Beef Pâté	1.71	54.50	2.07	27.10	5.54	26.20	25-Oct-19
Instinct Grain-Free Limited Ingredient Diet Real Salmon Pâté	1.71	54.69	1.14	26.12	5.71	29.09	8-Nov-19
Lovibles Over the Moo-n	1.71	56.20	0.94	26.80	5.40	29.00	21-Jan-20
Grandma Mae's Country Naturals Grain-Free Dog & Cat Lamb Soft Stew*	1.71	57.14	0.34	34.29	na	29.92	23-Nov-19
Grandma Mae's Country Naturals Grain-Free Whitefish & Chicken Slices in Gravy*	1.72	44.44	2.00	25.00	na	24.73	23-Nov-19
Fromm Seafood & Shrimp Pâté	1.73	44.68	1.15	26.02	na	25.82	31-Jan-20
Best Feline Friend OMG Lots-O-Luck! Duck & Tuna Minced in Gravy	1.73	62.30	0.54	17.00	11.30	18.18	27-Jan-20
Lotus Grain-Free Salmon Pâté	1.74	40.83	0.91	21.11	23.94	26.56	28-Jan-20
Merrick Purrfect Bistro Grain-Free Chicken Casserole	1.74	49.13	2.13	22.04	13.26	25.64	26-Jun-19
Tiki Cat Grain-Free Aloha Friends Chicken, Beef & Pumpkin Pouch*	1.74	52.17	na	34.78	0.00	25.60	30-Jan-20
Solid Gold Triple Layer Grain-Free with Chicken & Pumpkin	1.74	59.00	0.34	23.00	8.00	31.27	22-Jan-20
Soulistic Duck & Tuna Pâté	1.74	62.50	0.85	23.10	5.20	0.00	27-Jan-20
Best Feline Friend PLAY Trickster Duck & Tuna Pâté	1.74	62.50	0.85	23.10	5.20	24.00	27-Jan-20
Canada Fresh Salmon*	1.75	40.00	0.70	37.50	na	31.45	17-Jan-20
Canada Fresh Beef*	1.75	47.50	0.50	42.50	na	31.45	17-Jan-20
RAWZ 96% Rabbit & Pumpkin Pâté	1.75	48.92	0.42	29.46	9.42	30.18	3-Dec-19
Weruva Meal or No Deal! Chicken & Beef Pâté	1.75	62.90	0.55	22.50	4.60	16.91	26-Jan-20
Dave's Cat's Meow Farmyard Fowl*	1.76	48.33	1.50	24.56	13.96	26.00	7-Nov-19
Tiki Cat Grain-Free Aloha Friends Chicken & Pumpkin Pouch*	1.76	52.38	na	33.33	0.00	25.60	30-Jan-20
Tiki Cat Grain-Free Aloha Friends Chicken, Lamb & Pumpkin Pouch*	1.76	52.38	na	33.33	0.00	26.80	30-Jan-20

Brand and Variety	Phos	Prot	Sod	Fat	Carb	Cals	Obtained
PureVita Grain-Free Turkey Entrée	1.77	55.86	0.45	43.05	na	35.49	28-Jan-20
ZiwiPeak New Zealand Mackerel	1.77	64.00	1.23	14.00	10.00	30.50	1-Feb-20
Nulo FreeStyle Grain-Free Turkey & Chicken	1.78	49.44	0.41	37.73	1.34	35.09	26-Nov-19
Nulo MedalSeries Grain-Free Turkey & Chicken	1.78	49.44	0.41	37.73	1.34	35.09	26-Nov-19
Best Feline Friend PLAY Tic Toc Beef & Tuna Pâté	1.78	65.80	0.87	19.00	4.80	23.09	27-Jan-20
Natural Balance L.I.D. Limited Ingredient Duck & Green Pea	1.79	41.21	0.52	31.61	15.20	35.33	9-Jan-17
Wellness Complete Health Beef & Salmon Pâté	1.79	46.45	1.22	36.50	4.60	34.00	1-Feb-20
Chicken Soup for the Soul Grain-Free Salmon, Red Potato & Spinach Pâté	1.79	49.80	1.49	26.94	9.95	31.00	28-Oct-19
Hound & Gatos Grain-Free 98% Duck & Liver	1.79	55.34	0.41	29.67	na	36.91	8-Nov-19
Wellness Complete Health Gravies Tuna Dinner	1.79	55.56	1.63	16.29	13.81	21.45	1-Feb-20
Weruva The Slice is Right Wild Caught Salmon Pâté Pouch	1.79	61.60	0.27	17.90	11.50	16.73	26-Jan-20
Against the Grain Chicken & Pumpkin Samba	1.79	61.90	0.37	10.00	20.00	24.29	30-Oct-19
Halo Grain-Free Turkey and Giblets Indoor Pâté	1.80	42.80	1.10	39.70	6.90	31.82	30-Jan-20
Solid Gold Wholesome Selects Grain-Free Chicken, Duck & Pumpkin Chunks in Gravy*	1.80	48.00	0.54	22.55	16.60	28.00	22-Jan-20
VeRUS Grain-Free Chicken Pâté	1.80	49.80	0.61	38.70	0.30	32.55	27-Jan-20
Koha Grain-Free Limited Ingredient Wild Kangaroo Pâté*	1.81	51.58	0.54	29.10	8.69	32.36	13-Aug-19
Chicken Soup for the Soul Grain-Free Beef, Carrot & Red Potato Pâté	1.82	46.12	1.14	33.49	8.18	36.00	28-Oct-19
Chicken Soup for the Soul Grain-Free Chicken, Sweet Potato & Spinach Pâté	1.82	46.37	1.14	35.10	6.20	36.00	28-Oct-19

Brand and Variety	Phos	Prot	Sod	Fat	Carb	Cals	Obtained
Fancy Feast Classic Pâté Tender Beef & Liver Feast*	1.82	52.00	0.50	33.80	3.30	32.33	26-Nov-19
Tiki Cat Grain-Free Aloha Friends Chicken, Duck & Pumpkin Pouch*	1.82	54.55	na	31.82	0.00	24.40	30-Jan-20
RAWZ 96% Rabbit Pâté	1.83	47.24	0.46	30.60	8.70	31.27	3-Dec-19
Instinct Original Grain-Free 95% Real Salmon Pâté	1.83	54.17	1.13	26.25	3.33	30.00	8-Nov-19
Wellness Complete Health Minced Tuna Dinner	1.84	55.07	1.74	19.52	11.03	24.73	1-Feb-20
Wellness Complete Health Salmon & Trout Pâté	1.85	42.03	1.21	40.85	4.91	37.27	1-Feb-20
Wellness Complete Health Turkey Pâté	1.85	48.57	1.14	35.05	4.80	32.73	1-Feb-20
Merrick Purrfect Bistro Grain-Free Duck Pâté	1.86	43.22	1.99	36.86	7.42	28.36	26-Jun-19
VeRUS Grain-Free Salmon Pâté	1.86	49.40	0.76	36.30	0.30	33.27	27-Jan-20
Koha L.I.D. Shredded Duck Entrée in Gravy*	1.86	51.54	1.22	24.63	9.73	24.91	27-Nov-19
Fancy Feast Classic Pâté Savory Salmon Feast*	1.86	54.10	0.62	31.40	2.60	30.67	26-Nov-19
AvoDerm Wild by Nature Grain-Free Salmon in Salmon Consommé	1.86	68.73	0.33	22.61	16.70	27.33	15-Oct-19
Hound & Gatos Grain-Free 98% Trout & Duck Liver	1.87	49.39	0.36	35.42	na	32.91	8-Nov-19
Fancy Feast Classic Pâté Tender Beef Feast*	1.87	54.50	0.60	29.90	4.90	30.67	26-Nov-19
Wellness Complete Health Morsels Tuna Entrée	1.87	55.69	1.78	20.16	9.75	24.73	1-Feb-20
Weruva Stewlander	1.88	43.30	0.71	34.30	14.20	29.27	26-Jan-20
Weruva Stick a Spork in It Pouch	1.89	42.90	0.68	35.30	13.50	31.00	26-Jan-20
Wellness Complete Health Gravies Chicken Dinner	1.89	50.26	1.58	21.47	15.03	23.27	1-Feb-20
Wellness Complete Health Beef & Chicken Pâté	1.89	50.88	1.16	33.65	3.00	31.27	1-Feb-20
Merrick Limited Ingredient Grain-Free Chicken	1.90	42.60	0.54	37.40	6.20	26.20	26-Jun-19
Halo Grain-Free Chicken and Beef Indoor Pâté	1.90	43.50	1.00	37.30	7.00	36.36	30-Jan-20

Brand and Variety	Phos	Prot	Sod	Fat	Carb	Cals	Obtained
Whole Earth Farms Grain-Free Healthy Kitten Pâté	1.90	48.76	0.70	27.37	12.97	31.20	25-Oct-19
Halo Grain-Free Whitefish Indoor Pâté	1.90	50.00	1.10	39.50	0.10	30.91	30-Jan-20
Halo Grain-Free Seafood Medley Indoor Pâté	1.90	57.90	1.40	19.60	10.00	27.82	30-Jan-20
Wellness Core Grain-Free Chicken, Turkey & Chicken Liver Pâté	1.91	47.53	0.87	30.80	9.77	38.73	1-Feb-20
Wellness Complete Health Morsels Chicken Entrée	1.91	47.90	1.63	27.10	11.76	26.00	1-Feb-20
Wellness Complete Health Minced Salmon Entrée	1.91	48.90	2.10	26.41	9.10	25.00	1-Feb-20
Soulistic Moist & Tender Duck Dinner in Gravy Canned	1.91	52.76	0.68	22.61	9.85	23.27	27-Jan-20
ZiwiPeak New Zealand Hoki	1.91	55.00	0.29	19.00	13.00	29.73	1-Feb-20
Fancy Feast Classic Cod, Sole & Shrimp Feast*	1.91	62.90	0.81	23.00	2.50	27.33	26-Nov-19
Wellness Complete Health Morsels Turkey & Salmon Entrée	1.92	49.59	1.63	26.09	10.60	26.33	1-Feb-20
Wellness Complete Health Turkey & Salmon Pâté	1.92	50.15	1.28	31.12	5.69	30.36	1-Feb-20
Dr Elsey's Clean Protein Salmon Pâté	1.92	51.71	0.71	34.79	5.13	36.55	22-Sep-19
Instinct Original Grain-Free 95% Real Venison Pâté	1.92	52.61	0.49	27.87	4.18	36.18	8-Nov-19
Wellness Complete Health Sliced Salmon Entrée	1.93	50.07	2.13	24.36	10.83	24.18	1-Feb-20
Lovibles Furrever and Always	1.93	55.90	0.92	24.90	6.20	28.67	21-Jan-20
Koha L.I.D. Shredded Beef Entrée in Gravy*	1.94	41.74	0.99	32.15	12.02	29.64	27-Nov-19
Merrick Purrfect Bistro Grain-Free Tuna Pâté	1.94	48.76	1.90	32.73	4.38	29.82	26-Jun-19
Solid Gold Wholesome Selects Grain-Free Chicken & Liver Chunks in Gravy*	1.94	50.00	0.21	22.70	17.00	28.00	22-Jan-20
Wellness Complete Health Morsels Salmon Dinner	1.94	50.12	2.13	24.63	10.40	23.67	1-Feb-20

Brand and Variety	Phos	Prot	Sod	Fat	Carb	Cals	Obtained
Wellness Complete Health Kitten Pâté	1.94	50.50	1.11	34.02	2.35	32.33	1-Feb-20
I and Love and You Whascally Wabbit Pâté	1.94	55.95	0.61	26.68	na	31.67	11-Nov-19
Wellness Complete Health Minced Turkey Entrée	1.95	48.86	1.57	24.93	12.30	25.64	1-Feb-20
Hound & Gatos Grain-Free 98% Rabbit	1.95	50.01	0.51	32.87	na	33.09	8-Nov-19
Soulistic Moist & Tender Beef Dinner in Gravy Canned	1.95	56.84	0.79	20.00	9.05	21.64	27-Jan-20
I and Love and You Chicken Me Out Pâté	1.96	48.76	0.55	34.30	na	37.00	11-Nov-19
Fancy Feast Classic Pâté Tender Beef & Chicken Feast*	1.96	51.40	0.55	32.90	4.30	33.67	26-Nov-19
Wellness Complete Health Minced Chicken Dinner	1.97	46.50	1.58	27.26	12.86	26.73	1-Feb-20
Wellness Complete Health Sliced Chicken Entrée	1.97	46.59	1.59	27.40	12.60	24.00	1-Feb-20
Wellness Complete Health Minced Turkey & Salmon Entrée	1.97	48.85	1.63	25.02	12.13	25.82	1-Feb-20
Instinct Grain-Free Ultimate Protein Real Rabbit Pâté	1.97	59.40	0.68	21.37	3.42	26.67	8-Nov-19
Instinct Original Grain-Free 95% Real Rabbit Pâté	1.97	59.40	0.68	21.37	3.42	26.73	8-Nov-19
Diamond Naturals Whitefish Dinner Cat and Kitten	1.99	44.29	0.67	24.91	17.72	31.27	11-Nov-19
Chicken Soup for the Soul Grain-Free Chicken & Turkey Pâté	1.99	46.34	1.01	35.81	5.47	36.55	28-Oct-19
Fancy Feast Classic Pâté Chicken Feast*	1.99	53.00	0.61	31.00	4.10	33.00	26-Nov-19
Fancy Feast Classic Pâté Ocean Whitefish & Tuna Feast*	1.99	62.20	0.76	24.60	3.50	28.33	26-Nov-19
Against the Grain Captain's Catch with Sardines & Mackerel	1.99	64.30	0.58	14.90	0.00	21.43	30-Oct-19
Feline Natural New Zealand Beef Feast*	2.00	41.67	0.67	41.67	na	31.83	1-Feb-20
Nulo MedalSeries Limited Ingredient Diet 95% Salmon in Broth	2.00	47.66	0.24	28.07	11.05	37.09	26-Nov-19

Brand and Variety	Phos	Prot	Sod	Fat	Carb	Cals	Obtained
Wellness Complete Health Sliced Turkey & Salmon Dinner	2.00	48.61	1.66	25.48	11.59	25.27	1-Feb-20
Merrick Purrfect Bistro Grain-Free Salmon Pâté	2.01	48.47	2.10	34.67	2.93	31.82	26-Jun-19
Weruva The Newly Feds Beef & Salmon Pâté Pouch	2.03	66.40	0.43	16.80	5.40	18.73	26-Jan-20
Koha Grain-Free Limited Ingredient Duck Pâté*	2.04	41.67	0.36	45.07	2.36	37.67	13-Aug-19
Wellness Complete Health Sliced Turkey Entrée	2.06	48.94	1.62	25.26	11.30	23.67	1-Feb-20
Merrick Purrfect Bistro Grain-Free Tuna Niçoise	2.06	51.67	2.39	18.47	13.49	25.64	26-Jun-19
Halo Grain-Free Turkey and Duck Indoor Pâté	2.10	44.10	1.10	44.80	0.10	33.64	30-Jan-20
Halo Grain-Free Chicken Indoor Pâté	2.10	50.00	1.20	33.00	4.30	36.55	30-Jan-20
Fancy Feast Classic Pâté Seafood Feast*	2.10	58.40	0.70	26.70	3.20	29.33	26-Nov-19
Merrick Purrfect Bistro Grain-Free Chicken Pâté	2.11	47.41	1.94	37.24	2.59	33.64	26-Jun-19
Feline Natural New Zealand Beef & Hoki Feast*	2.11	47.89	na	33.16	na	26.83	1-Feb-20
Lovibles Simply Irresistable	2.11	64.30	0.93	15.40	4.90	25.00	21-Jan-20
Nulo MedalSeries Limited Ingredient Diet 95% Chicken & Chicken Liver in Broth	2.12	47.60	0.37	38.77	0.00	39.45	26-Nov-19
Wellness Core Indoor Chicken & Chicken Liver Pâté	2.12	52.42	1.12	20.48	12.10	26.91	1-Feb-20
President's Choice Extra Meaty Ocean Whitefish & Tuna	2.13	68.68	1.00	13.78	2.17	na	12-Dec-19
Fancy Feast Classic Pâté Chopped Grill Feast*	2.14	52.90	0.56	30.00	4.70	33.00	26-Nov-19
Dave's Cat's Meow 95% Chicken, Chicken Liver & Turkey*	2.15	55.98	0.48	27.14	8.09	35.82	7-Nov-19
Weruva Outback Grill	2.15	67.90	0.36	16.80	0.60	18.91	26-Jan-20
Fancy Feast Classic Pâté Tender Liver & Chicken Feast*	2.16	55.00	0.47	29.30	3.60	32.00	26-Nov-19
Chicken Soup for the Soul Grain-Free Salmon Pâté	2.17	51.93	1.27	30.45	5.09	32.73	28-Oct-19

Brand and Variety	Phos	Prot	Sod	Fat	Carb	Cals	Obtained
Wellness Complete Health Chicken & Herring Pâté	2.21	53.51	1.23	28.26	4.29	29.09	1-Feb-20
I and Love and You Oh My Cod! Pâté	2.22	52.23	0.66	28.41	na	27.33	11-Nov-19
Tiki Cat Grain-Free Mackerel & Sardine in Calamari Consommé (Makaha Luau)*	2.22	66.67	na	16.67	0.00	19.64	30-Jan-20
Health Extension Grain-Free Real Chicken Entrée for Kittens & Cats	2.23	42.00	0.59	40.00	3.00	36.00	7-Dec-16
Dave's Cat's Meow 95% Chicken & Chicken Liver*	2.23	58.52	0.26	27.37	5.38	35.45	7-Nov-19
Stella and Chewy's Purrfect Pâté Grain-Free Turkey*	2.27	39.90	0.93	20.00	4.37	34.00	3-Dec-19
Halo Grain-Free Salmon Indoor Pâté	2.30	51.10	1.10	33.70	2.40	38.36	30-Jan-20
Merrick Purrfect Bistro Grain-Free Turkey Pâté	2.31	54.33	2.26	24.42	4.76	31.82	26-Jun-19
Wellness Complete Health Chicken & Lobster Pâté	2.32	49.31	1.16	33.02	3.83	32.36	1-Feb-20
Friskies Extra Gravy Pâté with Salmon in Savory Gravy	2.40	47.50	na	na	na	na	7-Sep-18
President's Choice Extra Meaty Cod, Sole & Shrimp	2.44	65.38	0.77	11.92	5.56	na	12-Dec-19
Grandma Mae's Country Naturals Grain-Free Beef Pâté Entrée*	2.45	45.00	0.65	25.00	na	26.43	23-Nov-19
Best Feline Friend OMG Date Nite! Duck & Salmon in Gravy Pouch	2.47	59.50	0.52	20.40	9.00	19.29	27-Jan-20
Health Extension Grain-Free Real Turkey Entrée for Kittens & Cats	2.50	36.00	0.64	46.00	2.00	39.00	7-Dec-16
Friskies Extra Gravy Pâté with Tuna in Savory Gravy	2.50	48.10	na	na	na	na	7-Sep-18
Tiki Cat Grain-Free Sardine Cutlets (Tahitian Grill)*	2.50	73.68	na	15.79	0.00	21.43	30-Jan-20
Canada Fresh Lamb*	2.55	47.50	0.50	42.50	na	31.45	17-Jan-20
Canada Fresh Red Meat*	2.55	47.50	0.60	42.50	na	31.45	17-Jan-20
Koha L.I.D. Shredded Turkey Entrée in Gravy*	2.65	40.54	0.76	24.48	12.42	28.36	27-Nov-19
Canada Fresh Duck*	2.75	42.50	0.50	37.50	na	31.45	17-Jan-20

Brand and Variety	Phos	Prot	Sod	Fat	Carb	Cals	Obtained
Canada Fresh Chicken*	2.75	45.00	0.50	37.50	na	31.45	17-Jan-20
Koha Grain-Free Duck Stew*	2.76	52.80	1.40	28.60	3.46	24.36	13-Aug-19
Feline Natural New Zealand Chicken Feast*	2.78	52.78	0.56	30.56	na	28.67	1-Feb-20
Tiki Cat Grain-Free Sardine Cutlets in Lobster Consomme (Bora Bora Luau)*	2.85	72.22	na	16.67	0.00	20.71	30-Jan-20
Friskies Extra Gravy Pâté with Turkey in Savory Gravy	2.90	50.80	na	na	na	na	7-Sep-18
Merrick Purrfect Bistro Grain-Free Surf N Turf Pâté	3.25	54.37	2.18	29.71	6.21	28.18	26-Jun-19
Koha Grain-Free Limited Ingredient Rabbit au Jus*	3.98	53.81	0.48	25.87	0.00	25.33	13-Aug-19
Wellness Core Kitten Chicken & Turkey Pâté[7]	4.72	49.30	1.89	31.69	4.75	36.18	1-Feb-20

---

[7] The phosphorus content is extremely high, but Wellness has told me it is accurate

DRY FOODS IN ORDER OF PHOSPHORUS CONTENT

Please see pages 3 and 15 for information on how to use these tables. All data are on a dry matter analysis basis, except calories, which are provided per kg (2.2lbs) on an ME as fed basis.

Foods marked * show minimum values for protein and fat and in some cases phosphorus — the actual values could be much higher. Page 13 explains more about this.

"na" means the information was not available.

Brand and Variety	Phos	Prot	Sod	Fat	Carb	Cals	Obtained
NOW FRESH Grain-Free Senior/Weight Management Recipe	0.50	34.00	0.31	15.00	39.00	3571	31-Oct-19
Young Again ZERO Mature TruCarnivore 54/24	0.50	57.90	0.31	28.80	0.00	4510	01-Feb-20
Young Again LID (Limited Ingredient) ZERO Mature TruCarnivore 54/25	0.52	59.50	0.38	27.40	0.00	4446	01-Feb-20
NOW FRESH Grain-Free Fish	0.60	34.00	0.33	22.00	35.00	3988	31-Oct-19
Hill's Science Diet Adult Urinary Hairball Control	0.62	34.20	0.35	18.80	32.20	3681	01-Feb-20
Young Again Mature Health CalPhosMag 54/22	0.65	57.60	0.31	28.60	6.00	4657	01-Feb-20
Hill's Science Diet Adult Oral Care	0.66	33.50	0.39	21.10	30.60	3762	01-Feb-20
Hill's Science Diet Adult 7+ Youthful Vitality Chicken & Rice	0.67	35.40	0.39	16.50	41.00	3870	01-Feb-20
Hill's Science Diet Adult 7+ Chicken	0.68	32.10	0.35	21.30	38.70	4006	01-Feb-20
Hill's Science Diet Adult 11+ Indoor	0.68	34.70	0.33	20.90	29.90	3790	01-Feb-20
NOW Fresh Grain-Free Adult	0.68	35.73	0.35	21.59	34.00	3862	31-Oct-19
Hill's Science Diet Adult 11+ Chicken	0.69	32.70	0.33	22.50	37.00	4089	01-Feb-20
Performatrin Ultra Grain-Free Senior	0.69	33.00	0.28	17.00	30.80	4021	21-Jan-20
Hill's Healthy Advantage Adult Oral+ Feline Nutrition	0.69	33.40	0.41	22.30	30.10	4120	01-Feb-20

Brand and Variety	Phos	Prot	Sod	Fat	Carb	Cals	Obtained
Hill's Science Diet Adult 7+ Indoor	0.69	34.10	0.35	17.00	33.80	3593	01-Feb-20
Hill's Healthy Advantage Adult	0.69	34.20	0.48	22.70	35.70	4117	01-Feb-20
Hill's Science Diet Adult 7+ Hairball Control	0.70	33.90	0.35	19.10	31.40	3674	01-Feb-20
Hill's Science Diet Adult Chicken	0.70	35.00	0.45	21.40	35.20	4021	01-Feb-20
Hill's Science Diet Adult Multiple Benefit	0.72	34.60	0.41	13.00	37.00	3325	01-Feb-20
Hill's Science Diet Adult Indoor	0.76	36.10	0.55	16.10	31.70	3515	01-Feb-20
Hill's Science Diet Adult Perfect Weight	0.76	40.20	0.35	12.00	33.20	3409	01-Feb-20
Diamond Maintenance	0.77	34.30	0.36	16.70	42.00	3742	12-Nov-19
Hill's Science Diet Adult Light	0.78	38.00	0.53	9.10	39.50	3179	01-Feb-20
Hill's Science Diet Adult Hairball Control	0.79	33.90	0.45	19.30	31.00	3673	01-Feb-20
Hill's Science Diet Adult Sensitive Stomach & Skin	0.79	35.00	0.45	22.00	36.30	4104	01-Feb-20
Hill's Science Diet Adult Hairball Control Light	0.79	40.00	0.44	9.60	35.10	3172	01-Feb-20
Wysong Vegan (*I do not recommend vegan foods for cats*)	0.80	29.50	0.20	11.40	40.80	3312	16-Oct-19
Red Flannel Cat Formula	0.80	33.30	0.35	15.30	33.65	3776	12-Nov-19
Hill's Science Diet Adult Sensitive Stomach & Skin Grain-Free	0.80	35.00	0.45	21.90	35.20	4068	01-Feb-20
Organix Organic Chicken & Sweet Potato	0.80	36.90	0.23	15.40	39.90	3739	29-Oct-19
Lotus Grain-Free Oven-Baked Sardines & Herring	0.80	38.00	0.53	15.78	33.43	3457	28-Jan-20
Natural Planet Organic Chicken & Pea All Life Stages	0.81	34.02	0.66	15.75	na	3980	28-Jan-20
Regal Kitten Bites	0.81	37.28	0.30	23.44	na	3993	05-Jan-17
Young Again ZERO Cat & Kitten Trucarnivore 54/26	0.81	57.60	0.25	28.60	0.00	4482	01-Feb-20
Organix Grain-Free Organic Chicken & Brown Rice	0.83	32.60	0.24	15.60	41.10	3726	29-Oct-19
Trader Joe's Premium Chicken*	0.83	33.33	0.27	20.00	na	3832	28-Nov-16
Blackwood Indoor Chicken Meal & Brown Rice*	0.83	33.33	0.29	13.33	43.93	3824	27-Nov-19

Brand and Variety	Phos	Prot	Sod	Fat	Carb	Cals	Obtained
Solid Gold Winged Tiger with Quail & Pumpkin*	0.83	33.33	0.30	11.11	41.11	3560	08-Nov-19
Performatrin Ultra Limited Potato & Turkey	0.84	36.30	0.37	19.00	30.10	3835	28-Nov-19
Blackwood Adult Chicken Meal & Brown Rice*	0.86	33.33	0.28	18.89	37.46	3913	27-Nov-19
Life's Abundance All Life Stages	0.86	35.48	0.46	22.58	31.20	4023	27-Nov-19
Nulo MedalSeries Adult Hairball Management Chicken & Cod	0.86	43.78	0.42	17.57	23.26	3534	26-Nov-19
Annamaet Original Chicken Meal & Brown Rice	0.87	33.00	0.36	15.00	31.50	4022	26-Nov-19
Adirondack Kitten*	0.87	34.44	0.30	20.00	na	3643	09-Jan-17
Blackwood Kitten Chicken Meal & Brown Rice*	0.87	36.67	0.30	23.33	29.20	4204	27-Nov-19
Blackwood Special Diet Grain-Free Duck Meal, Salmon Meal & Field Pea*	0.87	42.22	0.30	20.00	29.18	3763	27-Nov-19
Performatrin Ultra Limited Green Pea & Duck	0.88	33.20	0.44	13.20	37.30	3630	28-Nov-19
PetGuard LifeSpan Cat & Kitten	0.88	35.55	0.40	15.55	47.70	3485	18-Dec-19
Performatrin Ultra Limited Sweet Potato & Chicken	0.89	33.30	0.34	13.40	37.80	3630	28-Nov-19
Blackwood Lean/Senior Chicken Meal & Brown Rice*	0.89	33.33	0.32	12.22	47.04	3594	27-Nov-19
Grandma Mae's Country Naturals Grain-Free Salmon*	0.89	34.44	0.24	21.11	na	3820	23-Nov-19
Grandma Mae's Country Naturals Grain-Free Chicken Meal & Brown Rice*	0.89	37.78	0.29	22.22	na	3900	23-Nov-19
Fussie Cat Market Fresh Salmon*	0.89	38.89	0.22	16.67	29.00	3550	17-Jan-20
Grandma Mae's Country Naturals Grain-Free Chicken & Herring*	0.89	38.89	0.26	18.89	na	3700	23-Nov-19
Acana Meadowland	0.89	39.00	0.33	22.00	27.00	4060	29-Oct-19
Acana Wild Atlantic	0.89	39.00	0.66	22.00	25.00	4020	29-Oct-19
Fussie Cat Market Fresh Salmon & Chicken*	0.89	40.00	0.36	17.78	27.00	3604	17-Jan-20
Fussie Cat Market Fresh Chicken & Turkey*	0.89	40.00	0.39	17.78	27.00	3598	17-Jan-20

Brand and Variety	Phos	Prot	Sod	Fat	Carb	Cals	Obtained
NutriSource Senior/Weight Management	0.90	28.92	0.63	9.06	na	3250	28-Jan-20
Diamond Care Urinary Support	0.90	32.90	0.49	16.30	43.90	3728	12-Nov-19
Gather Free Acres Organic Free Run Chicken	0.90	33.00	0.49	18.00	37.00	3664	31-Oct-19
Solid Gold Fit as a Fiddle with Alaskan Pollock*	0.90	33.33	na	11.11	na	3110	08-Nov-19
Halo Holistic Grain-Free Chicken & Chicken Liver Senior	0.90	33.50	0.60	14.20	40.40	3520	30-Jan-20
NutriSource Cat & Kitten Chicken Meal, Salmon & Liver	0.90	33.70	0.60	19.70	na	4170	28-Jan-20
Halo Holistic Grain-Free Wild Salmon & Whitefish Senior	0.90	34.00	0.70	13.70	39.40	3470	30-Jan-20
Halo Holistic Sensitive Stomach Seafood Medley	0.90	34.80	0.50	18.60	36.70	3760	30-Jan-20
Halo Holistic Chicken & Chicken Liver Adult	0.90	34.80	0.51	21.60	30.50	3780	30-Jan-20
Halo Holistic Wild Salmon & Whitefish Adult	0.90	35.00	0.60	16.80	36.30	3730	30-Jan-20
Fromm Chicken À La Veg	0.90	35.04	0.41	20.90	34.99	3871	31-Jan-20
Halo Holistic Sensitive Stomach Turkey & Turkey Liver	0.90	35.20	0.50	21.30	32.30	3770	30-Jan-20
Halo Holistic Healthy Weight Grain-Free Wild Salmon & Whitefish Indoor	0.90	36.80	0.60	17.20	33.60	3550	30-Jan-20
Now FRESH Grain-Free Kitten	0.90	38.00	0.31	24.00	30.00	3947	31-Oct-19
Halo Holistic Grain-Free Wild Salmon & Whitefish Kitten	0.90	38.50	0.40	20.90	29.70	3870	30-Jan-20
Wysong Uretic	0.90	46.20	0.80	18.00	20.50	3528	16-Oct-19
Feline Medley Chicken, Turkey & Fish	0.91	31.60	0.26	16.30	40.77	na	19-Nov-19
Star Pro Premium Feline Formula	0.91	33.41	0.33	17.03	33.33	3705	01-Feb-20
Performatrin Adult Grain-Free Chicken & Potato	0.91	35.70	0.37	20.10	28.80	4095	16-Jan-20
Young Again Original Cat & Kitten 50/22	0.91	56.50	0.21	26.80	6.00	4465	01-Feb-20
Young Again Li'l Bites Kitten 50/22	0.91	56.50	0.21	26.80	6.00	4465	01-Feb-20

80

Brand and Variety	Phos	Prot	Sod	Fat	Carb	Cals	Obtained
Infinia Holistic Chicken & Pea	0.93	36.70	0.45	18.90	23.87	3765	14-Nov-19
Fromm Beef Liváttini Veg	0.93	38.80	0.39	21.22	29.24	3802	31-Jan-20
Performatrin Ultra Limited Potato & Salmon	0.95	36.30	0.27	19.00	30.50	3835	28-Nov-19
Performatrin Ultra Grain-Free Ocean	0.95	42.00	0.53	20.00	20.60	4186	21-Jan-20
Regal Lean Cat Bites	0.96	31.49	0.30	9.10	na	3276	05-Jan-17
Wellness Complete Health Indoor Chicken & Chicken Meal	0.96	35.11	0.33	13.70	41.08	3532	01-Feb-20
Performatrin Senior	0.96	35.20	0.35	18.40	35.20	3920	28-Nov-19
Nulo Freestyle Freeze-Dried Raw Cat & Kitten Turkey & Duck	0.96	46.90	0.36	43.62	1.02	5214	26-Nov-19
Adirondack Lean /Senior*	0.97	31.11	0.27	11.11	na	3269	09-Jan-17
AvoDerm Grain-Free Tuna with Lobster & Crab Meal	0.97	34.70	0.51	18.30	39.00	3595	24-Jul-19
Whole Earth Farms Grain-Free Real Salmon	0.97	40.50	1.06	30.84	15.60	3458	25-Oct-19
Adirondack Adult*	0.98	33.33	0.26	15.56	na	3858	09-Jan-17
Artemis Fresh Mix	0.98	35.80	0.40	23.00	31.30	3922	23-Nov-16
AvoDerm Kitten Chicken & Herring Meal	0.98	39.13	0.35	23.91	23.00	4027	24-Jul-19
Blackwood Special Diet Grain-Free Chicken Meal & Field Pea*	0.98	44.44	0.31	20.00	27.30	3823	27-Nov-19
Regal Cat Bites	0.99	33.86	0.34	19.96	na	3813	05-Jan-17
Chicken Soup for the Soul Grain-Free Chicken & Legumes	0.99	35.70	0.35	17.19	35.11	3585	28-Oct-19
Authority Adult Chicken & Rice	0.99	36.10	0.20	18.60	37.70	4163	13-Dec-16
Grandma Mae's Country Naturals Grain-Free Indoor & Weight Control*	1.00	33.33	0.21	8.89	na	2950	23-Nov-19
GO! Solutions Skin + Coat Care Grain-Free Salmon	1.00	34.00	0.32	16.00	39.00	4122	31-Oct-19
Go! Solutions Sensitivities Limited Ingredient Grain-Free Pollock	1.00	34.00	0.38	17.00	41.00	4232	31-Oct-19
Halo Holistic Healthy Weight Grain-Free Game Bird Medley Indoor	1.00	34.00	0.70	18.20	35.70	3630	30-Jan-20

Brand and Variety	Phos	Prot	Sod	Fat	Carb	Cals	Obtained
Lotus Grain-Free Oven-Baked Low Fat Chicken	1.00	34.61	0.37	11.06	40.33	3206	28-Jan-20
Newman's Own Adult Cat	1.00	35.00	0.30	18.00	32.00	na	14-Nov-19
Go! Solutions Sensitivities Limited Ingredient Duck	1.00	35.00	0.45	18.00	36.00	4222	31-Oct-19
Halo Holistic Healthy Weight Grain-Free Chicken & Chicken Liver Indoor	1.00	35.20	0.70	17.10	36.30	3610	30-Jan-20
Go! Solutions Skin + Coat Care Chicken	1.00	36.00	0.28	22.00	33.00	4604	31-Oct-19
Solid Gold Let's Stay In with Salmon, Lentil & Apple*	1.00	36.00	0.38	16.00	25.00	na	23-Jan-20
Halo Holistic Grain-Free Chicken & Chicken Liver Kitten	1.00	36.00	0.40	22.90	29.40	3870	30-Jan-20
Rachael Ray Nutrish Real Chicken & Brown Rice*	1.00	37.36	0.50	15.38	na	3635	06-Jan-20
Solid Gold Katz-N-Flocken with Lamb & Brown Rice & Pearled Barley*	1.00	37.78	0.32	13.33	37.78	3525	08-Nov-19
Supreme Source Chicken Meal & Turkey Meal*	1.00	38.89	0.33	16.67	33.33	3650	03-Dec-19
Supreme Source Grain-Free Whitefish Meal & Salmon Meal*	1.00	38.89	0.33	16.67	33.33	3660	03-Dec-19
Solid Gold Touch of Heaven with Chicken & Sweet Potato*	1.00	40.00	0.30	20.00	27.78	3810	08-Nov-19
FirstMate Grain-Free Chicken Meal with Blueberries	1.00	40.00	0.40	18.00	29.00	3530	25-Nov-19
Solid Gold Indigo Moon with Peas, Chicken & Egg*	1.00	42.00	0.30	20.00	17.00	3860	22-Jan-20
Solid Gold Indigo Moon with Alaskan Pollock & Egg*	1.00	42.00	0.30	20.00	17.00	na	23-Jan-20
Instinct Ultimate Protein Duck	1.00	52.00	0.56	18.89	18.89	4510	08-Nov-19
Rayne Clinical Nutrition Growth/Sensitive-GI	1.01	36.93	0.54	14.60	36.30	3500	27-Nov-19
Annamaet No 29 Sustain Grain-Free	1.01	37.00	0.43	16.00	26.50	3618	26-Nov-19
Rachael Ray Nutrish Indoor Chicken With Lentils & Salmon*	1.01	37.36	0.48	13.19	na	3499	06-Jan-20

Brand and Variety	Phos	Prot	Sod	Fat	Carb	Cals	Obtained
Catered Bowl Antibiotic-free Chicken & Brown Rice*	1.02	33.33	0.27	17.06	37.00	3500	11-Nov-19
Tender & True Antibiotic-free Chicken & Brown Rice*	1.02	33.33	0.27	17.06	37.00	3500	11-Nov-19
AvoDerm Adult Chicken & Herring Indoor Hairball Care	1.02	34.78	0.33	17.39	29.00	3564	24-Jul-19
AvoDerm Adult Chicken & Herring Meal	1.02	34.78	0.33	21.74	28.50	3753	24-Jul-19
Solid Gold Let's Stay In with Chicken, Lentil & Apple*	1.02	36.00	0.38	16.00	25.00	na	22-Jan-20
Nulo MedalSeries Grain-Free Limited Ingredient Diet Cat & Kitten Chicken	1.02	41.57	0.65	19.73	27.85	3799	26-Nov-19
Nutrisca Grain-Free Chicken Recipe*	1.02	42.80	0.46	16.60	24.60	3645	21-Jan-20
VeRUS Feline Life Advantage	1.03	34.10	0.26	20.66	29.21	4785	27-Jan-20
Performatrin Hairball Formula	1.03	36.30	0.52	21.00	21.10	3830	28-Nov-19
Catered Bowl Antibiotic-free Turkey & Brown Rice*	1.04	33.33	0.34	17.06	37.00	3750	11-Nov-19
Tender & True Antibiotic-free Turkey & Brown Rice*	1.04	33.33	0.34	17.06	37.00	3750	11-Nov-19
Chicken Soup for the Soul Grain-Free Salmon & Legumes	1.04	35.75	0.30	17.19	35.42	3596	28-Oct-19
Dr Pol's Grain-Free 34/15 Cat & Kitten	1.04	37.78	0.29	16.67	34.59	3715	17-Jan-20
Rayne Clinical Nutrition Rabbit Maintenance	1.04	38.72	0.64	14.62	35.41	3530	27-Nov-19
Stella and Chewy's Raw Blend Cage-Free Recipe*	1.04	44.30	0.25	17.60	35.10	3818	21-Jan-20
Fromm Duck À La Veg	1.05	37.16	0.43	21.66	32.95	3757	31-Jan-20
Performatrin Ultra Healthy Weight with Salmon Recipe	1.05	37.20	0.49	13.20	30.70	3380	28-Nov-19
Hill's Healthy Advantage Kitten	1.05	37.30	0.43	24.80	28.30	4139	01-Feb-20
Annamaet Grain-Free Chicken Meal & Whitefish Meal	1.05	44.00	0.41	20.00	15.50	4149	26-Nov-19
NutriSource Cat & Kitten Chicken & Rice	1.06	32.40	0.59	19.25	na	4098	28-Jan-20
Hill's Science Diet Kitten Chicken	1.06	37.80	0.56	23.50	30.00	4152	01-Feb-20

Brand and Variety	Phos	Prot	Sod	Fat	Carb	Cals	Obtained
Nature's Harvest Adult Grain-Free Chicken*	1.06	38.89	na	22.22	23.33	4260	02-Dec-19
Farmina Natural and Delicious Low Ancestral Grain Chicken & Pomegranate Neutered	1.06	40.43	0.74	10.64	34.26	3877	11-Dec-16
Nulo MedalSeries Grain-Free Limited Ingredient Diet Cat & Kitten Turkey	1.06	41.57	0.28	19.73	25.60	3726	26-Nov-19
Stella and Chewy's Raw-Coated Cage-Free Chicken*	1.06	43.20	0.25	18.20	31.00	3837	21-Jan-20
Performatrin Ultra Chicken & Brown Rice Recipe	1.07	36.10	0.45	22.00	29.30	3865	28-Nov-19
Wellness Complete Health Chicken, Chicken Meal & Rice	1.07	42.07	0.30	21.14	26.96	3952	01-Feb-20
Life's Abundance All Life Stages Grain-Free	1.08	40.86	0.63	20.43	30.10	3961	27-Nov-19
Nature's Logic Chicken Meal Feast	1.08	40.90	0.36	22.40	28.62	3964	20-Feb-20
RAWZ Meal Free Salmon, Dehydrated Chicken & Whitefish	1.08	45.30	0.41	16.46	28.56	3710	03-Dec-19
Dr Elsey's Clean Protein Chicken Recipe	1.08	62.60	0.58	19.46	4.69	4008	22-Sep-19
Performatrin Adult	1.09	35.90	0.53	20.10	30.20	4110	28-Nov-19
Lovibles Kitten	1.09	36.10	0.48	16.60	33.00	4185	22-Jan-20
Performatrin Healthy Weight	1.09	36.20	0.46	14.30	24.40	3360	28-Nov-19
Taste of the Wild Prey Limited Ingredient Turkey	1.09	36.80	0.44	14.20	37.50	3689	18-Oct-19
Performatrin Indoor	1.09	36.80	0.51	16.70	29.70	3740	28-Nov-19
AvoDerm Salmon & Brown Rice	1.09	36.96	0.33	19.57	27.00	3793	24-Jul-19
Fromm Gold Kitten	1.09	37.16	0.43	21.66	32.76	4410	31-Jan-20
PureVita Grain-Free Salmon & Green Pea Entrée	1.10	31.40	0.90	18.30	na	4068	28-Jan-20
Exclusive Chicken & Brown Rice Weight Management/Hairball Care	1.10	32.50	0.66	10.08	31.94	3320	12-Nov-19
Exclusive Chicken & Brown Rice	1.10	32.50	0.67	21.30	25.56	3860	12-Nov-19
PureVita Grain-Free Chicken & Peas Entrée	1.10	32.70	0.70	18.80	na	3992	28-Jan-20

Brand and Variety	Phos	Prot	Sod	Fat	Carb	Cals	Obtained
Lone Star Meow for More	1.10	34.16	0.49	11.44	na	3370	01-Feb-20
Pro Pac Ultimates Deep Sea Select	1.10	34.80	0.40	16.30	39.10	3705	11-Nov-19
Lovibles Seafood	1.10	34.80	0.48	14.50	35.80	4060	22-Jan-20
NutriSource Grain-Free Country Select Entrée	1.10	36.00	0.30	16.00	na	4036	28-Jan-20
Pro Pac Ultimates Savanna Pride	1.10	37.00	0.30	16.30	39.10	3730	11-Nov-19
Fromm Hasen Duckenpfeffer	1.10	37.32	0.41	19.37	21.16	3708	31-Jan-20
Instinct Limited Ingredient Diet Rabbit	1.10	38.00	0.55	20.88	24.18	3890	08-Nov-19
Orijen Cat & Kitten	1.10	44.00	0.44	22.00	21.00	4060	23-Sep-19
GO! Solutions Carnivore 74% Grain-Free Salmon & Cod	1.10	46.00	0.45	18.00	25.00	4239	31-Oct-19
Wellness Complete Health Grain-Free Adult Chicken & Chicken Meal	1.10	47.12	0.29	19.67	21.83	3907	01-Feb-20
Wellness Complete Health Grain-Free Kitten Chicken & Chicken Meal	1.10	47.12	0.29	19.67	21.83	3907	01-Feb-20
Catered Bowl Salmon & Sweet Potato*	1.11	28.33	na	11.67	na	4700	11-Nov-19
Tender & True Salmon & Sweet Potato*	1.11	28.33	na	11.67	na	4700	11-Nov-19
Nature's Harvest Senior/Weight Management*	1.11	32.22	na	13.33	40.00	3870	02-Dec-19
Nature's Harvest Adult/Kitten Grain-Free *	1.11	35.56	na	21.11	28.89	3690	02-Dec-19
Nature's Harvest Grain-Free Cod*	1.11	40.00	0.44	22.22	na	na	03-Feb-20
Wellness Complete Health Healthy Weight Chicken, Chicken Meal & Turkey Meal	1.12	33.97	0.24	13.48	43.58	3520	01-Feb-20
Fromm Gold Mature	1.13	33.28	0.40	13.77	43.79	4017	31-Jan-20
Fromm Salmon À La Veg	1.13	35.18	0.47	17.20	39.20	3679	31-Jan-20
DAD'S Special Mix*	1.13	37.17	0.74	10.75	49.34	3350	25-Nov-19
Performatrin Kitten	1.13	38.60	0.57	23.30	25.80	4230	28-Nov-19
Performatrin Ultra Lamb & Brown Rice Adult Recipe	1.14	35.90	0.49	21.10	29.00	3865	28-Nov-19

Brand and Variety	Phos	Prot	Sod	Fat	Carb	Cals	Obtained
Organix Grain-Free Organic Healthy Kitten	1.14	37.50	0.31	16.30	37.57	3590	17-Nov-16
Wellness Complete Health Senior Chicken & Chicken Meal	1.14	43.10	0.32	16.14	29.40	3738	01-Feb-20
Fromm Game Bird Recipe	1.16	38.60	0.44	20.09	30.81	3654	31-Jan-20
Nulo Freestyle Grain-Free Indoor Adult Duck & Lentils	1.16	43.78	0.45	19.73	23.21	3724	26-Nov-19
Farmina Natural and Delicious Low Ancestral Grain Chicken & Pomegranate	1.17	38.30	0.53	21.28	29.79	4383	11-Dec-16
Stella and Chewy's Raw-Coated Cage-Free Salmon*	1.17	39.80	0.25	15.90	36.40	3687	21-Jan-20
Lovibles Chicken	1.18	35.00	0.50	14.50	34.70	4021	22-Jan-20
Hill's Science Diet Kitten Indoor	1.18	38.40	0.54	20.70	31.50	3997	01-Feb-20
Fromm Salmon Tunachovy	1.18	38.70	0.45	17.18	33.57	3621	31-Jan-20
Fromm Gold Adult	1.19	34.96	0.44	19.68	36.93	4318	31-Jan-20
Nulo MedalSeries Grain-Free Adult Salmon & Lentils	1.19	43.51	0.36	21.89	22.65	3881	26-Nov-19
Nulo MedalSeries Grain-Free Indoor Adult Duck & Cod	1.19	43.78	0.39	16.49	26.34	3493	26-Nov-19
Canidae All Life Stages Indoor Adult with Chicken, Turkey, Lamb & Fish Meals	1.20	33.15	0.33	15.76	39.00	4198	23-Jul-19
AvoDerm Adult Grain-Free Turkey Meal	1.20	33.70	0.43	18.48	30.00	3685	24-Jul-19
AvoDerm Adult Grain-Free Ocean Fish & Chicken Meal	1.20	33.70	0.54	17.39	31.00	3635	24-Jul-19
Evanger's Grain-Free Meat Lover's Medley with Rabbit	1.20	35.60	0.20	15.10	31.00	na	16-Sep-16
Taste of the Wild Canyon River with Trout & Smoked Salmon	1.20	36.00	0.38	17.50	36.40	3741	23-Sep-19
FirstMate Cat/Kitten	1.20	36.00	0.80	21.00	29.00	3660	25-Nov-19
Earthborn Holistic Feline Vantage	1.20	39.10	0.30	15.20	39.10	3770	15-Jan-20
GO! Solutions Carnivore 70% Grain-Free Lamb & Wild Boar	1.20	47.00	0.47	16.00	26.00	4147	31-Oct-19
Dr Elsey's Clean Protein with Salmon	1.20	58.35	0.65	19.02	9.06	3976	22-Sep-19

Brand and Variety	Phos	Prot	Sod	Fat	Carb	Cals	Obtained
AvoDerm Grain-Free Duck with Turkey Meal	1.21	35.80	0.39	17.70	39.00	3563	24-Jul-19
Chicken Soup for the Soul Classic Adult Chicken & Brown Rice	1.21	37.76	0.50	20.28	30.15	3732	28-Oct-19
Nulo MedalSeries Grain-Free Cat & Kitten Turkey & Cod	1.21	44.86	0.37	21.89	21.54	3953	26-Nov-19
Catered Bowl Ocean Whitefish & Potato*	1.22	33.33	0.38	17.06	35.00	3750	11-Nov-19
Tender & True Ocean Whitefish & Potato*	1.22	33.33	0.38	17.06	35.00	3750	11-Nov-19
Chicken Soup for the Soul Classic Indoor Chicken & Brown Rice	1.22	36.05	0.49	14.89	35.33	3425	28-Oct-19
Farmina Natural and Delicious Low Ancestral Grain Codfish & Orange	1.22	38.30	0.85	21.28	29.89	4476	11-Dec-16
Lotus Oven-Baked Chicken Adult	1.22	39.17	0.41	21.39	26.27	3697	28-Jan-20
Nulo MedalSeries Grain-Free Indoor Adult Turkey & Chicken	1.22	41.71	0.35	18.41	27.13	3632	26-Nov-19
Nulo MedalSeries Grain-Free Indoor Adult Trout & Duck	1.22	41.89	0.35	15.75	28.50	3428	26-Nov-19
Nulo MedalSeries Grain-Free Senior Cat Turkey, Alaska Pollock & Red Lentils	1.22	42.31	0.35	15.66	28.61	3454	26-Nov-19
Nulo MedalSeries Grain-Free Cat & Kitten Cod & Duck	1.22	43.10	0.36	17.84	27.22	3685	26-Nov-19
Open Farm Homestead Turkey & Chicken	1.22	44.57	0.37	21.74	21.74	3840	17-Jan-20
Country Vet Choice 30/11 Kitten & Adult	1.23	33.34	0.27	12.23	37.03	3280	17-Jan-20
Nulo MedalSeries Grain-Free Adult Chicken & Peas	1.23	43.51	0.37	21.89	22.71	3868	26-Nov-19
Horizon Complete All Life Stages	1.24	33.52	0.46	18.05	31.36	3680	25-Nov-19
Health Extension Chicken & Brown Rice	1.24	38.00	0.26	20.00	31.00	3719	07-Dec-16
Dr Tim's Chase	1.24	38.00	0.74	22.00	20.00	4140	29-Oct-19
Health Extension Grain-Free Turkey & Salmon Recipe	1.24	39.00	0.23	20.00	33.00	3744	07-Dec-16
Merrick Limited Ingredient Grain-Free Turkey	1.24	39.20	0.78	15.60	34.62	3588	18-Nov-16

Brand and Variety	Phos	Prot	Sod	Fat	Carb	Cals	Obtained
Fromm Surf & Turf	1.24	41.99	0.48	21.79	23.80	3696	31-Jan-20
DAD'S Original*	1.25	36.24	0.41	11.51	47.76	3370	25-Nov-19
Dave's Naturally Healthy Adult*	1.25	41.81	0.32	20.80	na	3777	30-Dec-19
Nulo Freestyle Grain-Free Cat and Kitten Chicken & Cod	1.25	44.23	0.33	22.25	21.44	3868	26-Nov-19
Nulo Freestyle Grain-Free Adult Trim Salmon & Lentils	1.25	45.86	0.37	13.76	23.89	3538	26-Nov-19
Chicken Soup for the Soul Classic Weight & Mature Care Chicken & Brown Rice	1.26	37.81	0.49	9.38	37.15	3113	28-Oct-19
Fromm Chicken au Frommage	1.27	38.10	0.52	21.02	na	3752	31-Jan-20
Wellness Natural Hairball Control Chicken Meal & Rice	1.27	41.63	0.28	18.29	27.72	3614	01-Feb-20
Wellness Complete Health Grain-Free Indoor Chicken & Chicken Meal	1.27	41.91	0.30	13.91	29.91	3451	01-Feb-20
Wellness Complete Health Grain-Free Indoor Healthy Weight Chicken & Turkey	1.27	41.91	0.30	13.91	29.91	3451	01-Feb-20
Farmina Natural and Delicious Low Ancestral Grain Lamb & Blueberry	1.28	38.30	0.64	21.28	29.79	4240	11-Dec-16
Open Farm Catch-of-the-Season Whitefish	1.28	44.57	0.37	21.74	21.74	3840	17-Jan-20
Nulo MedalSeries Grain-Free Adult Weight Management Salmon & Sweet Potato	1.29	43.51	0.41	14.05	28.79	3446	26-Nov-19
Wysong Anergen	1.30	30.30	0.20	13.50	37.20	3301	16-Oct-19
Canidae Grain-Free PURE Stream with Real Trout	1.30	34.78	0.33	17.39	35.00	3670	07-Dec-16
Canidae Grain-Free PURE Sea with Real Salmon	1.30	34.78	0.33	18.48	34.00	3750	07-Dec-16
PureVita Grain-Free Duck & Red Lentils Entrée	1.30	35.00	0.40	14.50	na	3880	28-Jan-20
Evanger's Grain-Free Catch of the Day	1.30	35.60	0.20	18.60	29.50	3758	16-Sep-16
Wysong Geriatrx	1.30	36.90	0.40	16.30	27.30	3528	16-Oct-19

88

Brand and Variety	Phos	Prot	Sod	Fat	Carb	Cals	Obtained
Canidae Grain-Free PURE Elements with Real Chicken	1.30	38.04	0.33	19.57	29.00	3750	07-Dec-16
FirstMate indoor Formula	1.30	39.00	0.80	13.00	33.00	3295	25-Nov-19
Canidae Grain-Free PURE Ocean Indoor Cat with Fresh Tuna	1.30	39.13	0.33	13.04	33.00	3400	07-Dec-16
Nulo MedalSeries Grain-Free Limited Ingredient Diet Cat & Kitten Cod	1.30	39.19	0.37	17.57	31.10	3657	26-Nov-19
Instinct Limited Ingredient Diet Salmon	1.30	41.00	0.88	18.70	28.57	4400	08-Nov-19
Open Farm Wild Caught Salmon	1.30	44.57	0.37	21.74	21.74	3840	17-Jan-20
FirstMate Grain-Free Pacific Ocean Fish Meal with Blueberries	1.30	47.00	1.70	20.00	22.00	3700	25-Nov-19
GO! Sensitivity + Shine Grain-Free Freshwater Trout & Salmon	1.30	50.00	0.65	21.00	20.00	4444	31-Oct-19
Country Vet Premium 30/15 Kitten & Adult	1.31	33.34	0.26	16.67	33.52	3570	17-Jan-20
Rancher's Choice 31.5/11 Cat & Kitten	1.31	35.00	0.29	12.23	36.93	3325	17-Jan-20
Taste of the Wild Rocky Mountain with Roasted Venison & Smoked Salmon	1.31	47.00	0.44	19.70	21.50	3745	23-Sep-19
Nulo Freestyle Freeze-Dried Raw Cat & Kitten Chicken & Salmon	1.31	60.62	0.45	30.10	0.78	4437	26-Nov-19
Azmira Classic Cat Formula*	1.32	33.08	0.33	11.38	na	3425	16-Jan-20
Lotus Grain-Free Oven-Baked Duck Adult	1.32	38.60	0.59	17.22	31.69	3531	28-Jan-20
Catered Bowl Organic Chicken & Liver*	1.33	33.33	0.23	18.89	30.00	3500	11-Nov-19
Tender & True Organic Chicken & Liver*	1.33	33.33	0.23	18.89	30.00	3500	11-Nov-19
Catered Bowl Organic Turkey & Liver*	1.33	33.33	0.29	18.00	30.00	3650	11-Nov-19
Tender & True Organic Turkey & Liver*	1.33	33.33	0.29	18.00	30.00	3650	11-Nov-19
Country Vet Naturals 34/15 Grain-Free	1.33	37.78	0.29	16.67	30.47	3588	17-Jan-20
Nature's Logic Turkey Meal Feast	1.33	41.50	0.32	15.60	27.50	3957	20-Feb-20

Brand and Variety	Phos	Prot	Sod	Fat	Carb	Cals	Obtained
Open Farm Pasture Raised Lamb	1.33	44.57	0.37	21.74	21.74	3840	17-Jan-20
Nulo Freestyle Adult Hairball Management Turkey & Cod	1.33	44.98	0.40	17.57	21.75	3534	26-Nov-19
RAWZ Meal Free Dehydrated Chicken, Turkey & Chicken	1.33	48.12	0.36	14.48	25.69	3710	03-Dec-19
AvoDerm Grain-Free Salmon with Tuna Meal	1.34	37.80	0.53	19.60	35.00	3595	24-Jul-19
DAD'S Gourmet Blend Natural*	1.35	37.33	0.74	11.49	47.93	3380	25-Nov-19
Canidae All Life Stages Cat Food with Chicken Meal & Rice	1.36	34.78	0.33	21.74	34.00	4400	23-Jul-19
Canidae All Life Stages with Chicken, Turkey, Lamb & Fish Meals	1.36	34.78	0.33	21.74	34.00	4585	23-Jul-19
Holistic Select Grain-Free Indoor Health/Weight Control (Turkey, Chicken & Herring Meal)	1.37	36.80	0.33	14.84	35.03	3547	01-Feb-20
Holistic Select Grain-Free Adult & Kitten Health Chicken Meal	1.37	38.80	0.41	20.98	28.63	3851	01-Feb-20
Petkind Green Tripe & High Seas*	1.38	37.78	1.01	17.78	25.50	3705	17-Jan-20
Nature's Logic Rabbit Meal Feast	1.38	41.60	0.36	16.00	23.90	4041	20-Feb-20
Farmina Natural and Delicious Grain-Free Lamb & Blueberry	1.38	44.68	0.64	21.28	22.66	4417	11-Dec-16
Farmina Natural and Delicious Grain-Free Boar & Apple	1.38	46.81	0.64	21.28	20.74	4396	11-Dec-16
Farmina Natural and Delicious Grain-Free Kitten Chicken & Pomegranate	1.38	46.81	0.64	21.28	20.96	4344	11-Dec-16
Farmina Natural and Delicious Grain-Free Adult Chicken & Pomegranate	1.38	46.81	0.64	21.28	20.96	4448	11-Dec-16
Farmina Natural and Delicious Grain-Free Fish & Orange	1.38	46.81	0.85	21.28	20.96	4456	11-Dec-16
Farmina Natural and Delicious Grain-Free Chicken & Pomegranate Neutered	1.38	48.94	0.64	11.70	24.47	3904	11-Dec-16
Performatrin Ultra Original Grain-Free Kitten Recipe	1.39	44.60	0.37	20.20	20.20	3915	16-Jan-20
Performatrin Ultra Grain-Free Recipe	1.39	44.60	0.37	20.20	20.20	3915	28-Nov-19

Brand and Variety	Phos	Prot	Sod	Fat	Carb	Cals	Obtained
Summit	1.40	31.00	0.37	18.00	40.00	3499	31-Oct-19
Diamond Care Weight Management	1.40	35.80	0.51	10.30	34.50	3080	12-Nov-19
NutriSource Grain-Free Ocean Select Entrée	1.40	36.70	1.50	16.00	na	4004	28-Jan-20
Wysong Vitality	1.40	38.70	0.40	17.20	23.80	3552	16-Oct-19
Acana Appalachian Ranch	1.40	39.00	0.39	22.00	24.00	3980	29-Oct-19
Acana Grasslands	1.40	39.00	0.44	22.00	24.00	3980	29-Oct-19
Wysong Nurture	1.40	40.40	0.40	15.90	23.30	3584	16-Oct-19
Wysong Fundamentals	1.40	42.10	0.40	15.80	24.60	3480	16-Oct-19
Wysong Nurture with Quail	1.40	43.70	0.40	17.10	22.30	3608	16-Oct-19
Orijen Six Fish	1.40	44.00	0.78	22.00	20.00	4060	23-Sep-19
Wellness Complete Health Grain-Free Senior Chicken & Chicken Meal	1.40	46.66	0.43	14.75	26.12	3392	01-Feb-20
Instinct Ultimate Protein Chicken	1.40	52.00	0.67	18.89	13.33	4470	08-Nov-19
Wellness RawRev indoor with 100% Raw Freeze-Dried Turkey Liver	1.41	42.55	0.29	15.49	31.47	3627	01-Feb-20
Wellness CORE Indoor Cat Chicken & Turkey	1.41	43.26	0.29	14.95	29.35	3561	01-Feb-20
Taste of the Wild Prey Limited Ingredient Angus Beef	1.42	33.60	0.42	14.20	41.30	3650	18-Oct-19
Wellness Complete Health Grain-Free Salmon & Salmon Meal	1.42	42.17	0.61	17.42	26.18	3672	01-Feb-20
Rachael Ray Nutrish PEAK Rustic Woodlands Indoor with Chicken, Turkey, & Duck*	1.42	43.96	0.58	15.38	na	3551	06-Jan-20
Wellness CORE Grain-Free Indoor Salmon & Herring	1.43	43.04	0.41	11.32	30.39	3277	01-Feb-20
ZiwiPeak New Zealand Air-Dried Venison	1.43	54.00	0.77	32.00	7.00	4700	01-Feb-20
Fussie Cat Quail & Duck Meal*	1.44	36.67	na	16.67	na	3598	17-Jan-20
Whole Earth Farms Grain-Free Real Turkey & Duck	1.45	39.87	0.70	16.80	30.27	3515	25-Oct-19
Nulo Freestyle Grain-Free Cat and Kitten Turkey & Duck	1.45	43.78	0.45	19.73	23.36	3696	26-Nov-19

Brand and Variety	Phos	Prot	Sod	Fat	Carb	Cals	Obtained
Merrick Limited Ingredient Grain-Free Chicken	1.46	41.02	0.64	16.16	29.65	3588	18-Nov-16
Whole Earth Farms Grain-Free Real Chicken	1.46	41.02	0.83	16.16	29.65	3459	25-Oct-19
I and Love and You Nude Food Surf n' Chick	1.46	49.95	na	23.33	na	3817	08-Nov-19
Holistic Select Grain-Free Adult Anchovy & Sardine and Salmon Meal	1.47	38.12	0.46	21.68	28.04	3921	01-Feb-20
I and Love and You Nude Food Poultry & Plenty	1.47	49.90	na	21.85	na	3732	08-Nov-19
Chicken Soup for the Soul Classic Kitten Chicken, Brown Rice & Pea	1.48	40.06	0.37	22.42	24.72	3797	28-Oct-19
Artemis OSOPure Grain-Free Salmon and Garbanzo Bean	1.50	40.40	0.39	21.90	25.60	3861	09-Dec-16
Instinct Raw Boost Indoor Health Chicken	1.50	41.00	0.66	14.29	26.37	3861	08-Nov-19
Instinct Raw Boost Healthy Weight Chicken	1.50	41.00	0.77	13.19	25.27	3709	08-Nov-19
I and Love and You Naked Essentials Salmon & Trout	1.50	42.87	0.50	17.37	na	3421	08-Nov-19
Merrick Purrfect Bistro Grain-Free Healthy Kitten Recipe Kitten	1.50	43.63	0.38	20.06	22.52	3755	26-Jun-19
Orijen Regional Red	1.50	44.00	0.56	22.00	19.00	4060	23-Sep-19
Earthborn Holistic Grain-Free Primitive Feline	1.50	47.80	0.30	21.70	20.10	3925	15-Jan-20
ZiwiPeak New Zealand Free Range Chicken	1.50	48.00	0.68	39.00	1.00	5500	01-Feb-20
GO! Solutions 84% Carnivore Grain-Free Chicken, Turkey & Duck	1.50	51.00	0.49	21.00	17.00	4298	31-Oct-19
Wellness Complete Health Grain-Free Indoor Salmon & Herring	1.52	38.21	0.53	12.55	31.77	3432	01-Feb-20
Nutrisca Grain-Free Salmon Recipe*	1.52	40.30	0.93	15.70	30.20	3560	21-Jan-20
Feline Natural Lamb & King Salmon Feast Freeze Dried*	1.52	47.83	na	40.22	na	5197	01-Feb-20
Only Natural Pet Feline Powerfood Kitten Power Dinner*	1.53	50.89	0.52	23.44	na	3750	29-Jan-20

Brand and Variety	Phos	Prot	Sod	Fat	Carb	Cals	Obtained
Rachael Ray Nutrish PEAK Woodland Catch with Chicken, Trout & Salmon*	1.54	43.96	0.88	19.78	na	3756	06-Jan-20
Merrick Purrfect Bistro Grain-Free Healthy Weight Recipe Adult	1.54	46.60	0.55	15.50	28.64	3215	26-Jun-19
ZiwiPeak New Zealand Air-Dried Lamb	1.56	43.00	0.77	41.00	3.00	5600	01-Feb-20
Orijen Tundra	1.56	44.00	0.44	22.00	20.00	4120	23-Sep-19
Diamond Naturals Chicken & Rice Indoor	1.60	36.40	0.58	15.80	30.90	3350	12-Nov-19
Diamond Naturals Chicken & Rice Kitten	1.60	38.90	0.47	24.60	24.50	4052	12-Nov-19
Earthborn Holistic Grain-Free Wild Sea Catch	1.60	47.80	0.40	21.70	19.00	3895	15-Jan-20
I and Love and You Naked Essentials Chicken & Duck	1.63	42.21	0.54	17.33	na	3502	08-Nov-19
Merrick Purrfect Bistro Grain-Free Healthy Senior Recipe Senior	1.63	44.44	0.62	16.56	29.13	3431	26-Jun-19
Feline Natural Chicken & LambFeast Freeze Dried*	1.63	52.17	na	33.70	na	4857	01-Feb-20
I and Love and You Lovingly Simple Salmon & Sweet Potato	1.65	42.13	0.87	15.70	na	3538	08-Nov-19
Wellness CORE Grain-Free Adult Turkey, Turkey Meal & Duck	1.66	44.29	0.28	20.74	21.14	3902	01-Feb-20
Fussie Cat Guinea Fowl & Turkey Meal*	1.67	38.89	na	16.67	na	3598	17-Jan-20
ZiwiPeak New Zealand Air-Dried Mackerel & Lamb	1.67	51.00	0.77	33.00	4.00	4800	01-Feb-20
Merrick Purrfect Bistro Grain-Free Real Salmon & Sweet Potato	1.68	46.81	0.57	18.38	26.43	3748	26-Jun-19
Wellness CORE Grain-Free Original Turkey & Chicken	1.68	51.36	0.51	21.30	14.17	3977	01-Feb-20
Wellness CORE Grain-Free Kitten Turkey & Chicken	1.68	51.36	0.51	21.30	14.17	3977	01-Feb-20
Wellness RawRev Original with 100% Raw Freeze-Dried Turkey Liver	1.68	52.66	0.51	21.36	12.76	3871	01-Feb-20
Orijen Fit & Trim	1.70	48.90	0.42	16.70	17.80	3710	23-Sep-19

Brand and Variety	Phos	Prot	Sod	Fat	Carb	Cals	Obtained
Natural Balance Original Ultra Whole Body Health Chicken & Salmon	1.71	38.84	0.59	18.61	31.13	na	07-Oct-19
Wellness Complete Health Salmon & Salmon Meal	1.72	42.07	0.61	19.84	26.03	3873	01-Feb-20
Nulo Freestyle Grain-Free Senior Cat Grain-Free Alaska Pollock, Duck & Sweet Potato	1.73	42.75	0.35	15.41	27.48	3454	26-Nov-19
Only Natural Pet Feline Powerfood High Protein Grain-Free Rabbit*	1.76	42.22	0.54	22.22	na	3650	29-Jan-20
Victor Mers Classic	1.78	35.34	0.35	18.29	38.39	3596	23-Nov-19
Merrick Purrfect Bistro Grain-Free Real Chicken & Sweet Potato	1.80	47.51	0.54	17.39	25.66	3731	26-Jun-19
Taste of the Wild Lowland Creek with Roasted Quail and Roasted Duck	1.86	40.30	0.55	17.50	29.10	3558	18-Oct-19
Nature's Logic Sardine Meal Feast	1.88	42.20	0.60	15.50	25.80	3504	20-Feb-20
ZiwiPeak New Zealand Air-Dried Beef	1.88	47.80	0.86	38.00	2.20	5500	01-Feb-20
Horizon Legacy Cat & Kitten Grain-Free	1.89	42.51	0.40	19.38	20.44	3870	25-Nov-19
Instinct Raw Boost Indoor Health Rabbit	1.90	43.00	0.55	15.93	26.37	3913	08-Nov-19
Only Natural Pet Feline Powerfood High Protein Grain-Free Poultry*	1.92	52.22	0.43	20.00	18.89	3630	29-Jan-20
Whole Earth Farms Grain-Free Healthy Kitten	1.95	42.50	1.30	17.20	28.03	3500	25-Oct-19
Instinct Raw Boost Grain-Free Real Salmon	2.00	46.00	0.88	20.30	17.58	4488	08-Nov-19
Diamond Naturals Chicken & Rice Active Cat	2.00	46.40	0.66	22.40	17.20	4000	12-Nov-19
Instinct Original Grain-Free Salmon Meal	2.00	47.00	0.66	19.78	17.58	4470	08-Nov-19

Brand and Variety	Phos	Prot	Sod	Fat	Carb	Cals	Obtained
Only Natural Pet Feline Powerfood High Protein Grain-Free Fish & Fowl	2.00	50.00	0.44	21.11	17.78	3665	29-Jan-20
Feline Natural Beef & Hoki Feast Freeze Dried*	2.17	51.09	na	34.78	na	4762	01-Feb-20
Instinct Limited Ingredient Diet Turkey	2.20	39.00	0.55	18.13	26.37	4070	08-Nov-19
Instinct Raw Boost Duck	2.20	44.00	0.77	25.82	12.09	4387	08-Nov-19
Instinct Original Grain-Free Duck	2.20	44.00	0.77	25.82	13.19	4397	08-Nov-19
Instinct Kitten Chicken	2.20	47.00	0.66	24.73	13.19	4456	08-Nov-19
Instinct Original Grain-Free Rabbit Meal	2.30	45.00	0.66	24.73	13.19	4346	08-Nov-19
Instinct Original Grain-Free Chicken Meal	2.60	45.00	0.66	23.08	15.38	4300	08-Nov-19
Instinct Raw Boost Grain-Free Real Chicken	2.60	45.00	0.66	24.18	14.29	4327	08-Nov-19

WET FOODS IN BRAND ORDER

Please see pages 3 and 15 for information on how to use these tables. All data are on a dry matter analysis basis, except calories, which are provided on an as fed per ounce basis.

Foods marked * show minimum values for protein and fat and in some cases phosphorus — the actual values could be much higher. Page 13 explains more about this.

"na" means the information was not available.

A

AGAINST THE GRAIN*

	Phos	Prot	Sod	Fat	Carb	Cals	Obtained
Aloha Tuna with Seaweed & Crab	1.20	75.30	0.63	16.90	0.28	23.93	30-Oct-19
Bimini Brunch with Krill & Egg	1.22	79.10	0.41	12.60	0.00	25.00	30-Oct-19
Tuna Mango Tango with Duck	1.25	65.20	0.28	15.00	0.00	20.29	30-Oct-19
Tuna Aubergine with Snapper & Eggplant Dinner	1.25	73.70	0.23	14.70	0.00	24.29	30-Oct-19
Big Kahuna with Crab & Tilapia	1.25	78.80	0.72	11.20	2.61	23.93	30-Oct-19
Chicken & Polyhauai'I Berry Dinner	1.39	82.10	0.26	8.94	0.00	16.00	30-Oct-19
Tuna Toscano with Salmon & Tomato Dinner	1.40	65.00	0.32	15.70	0.00	22.14	30-Oct-19
Chicken Mayflower with Turnip	1.47	78.70	0.52	9.26	0.00	13.71	30-Oct-19
Caribbean Club with Chicken & Cheese	1.54	84.00	0.21	10.50	0.00	26.43	30-Oct-19
Chicken & Pumpkin Samba	1.79	61.90	0.37	10.00	20.00	24.29	30-Oct-19
Captain's Catch with Sardines & Mackerel	1.99	64.30	0.58	14.90	2.41	21.43	30-Oct-19

ARTEMIS

	Phos	Prot	Sod	Fat	Carb	Cals	Obtained
OSOPure Tuna & Pumpkin	1.13	70.71	0.65	12.05	1.62	21.33	23-Nov-16
OSOPure Tuna	1.13	71.70	0.56	12.43	1.42	21.67	23-Nov-16
OSOPure Tuna & Shrimp	1.13	71.94	0.67	12.03	1.40	22.00	23-Nov-16
OSOPure Tuna & Salmon	1.15	70.24	0.52	13.59	1.50	21.67	23-Nov-16

	Phos	Prot	Sod	Fat	Carb	Cals	Obtained
OSOPure Tuna & Chicken	1.15	71.60	0.52	12.57	1.42	21.67	23-Nov-16

AUJUS BY RAWZ

	Phos	Prot	Sod	Fat	Carb	Cals	Obtained
Aku Tuna & Mackerel in a Silky Broth Pouch	0.90	65.62	0.60	13.20	13.82	23.17	3-Dec-19
Chicken Breast & Pumpkin in a Silky Broth Pouch	0.90	80.33	0.30	9.00	1.86	24.39	3-Dec-19
Aku Tuna & Salmon in a Silky Broth Pouch	0.91	66.82	0.61	15.51	10.57	24.39	3-Dec-19
Chicken Breast & Chicken Liver in a Silky Broth Pouch	0.91	81.40	0.30	9.00	1.05	24.80	3-Dec-19
Chicken Breast & Duck in a Silky Broth Pouch	0.92	83.84	0.33	9.00	0.57	24.39	3-Dec-19

AVODERM

	Phos	Prot	Sod	Fat	Carb	Cals	Obtained
Grain-Free Chicken & Duck Entrée in Gravy	0.93	42.72	0.22	23.27	13.90	27.33	15-Oct-19
Indoor Weight Control	0.94	35.81	0.29	20.61	22.00	27.45	15-Oct-19
Grain-Free Chicken Chunks Entrée in Gravy	0.96	62.12	1.65	18.85	22.20	22.00	15-Oct-19
Grain-Free Salmon & Chicken Entrée in Gravy	0.97	46.04	0.22	21.62	13.90	25.00	15-Oct-19
Grain-Free Sardine, Shrimp & Crab Entrée in Gravy	0.97	58.89	0.37	11.87	5.60	22.66	15-Oct-19
Grain-Free Tuna & Chicken Entrée with Vegetables	1.00	69.80	0.50	19.33	16.70	27.00	15-Oct-19
Grain-Free Tuna & Crab Entrée in Gravy	1.01	59.77	0.90	13.26	8.30	23.33	15-Oct-19
Chicken Formula	1.08	47.80	0.85	38.30	13.50	33.82	15-Oct-19
Grain-Free Chicken & Duck Recipe in Gravy Pouch	1.10	44.00	0.45	16.00	13.90	19.13	15-Oct-19
Grain-Free Ocean Fish Recipe in Gravy Pouch	1.16	62.00	0.94	12.50	12.50	17.70	15-Oct-19
Salmon Formula	1.18	47.68	0.49	31.63	13.55	36.00	15-Oct-19

	Phos	Prot	Sod	Fat	Carb	Cals	Obtained
Wild by Nature Grain-Free Tuna with Prawns in Consommé	1.18	78.77	1.04	15.32	5.60	23.67	15-Oct-19
Grain-Free Tuna Recipe in Gravy Pouch	1.30	72.00	0.93	11.00	11.00	17.70	15-Oct-19
Grain-Free Salmon Recipe in Gravy Pouch	1.32	44.00	0.57	11.00	11.00	17.70	15-Oct-19
Ocean Fish Formula	1.33	47.68	0.42	33.12	10.53	33.09	15-Oct-19
Wild by Nature Grain-Free Chopped Sardines in Consommé	1.51	69.49	0.21	17.78	11.10	22.67	15-Oct-19
Wild by Nature Grain-Free Salmon in Salmon Consommé	1.86	68.73	0.33	22.61	16.70	27.33	15-Oct-19

AZMIRA*

	Phos	Prot	Sod	Fat	Carb	Cals	Obtained
Beef & Chicken	1.05	57.18	0.64	22.55	na	34.55	5-Dec-16
Ocean Fish	1.09	50.18	0.50	45.82	na	30.72	5-Dec-16

B

BALANCED BLENDS

	Phos	Prot	Sod	Fat	Carb	Cals	Obtained
Species Balanced Steamed Turkey	1.50	62.37	0.53	30.37	na	38.70	01-Dec-19
Species Balanced Steamed Chicken	1.57	62.16	0.54	29.89	na	37.90	01-Dec-19
Species Balanced Steamed Beef Heart & Offal	1.64	59.90	0.53	30.59	na	33.40	01-Dec-19

BEST FELINE FRIEND

	Phos	Prot	Sod	Fat	Carb	Cals	Obtained
OMG Live N' Love Chicken & Lamb Ground in Gravy	0.71	42.90	0.56	40.80	11.50	36.07	27-Jan-20
PLAY Cherish Chicken Pâté Pouch	0.71	47.10	0.60	40.70	7.60	31.33	27-Jan-20
PLAY Tiptoe Chicken & Turkey Pâté Pouch	0.71	47.50	0.60	40.10	7.70	31.00	27-Jan-20

	Phos	Prot	Sod	Fat	Carb	Cals	Obtained
PLAY Checkmate Chicken Pâté	0.71	47.70	0.61	40.00	7.70	30.73	27-Jan-20
PLAY Topsy Turvy Chicken & Turkey Pâté	0.71	48.10	0.61	39.40	7.80	30.55	27-Jan-20
OMG Shine Bright Chicken & Salmon in Gravy Pouch	0.72	42.10	0.55	42.40	11.20	37.14	27-Jan-20
OMG Stir It Up Chicken & Salmon Ground in Gravy	0.72	42.60	0.56	41.80	11.30	36.55	27-Jan-20
OMG Devour Me Tuna & Duck Pouch	0.72	62.60	0.64	16.10	14.60	21.00	27-Jan-20
OMG Text Me Chicken & Turkey in Gravy Pouch	0.73	42.20	0.55	42.20	11.20	37.50	27-Jan-20
OMG Charge Me Up Chicken in Gravy Pouch	0.73	43.80	0.56	40.90	10.90	36.79	27-Jan-20
OMG Cloud 9 Chicken Ground in Gravy	0.73	44.30	0.57	40.30	11.00	35.82	27-Jan-20
OMG Tell Me Tuna & Turkey Minced in Gravy	0.75	61.10	0.66	18.50	13.30	20.73	27-Jan-20
OMG Start Me Up Tuna & Salmon Minced in Gravy	0.75	61.40	0.65	18.60	13.00	20.73	27-Jan-20
OMG Chase Me Tuna & Chicken Minced in Gravy	0.75	61.50	0.64	18.60	12.90	20.73	27-Jan-20
OMG Be Happy Chicken & Beef Ground in Gravy	0.77	42.30	0.58	42.60	10.50	36.55	27-Jan-20
OMG Dream Team Chicken & Duck Ground in Gravy	0.77	42.60	0.57	41.80	11.20	36.55	27-Jan-20
OMG Lights Out Tuna & Lamb Minced in Gravy	0.78	60.70	0.66	18.50	13.40	20.73	27-Jan-20
OMG Baby Cakes Tuna & Beef in Gravy Pouch	0.78	62.90	0.64	13.40	17.00	20.00	27-Jan-20
OMG Tickles Tuna & Turkey in Gravy Pouch	0.79	62.70	0.61	15.30	15.70	23.67	27-Jan-20
OMG Charm Me Tuna & Chicken in Gravy Pouch	0.79	67.80	0.65	15.20	10.80	17.67	27-Jan-20
PLAY Take a Chance Chicken, Duck & Turkey Pâté	0.81	48.50	0.62	39.20	7.90	30.36	27-Jan-20
PLAY Laugh Out Loud Chicken & Lamb Pâté	0.82	47.60	0.62	40.20	7.70	31.09	27-Jan-20
OMG Luv Ya Tuna & Lamb in Gravy Pouch	0.83	62.80	0.60	14.00	17.50	19.00	27-Jan-20

100

	Phos	Prot	Sod	Fat	Carb	Cals	Obtained
OMG Crazy 4 U! Chicken & Salmon Minced in Gravy	0.84	59.70	0.47	25.00	9.70	20.18	27-Jan-20
OMG Seeya Sooner! Chicken & Tuna in Gravy Pouch	0.86	59.30	0.38	28.40	7.10	21.07	27-Jan-20
OMG Ciao Baby! Chicken & Shrimp in Gravy Pouch	0.86	60.70	0.49	24.80	9.00	20.00	27-Jan-20
PLAY Destiny Chicken & Duck Pâté Pouch	0.87	47.80	0.62	39.90	7.70	30.67	27-Jan-20
OMG QT Patootie! Chicken & Turkey Minced in Gravy	0.88	60.30	0.48	21.90	12.30	19.45	27-Jan-20
OMG Love Munchkin! Chicken & Pumpkin Minced in Gravy	0.89	59.10	0.45	25.20	10.00	19.45	27-Jan-20
OMG Belly Rubs Tuna & Beef Minced in Gravy	0.89	61.10	0.69	18.50	12.10	20.71	27-Jan-20
OMG Dilly Dally Tuna & Duck Minced in Gravy	0.89	61.70	0.67	18.60	13.10	20.73	27-Jan-20
Originals 4EVA Tuna & Chicken Minced in Gravy	0.90	75.50	0.58	13.10	2.50	23.27	27-Jan-20
PLAY Best Buds Chicken & Beef Pâté	0.91	49.30	0.66	37.80	7.90	30.00	27-Jan-20
OMG Purr-fect Plannin'! Chicken, Turkey & Salmon in Gravy Pouch	0.93	59.10	0.46	27.80	7.50	20.36	27-Jan-20
OMG Tuna & Salmon Sweet Cheeks in Gravy Pouch	0.94	66.10	0.67	10.50	14.00	17.33	27-Jan-20
Originals Soulmates Tuna & Salmon Minced in Geleé	0.96	77.00	0.61	15.10	2.70	23.27	27-Jan-20
Originals Be Mine Tuna & Bonito Minced in Geleé	0.96	77.50	0.61	14.20	2.70	23.82	27-Jan-20
Originals Sweethearts Tuna & Shrimp Minced in Gravy	0.97	75.30	0.62	16.10	2.70	22.91	27-Jan-20
Originals Too Cool Tuna Minced in Geleé	0.97	76.90	0.62	13.10	2.70	23.09	27-Jan-20
Originals Chuckles Tuna & Chicken Minced in Geleé	0.97	80.10	0.62	14.00	2.70	23.45	27-Jan-20
Originals Twosome Tuna & Tilapia Minced in Geleé	0.98	79.30	0.63	14.10	2.70	23.09	27-Jan-20
PLAY Tubular Chicken & Tuna Pâté Pouch	1.00	59.40	0.76	29.40	4.50	27.67	27-Jan-20

	Phos	Prot	Sod	Fat	Carb	Cals	Obtained
Originals Valentine Tuna & Pumpkin Minced in Gravy	1.00	75.00	0.64	15.20	5.60	23.64	27-Jan-20
PLAY 'Til Then Chicken & Tuna Pâté	1.01	60.50	0.80	28.10	4.60	26.18	27-Jan-20
PLAY Totes! Tuna & Turkey Pâté Pouch	1.01	66.70	0.60	24.00	2.90	27.33	27-Jan-20
PLAY Chill Out Tuna & Chicken Pâté Pouch	1.02	65.80	0.60	25.30	2.60	27.67	27-Jan-20
PLAY TTYL Tuna & Turkey Pâté	1.02	67.20	0.60	22.60	3.80	26.73	27-Jan-20
OMG Shazaam! Lamb & Tuna in Gravy Pouch	1.03	48.00	0.40	34.20	12.70	26.43	27-Jan-20
PLAY Check Please! Tuna & Chicken Pâté	1.03	66.30	0.60	23.90	3.50	26.91	27-Jan-20
PLAY Shhh... Tuna & Salmon Pâté Pouch	1.05	62.60	0.59	27.90	3.60	30.00	27-Jan-20
OMG Selfie Cam! Chicken & Lamb Minced in Gravy	1.08	48.40	0.38	32.80	12.00	24.18	27-Jan-20
OMG Booya! Beef & Chicken in Gravy Pouch	1.08	60.70	0.46	23.40	9.70	18.57	27-Jan-20
PLAY Oh Snap Tuna & Salmon Pâté	1.10	63.20	0.59	26.40	4.30	29.82	27-Jan-20
PLAY Twinkles Turkey & Tuna Pâté Pouch	1.16	62.30	0.44	29.30	0.00	27.67	27-Jan-20
PLAY Tweet Me! Turkey & Tuna Pâté	1.19	58.40	0.45	28.10	5.00	26.36	27-Jan-20
PLAY Lovers' Lane Tuna & Lamb Pâté	1.22	65.30	0.61	24.30	3.60	27.86	27-Jan-20
PLAY Tuck Me In Salmon & Tuna Pâté	1.23	54.90	0.53	33.50	4.70	31.27	27-Jan-20
PLAY Blast Off! Tuna & Beef Pâté Pouch	1.34	68.10	0.64	21.30	2.80	26.00	27-Jan-20
PLAY Double Dare Tuna & Duck Pâté	1.35	67.20	0.63	21.70	3.70	26.00	27-Jan-20
PLAY Bodacious Tuna & Beef Pâté	1.39	68.60	0.64	19.80	3.50	25.82	27-Jan-20
PLAY Told Ya Lamb & Tuna Pâté	1.43	58.60	0.80	28.70	4.80	27.86	27-Jan-20
OMG Best Day Eva! Beef & Salmon Minced in Gravy	1.49	64.90	0.60	16.20	11.20	16.18	27-Jan-20
PLAY Tap Dance Duck & Tuna Pâté Pouch	1.70	61.30	0.82	24.60	5.00	25.33	27-Jan-20

	Phos	Prot	Sod	Fat	Carb	Cals	Obtained
PLAY Ta Da! Beef & Tuna Pâté Pouch	1.70	64.30	0.87	20.80	4.90	24.00	27-Jan-20
OMG Lots-O-Luck! Duck & Tuna Minced in Gravy	1.73	62.30	0.54	17.00	11.30	18.18	27-Jan-20
PLAY Trickster Duck & Tuna Pâté	1.74	62.50	0.85	23.10	5.20	24.00	27-Jan-20
PLAY Tic Toc Beef & Tuna Pate	1.78	65.80	0.87	19.00	4.80	23.09	27-Jan-20

C

CANADA FRESH

	Phos	Prot	Sod	Fat	Carb	Cals	Obtained
Salmon	1.75	40.00	0.70	37.50	na	31.45	17-Jan-20
Beef	1.75	47.50	0.50	42.50	na	31.45	17-Jan-20
Lamb	2.55	47.50	0.50	42.50	na	31.45	17-Jan-20
Red Meat	2.55	47.50	0.60	42.50	na	31.45	17-Jan-20
Duck	2.75	42.50	0.50	37.50	na	31.45	17-Jan-20
Chicken	2.75	45.00	0.50	37.50	na	31.45	17-Jan-20

CANIDAE

	Phos	Prot	Sod	Fat	Carb	Cals	Obtained
Under The Sun Witty Kitty Ruffle My Feathers Grain-Free Flaked Turkey & Turkey Liver in Broth	1.32	54.70	1.12	23.21	na	29.67	14-Dec-16
Under The Sun Witty Kitty Wingin' It Grain-Free Shredded with Chicken & Turkey in Broth	1.39	50.00	1.14	26.40	na	25.00	14-Dec-16
Under The Sun Witty Kitty The Big Catch Grain-Free Flaked Tuna & Sardines in Broth	1.47	59.42	1.33	20.53	na	26.67	14-Dec-16

CARU

	Phos	Prot	Sod	Fat	Carb	Cals	Obtained
Classics Natural Chicken Stew	0.85	46.08	0.23	22.31	12.79	25.50	28-Oct-19
Classics Natural Wild Salmon & Turkey Stew	0.88	65.40	0.53	12.20	14.38	22.33	28-Oct-19

	Phos	Prot	Sod	Fat	Carb	Cals	Obtained
Classics Natural Chicken & Crab Stew	0.91	43.06	0.25	20.53	20.32	25.00	28-Oct-19
Classics Natural Turkey Stew	0.97	64.30	0.31	22.30	13.78	29.33	28-Oct-19

CATERED BOWL*

	Phos	Prot	Sod	Fat	Carb	Cals	Obtained
Antibiotic-Free Turkey & Brown Rice	1.00	30.00	0.36	18.40	39.00	33.64	11-Nov-19
Ocean Whitefish & Potato	1.17	30.00	0.41	18.60	38.00	28.18	11-Nov-19
Organic Turkey & Liver	1.20	30.00	0.32	19.50	33.00	33.64	11-Nov-19
Organic Chicken & Liver	1.27	30.00	0.25	19.50	33.00	30.91	11-Nov-19
Antibiotic-Free Chicken & Brown Rice	1.30	30.00	0.29	18.40	39.00	33.64	11-Nov-19
Salmon & Sweet Potato	1.33	28.33	na	11.67	na	34.00	11-Nov-19

CATS IN THE KITCHEN

	Phos	Prot	Sod	Fat	Carb	Cals	Obtained
Chick Magnet Pouch	0.67	59.00	0.40	18.10	19.30	23.00	26-Jan-20
La Isla Bonita	0.77	66.50	0.56	24.90	4.50	18.17	26-Jan-20
Pumpkin Lickin' Chicken Pouch	0.77	70.60	0.23	11.50	13.90	20.00	26-Jan-20
1 if By Land, 2 if by Sea Pouch	0.80	62.70	0.68	13.80	18.90	20.00	26-Jan-20
Chicken Frick 'A Zee	0.81	67.40	0.21	25.80	2.70	23.83	26-Jan-20
Love Me Tender Pouch	0.82	63.90	0.22	12.50	19.50	21.33	26-Jan-20
Meowisss Bueller Pouch	0.85	53.90	0.44	31.30	9.70	23.00	26-Jan-20
Mack, Jack & Sam Pouch	0.85	61.00	0.40	13.60	21.00	21.00	26-Jan-20
Fowl Ball	0.89	57.10	0.28	32.20	5.80	22.33	26-Jan-20
Cattyshack Pouch	0.93	59.50	0.30	22.90	11.00	20.67	26-Jan-20
Pumpkin Jack Splash Pouch	0.96	72.00	0.31	8.40	14.40	19.00	26-Jan-20
Cat to the Future Pouch	0.99	61.10	0.29	22.90	9.50	21.33	26-Jan-20
Funk in the Trunk	0.99	72.00	0.38	13.50	8.90	17.83	26-Jan-20
The Breakfast Cat Pouch	1.01	59.10	0.30	21.40	11.90	19.33	26-Jan-20
Goldie Lox	1.01	75.40	0.39	14.10	4.60	18.50	26-Jan-20
Lamb Burger-ini	1.05	57.70	0.55	24.70	9.70	25.67	26-Jan-20
The Double Dip	1.10	61.00	0.28	23.30	9.70	16.67	26-Jan-20
Splash Dance	1.30	63.70	0.43	24.00	5.60	25.67	26-Jan-20

	Phos	Prot	Sod	Fat	Carb	Cals	Obtained
Cat Times at Fridgemont Pouch	1.39	64.80	0.54	19.60	7.70	18.33	26-Jan-20
Two Tu Tango	1.43	67.80	0.52	18.80	5.60	19.83	26-Jan-20
The Karate Kitty Pouch	1.58	68.80	0.71	9.90	10.00	15.33	26-Jan-20
Kitty Gone Wild	1.62	67.70	0.66	16.20	5.30	18.17	26-Jan-20

CHICKEN SOUP FOR THE SOUL

	Phos	Prot	Sod	Fat	Carb	Cals	Obtained
Classic Weight & Mature Care Ocean Fish, Chicken & Turkey Pâté	0.91	46.97	0.39	19.29	23.08	27.27	28-Oct-19
Classic Adult Chicken & Turkey Pâté	1.28	46.00	0.62	34.54	9.67	36.00	28-Oct-19
Classic Indoor Chicken & Salmon Pâté	1.30	42.39	0.50	30.49	11.26	36.73	28-Oct-19
Grain-Free Beef, Red Potato & Carrots Minced in Gravy	1.43	48.64	1.49	21.91	17.36	26.00	28-Oct-19
Grain-Free Salmon & Chicken Cuts in Gravy	1.47	49.73	1.58	20.96	17.51	25.67	28-Oct-19
Grain-Free Chicken, Sweet Potato & Spinach Minced	1.51	49.00	1.48	23.10	16.32	25.67	28-Oct-19
Classic Kitten Chicken & Turkey Pâté	1.57	45.81	0.62	34.11	8.91	38.18	28-Oct-19
Grain-Free Salmon, Red Potato & Spinach Pâté	1.79	49.80	1.49	26.94	9.95	31.00	28-Oct-19
Grain-Free Beef, Carrot & Red Potato Pâté	1.82	46.12	1.14	33.49	8.18	36.00	28-Oct-19
Grain-Free Chicken, Sweet Potato & Spinach Pâté	1.82	46.37	1.14	35.10	6.20	36.00	28-Oct-19
Grain-Free Chicken & Turkey Pâté	1.99	46.34	1.01	35.81	5.47	36.55	28-Oct-19
Grain-Free Salmon Pâté	2.17	51.93	1.27	30.45	5.09	32.73	28-Oct-19

D

DAVE'S*

	Phos	Prot	Sod	Fat	Carb	Cals	Obtained
Naturally Healthy Grain-Free Chicken and Herring Dinner	0.71	44.60	0.71	34.70	12.67	38.36	7-Nov-19
Naturally Healthy Grain-Free Turkey & Salmon Dinner	0.88	42.29	0.33	28.50	3.50	33.82	7-Nov-19
Naturally Healthy Grain-Free Tuna and Salmon Dinner in Aspic	0.90	58.50	0.62	26.10	5.70	27.09	7-Nov-19
95% Premium Meat Beef & Beef Liver Pâté	0.91	33.73	0.32	31.21	6.36	31.09	7-Nov-19
Cat's Meow Chicken with Lamb	0.91	42.56	1.73	26.65	16.91	32.00	7-Nov-19
Cat's Meow Beef with Lamb	0.92	44.21	1.55	25.31	18.51	33.64	7-Nov-19
95% Premium Meat Turkey & Turkey Liver Pâté	0.93	34.94	0.32	31.24	4.60	30.73	7-Nov-19
Naturally Healthy Grain-Free Beef & Chicken Pâté	0.96	46.15	0.38	41.08	1.50	35.36	11-Nov-19
Naturally Healthy Grain-Free Tuna Entrée in Gravy	0.97	62.00	0.46	17.70	11.20	26.36	7-Nov-19
Naturally Healthy Grain-Free Tuna & Mackerel Dinner In Gravy	1.00	62.40	0.44	17.50	11.20	17.64	7-Nov-19
Cat's Meow Chicken with Duck	1.03	38.24	1.78	26.85	21.10	32.36	7-Nov-19
Naturally Healthy Grain-Free Tuna & Shrimp Dinner In Gravy	1.03	63.70	0.51	18.00	10.00	24.91	7-Nov-19
Naturally Healthy Grain-Free Tuna and Chicken Dinner in Gravy	1.05	66.10	0.50	13.70	11.70	23.09	7-Nov-19
95% Premium Meat Chicken & Chicken Liver Pâté	1.08	35.20	0.60	29.12	10.70	37.09	7-Nov-19
Cat's Meow Beef with Duck	1.08	44.86	1.60	25.22	18.02	33.27	7-Nov-19
Cat's Meow 95% Turkey & Turkey Liver	1.09	58.68	0.47	27.95	9.22	35.82	7-Nov-19
Naturally Healthy Grain-Free Poultry Platter Dinner	1.10	38.09	0.52	29.39	6.16	36.73	7-Nov-19
Naturally Healthy Grain-Free Beef & Chicken Dinner	1.16	48.19	0.46	41.50	1.83	35.45	7-Nov-19
Naturally Healthy Grain-Free Ahi Tuna & Chicken Dinner	1.16	72.30	0.46	13.50	3.00	25.45	11-Nov-19

	Phos	Prot	Sod	Fat	Carb	Cals	Obtained
Naturally Healthy Grain-Free Turkey & Giblets Dinner	1.32	48.42	0.53	39.02	3.73	35.36	7-Nov-19
Naturally Healthy Grain-Free Shredded Salmon in Gravy	1.33	48.72	1.54	27.79	11.42	26.36	11-Nov-19
Cat's Meow Beef with Turkey	1.34	43.46	1.56	24.54	18.54	33.64	7-Nov-19
Cat's Meow 95% Beef & Beef Liver	1.38	52.37	0.92	31.89	9.19	38.00	7-Nov-19
Naturally Healthy Grain-Free Shredded Chicken in Gravy	1.40	50.38	1.65	24.96	11.73	25.64	7-Nov-19
Naturally Healthy Grain-Free Chicken & Whitefish Dinner	1.46	50.40	0.71	36.08	3.28	35.82	7-Nov-19
Naturally Healthy Grain-Free Gobbleicious	1.47	51.10	0.69	22.80	15.45	36.73	7-Nov-19
Naturally Healthy Grain-Free Fisherman's Stew in Gravy	1.50	50.27	1.61	24.38	12.67	25.09	7-Nov-19
Naturally Healthy Grain-Free Turkey	1.57	48.23	0.39	36.50	4.58	32.80	7-Nov-19
95% Premium Meat Tuna & Chicken Pâté	1.60	39.11	0.32	29.46	4.58	36.36	7-Nov-19
Naturally Healthy Grain-Free Chicken	1.66	49.87	0.39	34.54	4.33	33.95	7-Nov-19
Cat's Meow Farmyard Fowl	1.76	48.33	1.50	24.56	13.96	26.00	7-Nov-19
Cat's Meow 95% Chicken, Chicken Liver & Turkey	2.15	55.98	0.48	27.14	8.09	35.82	7-Nov-19
Cat's Meow 95% Chicken & Chicken Liver	2.23	58.52	0.26	27.37	5.38	35.45	7-Nov-19

DIAMOND

	Phos	Prot	Sod	Fat	Carb	Cals	Obtained
Naturals Indoor Cat Hairball Control Adult Dinner	1.18	42.58	0.43	26.98	15.74	29.64	11-Nov-19
Naturals Chicken Dinner Cat and Kitten	1.49	43.04	0.54	33.25	13.69	38.00	11-Nov-19
Naturals Whitefish Dinner Cat and Kitten	1.99	44.29	0.67	24.91	17.72	31.27	11-Nov-19

DR. ELSEY'S

	Phos	Prot	Sod	Fat	Carb	Cals	Obtained
Clean Protein Turkey Pâté	1.08	51.88	0.42	38.33	1.25	36.73	22-Sep-19
Clean Protein Beef Pâté	1.17	50.00	0.50	28.79	15.71	32.73	22-Sep-19
Clean Protein Chicken Pâté	1.25	50.00	0.38	39.75	2.08	35.82	22-Sep-19
Clean Protein Rabbit & Turkey Pâté	1.27	50.19	0.38	33.24	3.04	32.36	22-Sep-19
Clean Protein Single Source Pork Pâté	1.39	60.40	0.35	18.46	16.54	29.27	22-Sep-19
Clean Protein Duck & Turkey Pâté	1.42	50.46	0.40	36.66	3.29	35.82	22-Sep-19
Clean Protein Ocean Whitefish Pâté	1.50	57.75	0.63	35.25	0.00	34.55	22-Sep-19
Clean Protein Single Source Salmon Pâté	1.52	48.13	0.59	30.67	12.71	38.36	29-Oct-19
Clean Protein Single Source Duck Pâté	1.61	49.98	0.38	35.30	6.92	34.91	22-Sep-19
Clean Protein Salmon Pâté	1.92	51.71	0.71	34.79	5.13	36.55	22-Sep-19

DR. TIM'S

	Phos	Prot	Sod	Fat	Carb	Cals	Obtained
Nimble Chicken & Vegetable Pâté	1.34	41.50	0.93	27.30	20.20	31.19	29-Oct-19

E

EARTHBORN HOLISTIC

	Phos	Prot	Sod	Fat	Carb	Cals	Obtained
Chicken Fricatssee	0.95	52.55	0.26	14.48	29.41	29.40	15-Jan-20
Chicken Catcciatori	0.95	60.54	0.26	12.45	22.22	25.80	15-Jan-20
Monterey Medley	1.03	70.82	0.48	10.25	11.11	24.20	15-Jan-20
Chicken Jumble with Liver	1.06	48.33	0.29	20.83	29.41	25.00	15-Jan-20
Harbor Harvest	1.10	64.24	0.33	12.79	16.67	25.60	15-Jan-20
Catalina Catch	1.14	78.65	0.29	13.29	0.55	30.00	15-Jan-20
Ranch House Stew	1.48	45.71	0.87	24.09	23.53	27.60	15-Jan-20

EVANGER'S

	Phos	Prot	Sod	Fat	Carb	Cals	Obtained
Beef it Up	0.71	37.94	0.35	22.34	8.60	44.17	13-Jan-17
Chicken Lickin	0.75	37.97	0.38	22.56	7.60	38.00	13-Jan-17

F

FANCY FEAST*

	Phos	Prot	Sod	Fat	Carb	Cals	Obtained
Purely Natural White Meat Chicken and Flaked Tuna Entrée in a Delicate Broth	1.11	72.22	1.11	8.33	0.00	20.50	9-May-18
Purely Natural Wild Alaskan Salmon & White Meat Chicken in a Delicate Broth	1.11	75.00	0.28	8.33	0.00	23.50	9-May-18
Purely Natural White Meat Chicken Entrée in a Delicate Broth	1.11	80.56	0.28	8.33	0.00	22.50	9-May-18
Purely Natural Flaked Skipjack Tuna in a Delicate Broth	1.17	77.78	0.56	8.33	0.22	21.00	9-May-18
Purely Natural Tender Tongol Tuna Entrée in a Delicate Broth	1.17	83.33	0.44	8.33	0.00	22.50	9-May-18
Purely Natural Seabass and Shrimp in a Delicate Broth	1.22	77.78	0.67	11.11	0.00	22.50	9-May-18
Purely Natural White Meat Chicken and Shredded Beef Entrée in a Delicate Broth	1.28	77.78	0.56	13.89	0.00	22.50	9-May-18
Classic Salmon & Shrimp Pâté Feast	1.59	54.30	0.53	31.00	3.30	30.67	26-Nov-19
Classic Pâté Turkey & Giblets Feast	1.69	53.30	0.49	32.70	3.90	32.00	26-Nov-19
Classic Pâté Tender Beef & Liver Feast	1.82	52.00	0.50	33.80	3.30	32.33	26-Nov-19
Classic Pâté Savory Salmon Feast	1.86	54.10	0.62	31.40	2.60	30.67	26-Nov-19
Classic Pâté Tender Beef Feast	1.87	54.50	0.60	29.90	4.90	30.67	26-Nov-19
Classic Cod, Sole & Shrimp Feast	1.91	62.90	0.81	23.00	2.50	27.33	26-Nov-19
Classic Pâté Tender Beef & Chicken Feast	1.96	51.40	0.55	32.90	4.30	33.67	26-Nov-19

109

	Phos	Prot	Sod	Fat	Carb	Cals	Obtained
Classic Pâté Chicken Feast	1.99	53.00	0.61	31.00	4.10	33.00	26-Nov-19
Classic Pâté Ocean Whitefish & Tuna Feast	1.99	62.20	0.76	24.60	3.50	28.33	26-Nov-19
Classic Pâté Seafood Feast	2.10	58.40	0.70	26.70	3.20	29.33	26-Nov-19
Classic Pâté Chopped Grill Feast	2.14	52.90	0.56	30.00	4.70	33.00	26-Nov-19
Classic Pâté Tender Liver & Chicken Feast	2.16	55.00	0.47	29.30	3.60	32.00	26-Nov-19

FIRSTMATE

	Phos	Prot	Sod	Fat	Carb	Cals	Obtained
Limited Ingredient Wild Salmon	0.90	50.00	0.80	14.00	26.00	22.00	25-Nov-19
Wild Pacific Salmon & Rice	0.90	50.00	0.80	14.00	16.00	22.00	25-Nov-19
Wild Salmon & Wild Tuna 50/50	0.90	50.00	0.80	18.00	19.00	27.00	25-Nov-19
Cage-Free Turkey & Rice	1.20	31.00	0.70	31.00	29.00	31.00	25-Nov-19
Limited Ingredient Free Run Turkey	1.20	31.00	0.80	31.00	29.00	31.00	25-Nov-19
Limited Ingredient Free Run Chicken	1.40	41.00	0.80	23.00	24.00	26.00	25-Nov-19
Cage-Free Chicken & Wild Tuna 50/50	1.40	41.00	0.90	23.00	23.00	26.00	25-Nov-19
Cage-Free Chicken & Rice	1.40	41.00	0.90	23.00	24.00	26.00	25-Nov-19
Cage-Free Turkey & Wild Tuna 50/50	1.40	41.00	0.90	32.00	14.00	26.00	25-Nov-19
Limited Ingredient Wild Tuna	1.40	50.00	0.70	23.00	12.00	27.00	25-Nov-19

FROMM

	Phos	Prot	Sod	Fat	Carb	Cals	Obtained
Beef & Venison Pâté	0.96	49.74	0.96	25.83	na	28.18	31-Jan-20
Turkey & Duck Pâté	1.02	49.76	0.97	25.92	na	30.36	31-Jan-20
Beef Pâté	1.02	53.30	1.08	21.09	na	25.27	31-Jan-20
Turkey Pâté	1.09	43.28	0.97	29.67	na	29.64	31-Jan-20
Lamb Pâté	1.17	42.88	1.04	29.50	na	27.82	31-Jan-20
Chicken & Duck Pâté	1.26	46.75	0.95	38.96	na	30.73	31-Jan-20
Chicken Pâté	1.30	47.66	1.06	25.03	na	29.27	31-Jan-20

	Phos	Prot	Sod	Fat	Carb	Cals	Obtained
Chicken, Duck & Salmon Pâté	1.35	45.06	0.98	38.37	na	30.55	31-Jan-20
Turkey & Pumpkin Pâté	1.37	46.70	0.62	24.10	na	27.27	31-Jan-20
Salmon & Tuna Pâté	1.41	47.53	1.00	35.38	na	30.18	31-Jan-20
Duck À La Veg Pâté	1.42	49.30	0.80	32.40	na	30.18	31-Jan-20
Chicken & Salmon Pâté	1.45	43.37	1.00	38.88	na	27.45	31-Jan-20
Seafood & Shrimp Pate	1.73	44.68	1.15	26.02	na	25.82	31-Jan-20

FUSSIE CAT*

	Phos	Prot	Sod	Fat	Carb	Cals	Obtained
Super Premium Chicken with Sweet Potato	0.64	49.57	0.23	7.68	na	22.94	5-Dec-19
Super Premium Chicken with Vegetables	0.68	66.38	0.23	7.89	na	23.02	5-Dec-19
Super Premium Chicken in Gravy	0.72	68.56	0.26	8.87	na	23.79	5-Dec-19
Super Premium Chicken with Egg	0.74	67.38	0.26	10.90	na	25.23	5-Dec-19
Super Premium Chicken with Duck	0.75	65.21	0.27	12.95	na	25.57	5-Dec-19
Premium Tuna with Smoked Tuna	1.10	80.82	0.18	9.72	na	21.55	5-Dec-19
Super Premium Chicken & Beef in Pumpkin Soup	1.11	76.25	0.17	13.18	na	20.10	5-Dec-19
Premium Tuna with Threadfin Bream	1.11	76.50	0.18	9.15	na	21.18	5-Dec-19
Premium Tuna with Mussels	1.16	79.45	0.20	12.19	na	20.78	5-Dec-19
Premium Tuna with Clams	1.17	79.49	0.21	12.31	na	20.55	5-Dec-19
Premium Tuna with Chicken	1.17	81.73	0.20	11.22	na	21.26	5-Dec-19
Super Premium Chicken with Chicken Liver in Pumpkin Soup	1.18	76.27	0.12	12.13	na	18.71	5-Dec-19
Premium Tuna with Anchovies	1.18	79.16	1.53	11.08	na	22.28	5-Dec-19
Premium Tuna with Shrimp	1.18	80.42	0.44	11.61	na	21.09	5-Dec-19
Premium Tuna with Ocean Fish	1.19	77.14	0.41	11.40	na	20.87	5-Dec-19
Premium Tuna with Salmon	1.19	80.87	0.23	12.07	na	21.26	5-Dec-19
Premium Tuna with Prawns	1.20	80.20	0.37	11.86	na	20.84	5-Dec-19
Premium Tuna with Chicken Liver	1.22	76.05	0.18	11.33	na	17.83	5-Dec-19
Premium Tuna in Aspic	1.23	81.35	2.08	9.51	na	19.99	5-Dec-19

G

GO! SOLUTIONS

	Phos	Prot	Sod	Fat	Carb	Cals	Obtained
Sensitivities Limited Ingredient Grain-Free Pollock Pâté	0.90	42.00	0.36	18.00	33.00	23.94	31-Oct-19
Sensitivities Limited Ingredient Grain-Free Duck Pâté	1.00	36.00	0.64	26.00	31.00	28.66	31-Oct-19
98% Carnivore Grain-Free Salmon & Cod Pâté	1.40	43.00	0.77	30.00	18.00	24.47	31-Oct-19
Skin & Coat Care Salmon Pâté	1.50	38.00	0.77	29.00	25.00	29.13	31-Oct-19
96% Carnivore Chicken, Turkey & Duck Pâté	1.50	47.00	0.77	27.00	17.00	28.35	31-Oct-19
99% Carnivore Grain-Free Minced Lamb & Wild Boar	1.60	44.00	1.00	35.00	12.00	23.93	31-Oct-19
Skin + Coat Care Minced Chicken	1.60	45.00	0.90	26.00	20.00	26.25	31-Oct-19

GRANDMA MAE'S*

	Phos	Prot	Sod	Fat	Carb	Cals	Obtained
Country Naturals Grain-Free Beef & Chicken Chunks in Gravy	1.06	44.44	0.72	13.89	na	24.29	23-Nov-19
Country Naturals Grain-Free Chicken Chunks in Gravy	1.17	44.44	0.61	16.67	na	25.71	23-Nov-19
Country Naturals Grain-Free Dog & Cat Salmon Soft Stew	1.35	55.56	0.41	30.41	na	35.23	23-Nov-19
Country Naturals Grain-Free Dog & Cat Beef Soft Stew	1.38	47.62	0.29	24.29	na	31.06	23-Nov-19
Country Naturals Grain-Free Whitefish Pâté Entrée	1.38	50.00	1.25	12.50	na	19.29	23-Nov-19
Country Naturals Grain-Free Tuna & Chicken Pâté Entrée	1.38	56.25	0.69	12.50	na	20.36	23-Nov-19
Country Naturals Grain-Free Chicken Pâté Entrée	1.40	45.00	0.45	25.00	na	30.36	23-Nov-19
Country Naturals Grain-Free Tuna Pâté Entrée	1.44	56.25	0.69	12.50	na	20.36	23-Nov-19
Country Naturals Grain-Free Chicken Pâté in Gravy	1.45	52.27	0.41	31.82	na	32.55	23-Nov-19

	Phos	Prot	Sod	Fat	Carb	Cals	Obtained
Country Naturals Grain-Free Ocean Fish & Chicken Pâté	1.45	52.27	0.41	31.82	na	32.55	23-Nov-19
Country Naturals Grain-Free Chicken & Liver Pâté	1.45	52.27	0.41	31.82	na	32.55	23-Nov-19
Country Naturals Grain-Free Mackerel & Sardine Pâté	1.45	52.27	0.41	31.82	na	32.55	23-Nov-19
Country Naturals Grain-Free Sardine & Ocean Fish Pâté	1.45	52.27	0.41	31.82	na	32.55	23-Nov-19
Grandma Mae's Country Naturals Grain-Free Pork Liver & Chicken Pâté	1.45	52.27	0.41	31.82	na	32.55	23-Nov-19
Country Naturals Grain-Free Lamb Chunks in Gravy	1.50	44.44	0.67	16.67	na	29.64	23-Nov-19
Country Naturals Grain-Free Salmon Slices in Gravy	1.61	44.44	2.11	25.00	na	26.18	23-Nov-19
Country Naturals Grain-Free Duck Soft Stew	1.67	44.44	0.33	25.00	na	31.82	23-Nov-19
Country Naturals Grain-Free Chicken Slices in Gravy	1.67	44.44	1.94	25.00	na	25.82	23-Nov-19
Country Naturals Grain-Free Chicken Soft Stew	1.70	56.14	0.35	28.07	na	33.33	23-Nov-19
Country Naturals Grain-Free Dog & Cat Lamb Soft Stew	1.71	57.14	0.34	34.29	na	29.92	23-Nov-19
Country Naturals Grain-Free Whitefish & Chicken Slices in Gravy	1.72	44.44	2.00	25.00	na	24.73	23-Nov-19
Country Naturals Grain-Free Beef Pâté Entrée	2.45	45.00	0.65	25.00	na	26.43	23-Nov-19

H

HALO

	Phos	Prot	Sod	Fat	Carb	Cals	Obtained
Grain-Free Turkey and Chickpea Senior	0.70	39.30	0.30	35.00	na	32.73	30-Jan-20
Holistic Gluten-Free Turkey and Quail Indoor	0.70	41.20	0.50	43.50	5.31	33.64	30-Jan-20

	Phos	Prot	Sod	Fat	Carb	Cals	Obtained
Holistic Sensitive Stomach Grain-Free Chicken, Egg & Garden Greens Pâté	0.80	46.20	0.40	40.40	7.30	33.09	30-Jan-20
Grain-Free Chicken and Chickpeas Senior	0.90	40.50	0.40	29.60	18.20	33.09	30-Jan-20
Holistic Sensitive Stomach Grain-Free Guinea Fowl & Garden Greens Pâté	0.90	48.30	0.40	35.00	9.30	33.64	30-Jan-20
Gluten-Free Chicken and Trout Indoor	1.00	44.50	0.60	38.20	9.04	33.64	30-Jan-20
Holistic Grain-Free Turkey Adult	1.10	43.20	0.20	40.70	6.80	35.45	30-Jan-20
Holistic Grain-Free Chicken Kitten	1.20	44.90	0.40	37.70	8.60	35.33	30-Jan-20
Holistic Grain-Free Chicken Adult	1.20	46.60	0.30	35.10	7.80	29.09	30-Jan-20
Holistic Sensitive Stomach Grain-Free Quail and Garden Greens Recipe Pâté	1.20	46.90	0.40	32.00	10.10	33.64	30-Jan-20
Holistic Grain-Free Chicken and Beef Adult	1.20	47.70	0.30	38.50	4.80	34.36	30-Jan-20
Holistic Grain-Free Whitefish Kitten	1.30	47.80	0.50	38.50	1.50	35.00	30-Jan-20
Holistic Sensitive Stomach Grain-Free Rabbit & Garden Greens Pâté	1.30	49.40	0.50	36.10	6.00	32.73	30-Jan-20
Holistic Grain-Free Lamb Adult	1.30	50.00	0.60	34.60	4.10	27.64	30-Jan-20
Holistic Grain-Free Salmon Adult	1.50	45.80	0.30	37.40	6.80	34.18	30-Jan-20
Holistic Grain-Free Chicken, Shrimp & Crab Adult	1.50	51.20	0.40	33.30	4.90	30.00	30-Jan-20
Grain-Free Turkey and Giblets Indoor Pâté	1.80	42.80	1.10	39.70	6.90	31.82	30-Jan-20
Grain-Free Chicken and Beef Indoor Pâté	1.90	43.50	1.00	37.30	7.00	36.36	30-Jan-20
Grain-Free Whitefish Indoor Pâté	1.90	50.00	1.10	39.50	0.10	30.91	30-Jan-20
Grain-Free Seafood Medley Indoor Pâté	1.90	57.90	1.40	19.60	10.00	27.82	30-Jan-20
Grain-Free Turkey and Duck Indoor Pâté	2.10	44.10	1.10	44.80	0.10	33.64	30-Jan-20
Grain-Free Chicken Indoor Pâté	2.10	50.00	1.20	33.00	4.30	36.55	30-Jan-20
Grain-Free Salmon Indoor Pâté	2.30	51.10	1.10	33.70	2.40	38.36	30-Jan-20

HEALTH EXTENSION

	Phos	Prot	Sod	Fat	Carb	Cals	Obtained
Grain-Free Real Beef Entrée for Kittens & Cats	1.59	45.00	0.77	45.00	1.00	45.00	7-Dec-16
Grain-Free Real Chicken Entrée for Kittens & Cats	2.23	42.00	0.59	40.00	3.00	36.00	7-Dec-16
Grain-Free Real Turkey Entrée for Kittens & Cats	2.50	36.00	0.64	46.00	2.00	39.00	7-Dec-16

HILL'S

	Phos	Prot	Sod	Fat	Carb	Cals	Obtained
Science Diet Adult Tender Tuna Dinner	0.52	41.30	0.48	17.50	32.60	29.45	01-Feb-20
Science Diet Adult 7+ Tender Tuna Dinner	0.54	41.80	0.47	18.90	30.00	27.64	01-Feb-20
Science Diet Adult 11+ Healthy Cuisine Seared Tuna & Carrot Medley	0.57	37.60	0.38	19.90	35.50	23.57	01-Feb-20
Science Diet Adult Healthy Cuisine Roasted Chicken & Rice Medley	0.59	36.50	0.54	21.10	33.50	23.57	01-Feb-20
Science Diet Adult Tender Chicken Dinner	0.60	37.50	0.40	21.60	33.60	29.09	01-Feb-20
Science Diet Adult 7+ Healthy Cuisine Roasted Chicken & Rice Medley	0.63	38.00	0.37	19.10	34.30	22.86	01-Feb-20
Science Diet Youthful Vitality 7+ Tuna & Vegetable Stew	0.63	38.80	0.44	17.60	35.50	23.79	01-Feb-20
Science Diet Adult 7+ Savory Turkey Entrée	0.64	33.70	0.29	24.00	31.40	33.64	01-Feb-20
Science Diet Adult 7+ Savory Chicken Entrée	0.64	38.70	0.33	24.30	27.20	31.09	01-Feb-20
Science Diet Adult Indoor Cat Savory Chicken Entrée	0.65	33.60	0.50	23.80	25.30	30.91	01-Feb-20
Science Diet Youthful Vitality Adult 7+ Chicken & Vegetable Entrée	0.65	34.60	0.43	17.90	39.30	33.45	01-Feb-20
Science Diet Adult Savory Chicken Entrée	0.65	40.10	0.37	26.60	22.40	32.91	01-Feb-20

	Phos	Prot	Sod	Fat	Carb	Cals	Obtained
Science Diet Adult Indoor Cat Ocean Fish Entrée	0.67	38.30	0.46	21.00	26.20	31.64	01-Feb-20
Science Diet Adult Ocean Fish Entrée	0.67	38.30	0.46	21.20	29.50	33.27	01-Feb-20
Science Diet Youthful Vitality 7+ Salmon & Vegetable Stew	0.68	39.50	0.31	18.00	34.10	25.52	01-Feb-20
Science Diet Adult 7+ Tender Chicken Dinner	0.68	46.10	0.36	21.60	25.90	30.00	01-Feb-20
Science Diet Adult 7+ Savory Beef Entrée	0.69	39.50	0.38	22.70	27.60	28.91	01-Feb-20
Science Diet Adult Tender Ocean Fish Dinner	0.69	40.70	0.41	18.40	32.80	27.82	01-Feb-20
Science Diet Sensitive Stomach & Skin Chicken & Vegetable Entrée	0.70	35.20	0.40	23.90	34.60	30.00	01-Feb-20
Healthy Advantage Adult Chicken Entrée	0.72	40.40	0.40	18.00	35.20	29.27	01-Feb-20
Science Diet Sensitive Stomach & Skin Tuna & Vegetable Entrée	0.72	44.70	0.46	21.50	26.40	29.66	01-Feb-20
Science Diet Adult Hairball Control Ocean Fish Entrée	0.73	37.70	0.44	22.70	23.70	32.73	01-Feb-20
Science Diet Youthful Vitality Adult 7+ Chicken & Vegetable Stew	0.74	35.70	0.42	17.90	38.30	23.45	01-Feb-20
Science Diet Adult Healthy Cuisine Seared Tuna & Carrot Medley	0.74	39.10	0.53	20.80	30.40	25.36	01-Feb-20
Science Diet Adult Savory Turkey Entrée	0.76	33.90	0.30	26.10	29.30	33.64	01-Feb-20
Science Diet Adult Urinary Hairball Control Savory Chicken Entrée	0.76	36.30	0.34	21.10	26.30	28.91	01-Feb-20
Science Diet Adult Healthy Cuisine Poached Salmon & Spinach Medley	0.76	36.90	0.36	25.20	28.50	28.21	01-Feb-20
Science Diet Adult Perfect Weight Liver & Chicken Entrée	0.76	38.40	0.36	13.00	31.30	24.83	01-Feb-20
Science Diet Adult Turkey & Liver Entrée	0.78	35.30	0.33	29.50	24.10	34.00	01-Feb-20

TANYA'S CAT FOOD DATA

	Phos	Prot	Sod	Fat	Carb	Cals	Obtained
Science Diet Kitten Tender Chicken Dinner	0.78	45.50	0.33	25.30	19.20	28.18	01-Feb-20
Science Diet Adult Hairball Control Savory Chicken Entrée	0.79	33.70	0.46	24.20	24.90	30.36	01-Feb-20
Science Diet Adult Savory Salmon Entrée	0.79	36.60	0.34	25.90	27.40	33.64	01-Feb-20
Science Diet Perfect Weight Roasted Vegetables & Chicken Medley	0.79	38.80	0.45	11.90	33.30	21.38	01-Feb-20
Science Diet Adult Liver & Chicken Entrée	0.79	41.40	0.31	20.20	27.00	28.36	01-Feb-20
Science Diet Adult Light Liver & Chicken Entrée	0.80	36.70	0.45	15.00	34.60	26.73	01-Feb-20
Science Diet Kitten Healthy Cuisine Roasted Chicken & Rice Medley	0.87	38.00	0.55	24.10	28.90	25.36	01-Feb-20
Healthy Advantage Kitten Chicken Entree	1.12	43.40	0.39	22.90	25.60	31.45	01-Feb-20
Science Diet Kitten Savory Turkey Entrée	1.18	44.20	0.50	29.60	15.10	36.91	01-Feb-20
Science Diet Kitten Liver & Chicken Entrée	1.23	45.50	0.50	29.20	14.80	37.82	01-Feb-20
Science Diet Kitten Savory Salmon Entrée	1.32	44.20	0.56	28.40	16.30	37.45	01-Feb-20

HOLISTIC SELECT

	Phos	Prot	Sod	Fat	Carb	Cals	Obtained
Grain-Free Turkey Pâté	1.16	52.71	0.43	35.09	2.92	36.62	5-Oct-19
Grain-Free Ocean Fish & Tuna Pâté	1.19	55.49	0.68	30.89	4.21	35.31	5-Oct-19
Grain-Free Salmon & Shrimp Pâté	1.42	54.39	0.63	32.02	4.47	37.31	5-Oct-19
Grain-Free Chicken Pâté	1.43	52.02	0.43	33.68	4.60	36.54	5-Oct-19
Grain-Free Chicken Liver & Lamb Pâté	1.53	53.31	0.47	33.01	3.70	38.15	5-Oct-19

HOUND & GATOS

	Phos	Prot	Sod	Fat	Carb	Cals	Obtained
Grain-Free 98% Salmon, Mackerel & Sardine	1.04	52.95	0.48	47.26	na	39.82	8-Nov-19
Grain-Free 98% Pork	1.12	54.08	0.39	35.42	na	35.64	8-Nov-19
Grain-Free 98% Paleolithic	1.18	42.92	0.37	31.92	na	33.27	8-Nov-19
Grain-Free 98% Turkey & Liver	1.20	44.38	0.62	38.09	na	34.73	8-Nov-19
Grain-Free 98% Lamb & Liver	1.21	53.56	0.38	35.42	na	34.00	8-Nov-19
Grain-Free 98% Chicken & Liver	1.26	45.00	0.40	43.48	na	36.55	8-Nov-19
Grain-Free 98% Beef	1.26	45.00	0.63	36.85	na	35.64	8-Nov-19
Grain-Free 98% Lamb, Chicken & Salmon	1.33	45.01	0.55	39.60	na	36.18	8-Nov-19
Grain-Free 98% Gamebird Poultry	1.43	49.80	0.68	39.52	na	34.73	8-Nov-19
Grain-Free 98% Salmon	1.54	44.95	1.26	47.27	na	39.27	8-Nov-19
Grain-Free 98% Duck & Liver	1.79	55.34	0.41	29.67	na	36.91	8-Nov-19
Grain-Free 98% Trout & Duck Liver	1.87	49.39	0.36	35.42	na	32.91	8-Nov-19
Grain-Free 98% Rabbit	1.95	50.01	0.51	32.87	na	33.09	8-Nov-19

I

I AND LOVE AND YOU

	Phos	Prot	Sod	Fat	Carb	Cals	Obtained
Beef, Right Meow! Pâté	1.41	46.77	0.51	38.66	na	30.67	11-Nov-19
Purrky Turkey Pâté	1.53	47.42	0.54	33.05	14.30	33.33	11-Nov-19
Tuna Fintastic Canned Chunks in Gravy	1.54	58.26	1.58	17.03	28.50	24.00	11-Nov-19
Salmon Chanted Evening Canned Chunks in Gravy	1.55	49.90	1.37	26.07	30.49	25.00	11-Nov-19
Chicken Dalish Canned Chunks in Gravy	1.61	50.34	1.41	26.31	na	26.00	11-Nov-19
Savory Salmon Pâté	1.62	49.73	0.64	32.81	na	29.67	11-Nov-19
Whascally Wabbit Pâté	1.94	55.95	0.61	26.68	na	31.67	11-Nov-19
Chicken Me Out Pâté	1.96	48.76	0.55	34.30	na	37.00	11-Nov-19
Oh My Cod! Pâté	2.22	52.23	0.66	28.41	na	27.33	11-Nov-19

IDENTITY

	Phos	Prot	Sod	Fat	Carb	Cals	Obtained
95% Free-Range Canadian Duck	0.75	39.19	0.29	35.28	5.27	31.45	20-Jan-20
95% Free Range Quail & Turkey	0.77	41.92	0.32	26.63	8.03	26.55	20-Jan-20
95% Free-Range Heritage Turkey	0.77	46.46	0.35	24.42	10.01	27.45	20-Jan-20
95% Sustainable Atlantic Salmon & Herring	0.78	41.12	0.35	32.57	10.51	29.09	20-Jan-20
95% Grass-Fed Angus Beef	0.86	40.14	0.35	37.31	3.99	29.09	20-Jan-20
95% Free-Range Cobb Chicken	0.89	40.13	0.41	27.02	10.71	27.64	20-Jan-20
95% Free-Range Prairie Pork	1.05	44.22	0.42	10.86	10.41	23.64	20-Jan-20
95% Free-Range NZ Lamb	1.10	42.03	0.45	36.01	9.41	31.45	20-Jan-20

INSTINCT

	Phos	Prot	Sod	Fat	Carb	Cals	Obtained
Original Grain-Free 95% Real Beef Pâté	1.22	52.96	0.42	34.49	1.39	40.36	8-Nov-19
Grain-Free Minced Tuna in Savory Gravy Cup	1.26	62.60	1.21	13.00	12.09	23.14	8-Nov-19
Original Grain-Free 95% Real Lamb Pâté	1.28	48.06	0.58	39.53	0.78	37.45	8-Nov-19
Original Grain-Free 95% Real Duck Pâté	1.28	49.81	0.54	35.41	2.72	35.45	8-Nov-19
Grain-Free Limited Ingredient Diet Real Turkey Pâté	1.30	50.19	0.50	33.33	4.60	35.82	8-Nov-19
Grain-Free Limited Ingredient Diet Rabbit	1.37	51.56	0.51	16.02	19.53	28.36	8-Nov-19
Grain-Free 95% Real Chicken Pâté	1.40	49.80	0.60	35.60	2.40	35.09	8-Nov-19
Grain-Free Ultimate Protein Real Chicken Pâté	1.42	49.80	0.55	35.57	2.37	35.09	8-Nov-19
Original Kitten Grain-Free Real Chicken Pâté	1.45	53.91	0.63	33.20	1.17	34.55	8-Nov-19
Grain-Free Minced Salmon in Savory Gravy Cup	1.47	52.90	1.52	22.00	13.59	25.14	8-Nov-19
Grain-Free Minced Chicken in Savory Gravy Cup	1.53	50.50	1.25	24.00	13.76	27.71	8-Nov-19
Grain-Free Minced Rabbit in Savory Gravy Cup	1.68	55.00	1.29	15.00	14.85	21.14	8-Nov-19

	Phos	Prot	Sod	Fat	Carb	Cals	Obtained
Grain-Free Limited Ingredient Diet Duck	1.70	45.29	0.47	33.33	7.25	36.36	8-Nov-19
Grain-Free Limited Ingredient Diet Real Salmon Pâté	1.71	54.69	1.14	26.12	5.71	29.09	8-Nov-19
Original Grain-Free 95% Real Salmon Pâté	1.83	54.17	1.13	26.25	3.33	30.00	8-Nov-19
Original Grain-Free 95% Real Venison Pâté	1.92	52.61	0.49	27.87	4.18	36.18	8-Nov-19
Original Grain-Free 95% Real Rabbit Pâté	1.97	59.40	0.68	21.37	3.42	26.73	8-Nov-19
Grain-Free Ultimate Protein Real Rabbit Pâté	1.97	59.40	0.68	21.37	3.42	26.67	8-Nov-19

J

JUSTFOODFORCATS

	Phos	Prot	Sod	Fat	Carb	Cals	Obtained
Fish & Chicken	0.63	52.00	0.83	22.00	17.50	35.00	8-Nov-19

K

KASIKS

	Phos	Prot	Sod	Fat	Carb	Cals	Obtained
Grub Formula (Insect-based)	0.90	55.00	0.90	18.00	18.00	24.00	1-Dec-19
Wild Caught Coho Salmon	1.00	59.00	0.80	16.00	26.00	24.00	25-Nov-19
Cage-Free Turkey	1.20	31.00	0.80	31.00	30.00	29.00	25-Nov-19
Cage-Free Chicken	1.40	41.00	0.90	23.00	25.00	27.00	25-Nov-19

KOHA*

	Phos	Prot	Sod	Fat	Carb	Cals	Obtained
Poké Bowl Tuna & Duck Entrée in Gravy	0.62	56.19	1.90	15.71	17.67	25.09	27-Nov-19
Poké Bowl Tuna & Beef Entrée in Gravy	0.70	61.50	2.10	18.25	10.95	25.45	27-Nov-19

	Phos	Prot	Sod	Fat	Carb	Cals	Obtained
Poké Bowl Tuna & Pumpkin Entrée in Gravy	0.74	60.32	2.59	15.71	13.23	24.55	27-Nov-19
Poké Bowl Tuna & Salmon Entrée in Gravy	0.74	61.27	2.35	14.17	12.40	24.91	27-Nov-19
Grain-Free Limited Ingredient Beef Pâté	0.75	49.88	0.42	40.65	3.57	36.00	13-Aug-19
Poké Bowl Tuna & Chicken Entrée in Gravy	0.78	65.69	2.60	17.75	7.06	25.64	27-Nov-19
Poké Bowl Tuna & Lamb Entrée in Gravy	0.79	61.40	2.60	14.70	12.33	25.82	27-Nov-19
Poké Bowl Tuna & Shrimp Entrée in Gravy	0.80	65.83	2.46	15.18	8.59	24.73	27-Nov-19
Poké Bowl Tuna & Turkey Entrée in Gravy	0.91	61.54	2.12	18.46	9.13	25.64	27-Nov-19
L.I.D. Shredded Chicken Entrée in Gravy	1.00	68.98	1.12	21.34	1.12	23.82	27-Nov-19
Grain-Free Limited Ingredient Guineafowl Pâté	1.15	45.20	0.63	41.50	4.28	37.09	13-Aug-19
Grain-Free Turkey Stew	1.18	45.60	1.23	34.20	11.14	26.55	13-Aug-19
Grain-Free Chicken Stew	1.38	46.60	1.19	34.70	8.57	24.36	13-Aug-19
L.I.D. Shredded Lamb Entrée in Gravy	1.39	39.36	1.14	35.84	10.79	22.00	27-Nov-19
Grain-Free Limited Ingredient Turkey Pâté	1.44	47.80	0.42	40.44	2.05	38.67	13-Aug-19
Grain-Free Limited Ingredient Chicken Pâté	1.59	49.36	0.43	39.41	1.32	37.00	13-Aug-19
Grain-Free Limited Ingredient Wild Kangaroo Pâté	1.81	51.58	0.54	29.10	8.69	32.36	13-Aug-19
L.I.D. Shredded Duck Entrée in Gravy	1.86	51.54	1.22	24.63	9.73	24.91	27-Nov-19
L.I.D. Shredded Beef Entrée in Gravy	1.94	41.74	0.99	32.15	12.02	29.64	27-Nov-19
Grain-Free Limited Ingredient Duck Pâté	2.04	41.67	0.36	45.07	2.36	37.67	13-Aug-19
L.I.D. Shredded Turkey Entrée in Gravy	2.65	40.54	0.76	24.48	12.42	28.36	27-Nov-19
Grain-Free Duck Stew	2.76	52.80	1.40	28.60	3.46	24.36	13-Aug-19
Grain-Free Limited Ingredient Rabbit au Jus	3.98	53.81	0.48	25.87	0.00	25.33	13-Aug-19

L

LIFE'S ABUNDANCE

	Phos	Prot	Sod	Fat	Carb	Cals	Obtained
Instinctive Choice All Life Stage	1.17	50.00	0.45	33.33	na	36.00	27-Nov-19
Grain-Free Limited Ingredient Pork & Duck	1.29	54.55	1.31	22.73	3.06	32.67	30-Jan-20

LOTUS

	Phos	Prot	Sod	Fat	Carb	Cals	Obtained
Grain-Free Just Juicy Turkey Stew	0.88	68.01	0.84	13.61	12.65	26.98	28-Jan-20
Grain-Free Rabbit Pâté	0.96	37.23	0.64	33.36	20.61	34.88	28-Jan-20
Grain-Free Just Juicy Chicken Stew	0.98	66.24	0.68	15.96	12.88	27.36	28-Jan-20
Grain-Free Turkey Pâté	1.02	35.64	0.73	28.14	25.54	27.12	28-Jan-20
Grain-Free Just Juicy Pork Stew	1.13	68.28	1.17	16.43	7.45	24.55	28-Jan-20
Grain-Free Chicken Pâté	1.18	41.51	0.85	23.39	22.70	29.84	28-Jan-20
Grain-Free Pork Pâté	1.18	41.87	0.86	24.31	23.29	31.44	28-Jan-20
Grain-Free Just Juicy Venison Stew	1.18	61.91	0.82	21.36	7.79	32.26	28-Jan-20
Grain-Free Sardine Pâté	1.21	50.36	1.17	16.17	20.09	27.36	28-Jan-20
Grain-Free Duck Pâté	1.23	44.70	0.90	19.75	23.15	28.16	28-Jan-20
Grain-Free Just Juicy Salmon & Pollock Stew	1.28	54.92	0.92	25.13	9.03	24.15	28-Jan-20
Grain-Free Just Juicy Pollock Stew	1.50	45.33	1.50	26.17	10.72	21.32	28-Jan-20
Grain-Free Salmon Pâté	1.74	40.83	0.91	21.11	23.94	26.56	28-Jan-20

LOVIBLES

	Phos	Prot	Sod	Fat	Carb	Cals	Obtained
One Cool Chick	0.99	45.90	2.49	29.60	12.00	25.68	21-Jan-20
Put a Wing on It	1.22	51.60	0.45	33.10	4.10	32.14	21-Jan-20
Seashore Love	1.25	55.90	0.78	23.00	7.60	27.27	21-Jan-20
Love of my Life	1.28	53.60	0.91	31.60	5.30	31.67	21-Jan-20
Poetry in Motion	1.28	53.60	0.98	30.40	6.00	29.33	21-Jan-20
Key to My Heart	1.35	59.00	1.01	25.80	5.90	29.00	21-Jan-20

	Phos	Prot	Sod	Fat	Carb	Cals	Obtained
A-moo-zing Love	1.37	47.90	0.58	36.60	7.70	34.18	21-Jan-20
Tender Lovin'	1.42	53.20	0.92	32.30	3.40	33.27	21-Jan-20
Sizzling Summer Love	1.45	53.30	0.34	32.70	3.80	31.67	21-Jan-20
My One and Only	1.46	55.40	0.80	27.60	5.40	30.00	21-Jan-20
Feast of My Dreams	1.56	49.10	1.56	36.30	8.70	36.36	21-Jan-20
Beggin' for Love	1.70	48.20	0.59	39.50	4.00	39.09	21-Jan-20
Over the Moo-n	1.71	56.20	0.94	26.80	5.40	29.00	21-Jan-20
Furrever and Always	1.93	55.90	0.92	24.90	6.20	28.67	21-Jan-20
Simply Irresistable	2.11	64.30	0.93	15.40	4.90	25.00	21-Jan-20

M

MERRICK

	Phos	Prot	Sod	Fat	Carb	Cals	Obtained
Limited Ingredient Grain-Free Duck	0.80	30.40	0.30	52.40	5.54	26.20	26-Jun-19
Backcountry Real Duck Cuts	0.95	49.21	1.40	26.27	15.55	28.33	26-Nov-19
Backcountry Real Turkey Cuts	0.96	50.30	1.42	26.45	14.53	28.00	26-Nov-19
Backcountry Grain-Free Real Beef Cuts	1.06	51.06	1.38	25.11	14.17	26.67	26-Nov-19
Backcountry Grain-Free Real Whitefish Cuts	1.08	50.96	1.51	22.07	17.13	25.67	26-Nov-19
Limited Ingredient Grain-Free Salmon	1.09	39.90	0.30	39.40	5.84	26.20	26-Jun-19
Backcountry Real Rabbit Cuts	1.09	52.35	1.41	22.98	14.91	26.67	26-Nov-19
Backcountry Grain-Free Real Kitten Recipe Cuts	1.13	50.70	1.24	26.74	na	27.33	26-Nov-19
Backcountry Real Chicken Cuts	1.15	50.48	1.44	25.55	14.75	26.33	26-Nov-19
Purrfect Bistro Grain-Free Beef Wellington	1.23	54.50	1.71	21.33	9.81	25.10	26-Jun-19
Purrfect Bistro Grain-Free Grammy's Pot Pie	1.28	43.16	1.75	38.29	8.46	30.91	26-Jun-19
Purrfect Bistro Grain-Free Thanksgiving Day Dinner	1.28	43.16	1.75	38.29	8.46	30.91	26-Jun-19
Purrfect Bistro Grain-Free Cowboy Cookout	1.28	50.64	2.20	16.83	20.60	28.18	26-Jun-19

	Phos	Prot	Sod	Fat	Carb	Cals	Obtained
Backcountry Grain-Free Real Chicken + Trout Cuts Pouch	1.28	52.55	1.31	28.52	na	25.67	26-Nov-19
Limited Ingredient Grain-Free Turkey	1.37	44.80	0.42	36.70	5.77	27.80	26-Jun-19
Purrfect Bistro Grain-Free Chicken Divan	1.61	49.55	2.32	21.29	15.04	25.27	26-Jun-19
Purrfect Bistro Grain-Free Beef Pâté	1.71	54.50	2.07	27.07	5.68	30.55	26-Jun-19
Purrfect Bistro Grain-Free Chicken Casserole	1.74	49.13	2.13	22.04	13.26	25.64	26-Jun-19
Purrfect Bistro Grain-Free Duck Pâté	1.86	43.22	1.99	36.86	7.42	28.36	26-Jun-19
Limited Ingredient Grain-Free Chicken	1.90	42.60	0.54	37.40	6.20	26.20	26-Jun-19
Purrfect Bistro Grain-Free Tuna Pâté	1.94	48.76	1.90	32.73	4.38	29.82	26-Jun-19
Purrfect Bistro Grain-Free Salmon Pâté	2.01	48.47	2.10	34.67	2.93	31.82	26-Jun-19
Purrfect Bistro Grain-Free Tuna Niçoise	2.06	51.67	2.39	18.47	13.49	25.64	26-Jun-19
Purrfect Bistro Grain-Free Chicken Pâté	2.11	47.41	1.94	37.24	2.59	33.64	26-Jun-19
Purrfect Bistro Grain-Free Turkey Pâté	2.31	54.33	2.26	24.42	4.76	31.82	26-Jun-19
Purrfect Bistro Grain-Free Surf N Turf Pâté	3.25	54.37	2.18	29.71	6.21	28.18	26-Jun-19

MY PERFECT PET

	Phos	Prot	Sod	Fat	Carb	Cals	Obtained
Bengal's Beef Carnivore Grain-Free Blend	0.50	69.30	0.20	17.60	na	61.50	26-Jan-20
Toby's Turkey Carnivore Grain-Free Blend	0.80	58.10	1.30	15.30	na	50.75	26-Jan-20

N

NATURAL BALANCE

	Phos	Prot	Sod	Fat	Carb	Cals	Obtained
Delectable Delights O'Fishally Scampi Stew	0.93	60.69	0.55	19.74	10.79	24.00	9-Jan-17
L.I.D. Limited Ingredient Chicken & Pumpkin in Broth	0.96	76.29	0.69	13.49	3.01	24.36	9-Jan-17
Delectable Delights Sea Brûlée Stew	1.00	59.41	0.67	20.10	12.42	28.00	9-Jan-17
Delectable Delights Catatouille Stew	1.02	63.52	0.55	19.27	9.33	24.00	9-Jan-17
L.I.D. Limited Ingredient Tuna & Pumpkin in Broth	1.07	74.10	1.64	14.71	1.36	23.27	9-Jan-17
Delectable Delights Purrrfect Paella Stew	1.15	59.74	0.71	19.18	10.31	24.00	9-Jan-17
Platefulls Chicken & Pumpkin in Gravy Pouch	1.19	42.15	0.90	27.15	20.83	26.67	9-Jan-17
Platefulls Indoor Chicken & Chicken Liver in Gravy Pouch	1.24	42.29	0.85	23.50	24.36	24.33	9-Jan-17
Platefulls Tuna & Beef in Gravy Pouch	1.24	45.64	1.04	24.59	18.14	26.67	9-Jan-17
Ultra Premium Tuna with Shrimp	1.24	50.51	0.88	22.96	16.93	31.45	9-Jan-17
Original Ultra Whole Body Health Reduced Calorie Chicken, Salmon & Duck	1.25	40.73	0.61	37.67	12.24	33.33	9-Jan-17
Platefulls Indoor Turkey & Duck in Gravy Pouch	1.27	42.37	0.84	23.85	22.42	27.00	9-Jan-17
Platefulls Indoor Salmon, Tuna, Chicken & Shrimp in Gravy Pouch	1.27	43.54	0.89	21.80	23.85	23.33	9-Jan-17
Platefulls Salmon, Tuna & Crab in Gravy Pouch	1.28	45.20	1.12	23.58	20.00	26.67	9-Jan-17
Ultra Premium Indoor	1.29	40.67	0.58	30.29	19.36	35.83	9-Jan-17
Platefulls Indoor Duck, Chicken & Pumpkin in Gravy Pouch	1.29	43.11	0.83	25.06	20.10	27.33	9-Jan-17
Platefulls Indoor Mackerel & Sardine in Gravy Pouch	1.32	46.76	0.96	20.87	20.32	23.33	9-Jan-17
Ultra Premium Turkey & Giblets	1.33	45.83	0.60	31.67	11.93	30.00	9-Jan-17

	Phos	Prot	Sod	Fat	Carb	Cals	Obtained
Platefulls Chicken & Giblets in Gravy Pouch	1.34	42.69	0.83	25.93	21.31	23.33	9-Jan-17
Ultra Premium Ocean Fish	1.36	52.70	0.84	25.69	10.77	33.33	9-Jan-17
Platefulls Chicken & Salmon in Gravy Pouch	1.39	42.60	0.82	25.39	21.27	23.33	9-Jan-17
L.I.D. Limited Ingredient Salmon & Green Pea	1.42	46.44	0.64	26.54	14.83	37.00	9-Jan-17
Delectable Delights Land 'n Sea Cats-serole Pâté	1.42	58.13	0.71	20.16	11.63	30.00	9-Jan-17
Original Ultra Whole Body Health Chicken, Salmon & Duck	1.45	41.38	0.53	38.36	11.28	36.67	9-Jan-17
Platefulls Indoor Turkey, Salmon & Chicken in Gravy Pouch	1.47	42.72	0.91	24.08	20.89	23.33	9-Jan-17
L.I.D. Limited Ingredient Chicken & Green Pea	1.48	45.06	0.56	30.67	12.65	33.33	9-Jan-17
Original Ultra Whole Body Health Chicken, Salmon & Duck Kitten	1.50	41.57	0.54	36.54	10.48	36.67	9-Jan-17
Platefulls Cod, Chicken, Sole & Shrimp in Gravy Pouch	1.52	44.42	0.91	20.64	23.39	23.33	9-Jan-17
Ultra Premium Salmon	1.58	45.41	0.76	30.29	13.28	33.33	9-Jan-17
Ultra Premium Chicken & Liver Pâté	1.63	43.16	0.85	37.14	8.22	35.33	9-Jan-17
L.I.D. Limited Ingredient Venison & Green Pea	1.67	42.90	0.76	26.77	15.35	31.67	9-Jan-17
Delectable Delights Life's a Beach Pâté	1.67	60.24	0.55	18.51	9.65	28.00	9-Jan-17
Platefulls Turkey, Chicken & Duck n Gravy Pouch	1.68	41.01	0.83	23.85	22.56	23.33	9-Jan-17
L.I.D. Limited Ingredient Duck & Green Pea	1.79	41.21	0.52	31.61	15.20	35.33	9-Jan-17

NATURAL PLANET

	Phos	Prot	Sod	Fat	Carb	Cals	Obtained
Organic Turkey Dinner	1.38	45.00	0.42	45.79	na	34.18	5-Dec-19

NATURE'S HARVEST*

	Phos	Prot	Sod	Fat	Carb	Cals	Obtained
Adult Grain-Free Ocean Fish Pâté	0.92	38.05	0.32	30.36	18.21	29.09	2-Dec-19
Adult Grain-Free Duck Pâté	0.98	41.30	0.37	27.50	17.53	24.55	2-Dec-19
Kitten Grain-Free Chicken Pâté	1.00	40.64	0.38	34.10	12.73	31.27	2-Dec-19
Mature Grain-Free Chicken Pâté	1.02	38.24	0.38	32.05	16.24	29.09	2-Dec-19
Adult Grain-Free Chicken Pâté	1.06	40.16	0.65	34.72	12.16	26.36	2-Dec-19
Adult Grain-Free Turkey Pâté	1.07	38.29	0.43	35.18	14.23	26.36	2-Dec-19

NATURE'S LOGIC

	Phos	Prot	Sod	Fat	Carb	Cals	Obtained
Beef Feast	0.58	47.20	0.62	36.89	3.30	40.91	20-Feb-20
Rabbit Feast	0.92	52.11	0.63	30.17	4.80	38.55	20-Feb-20
Duck & Salmon Feast	0.95	43.64	0.62	37.82	4.02	41.82	20-Feb-20
Sardine Feast	1.28	59.63	0.56	16.90	3.40	31.09	20-Feb-20
Chicken Feast	1.40	45.44	0.60	35.60	4.00	41.82	20-Feb-20
Turkey Feast	1.41	45.50	0.59	35.49	4.69	39.82	20-Feb-20

NEWMAN'S OWN

	Phos	Prot	Sod	Fat	Carb	Cals	Obtained
Beef & Vegetable Grain-Free Stew	0.88	61.00	0.11	13.00	3.80	33.64	14-Nov-19
Beef Liver & Vegetable Grain-Free Stew	0.88	61.00	0.11	13.00	3.80	34.55	14-Nov-19
Lamb, Liver & Vegetable Stew	0.88	61.00	0.11	13.00	3.80	42.55	14-Nov-19
Premium Chicken & Brown Rice	1.15	40.00	0.47	35.00	16.00	32.00	14-Nov-19
Premium Chicken & Salmon	1.15	40.00	0.47	35.00	16.00	37.27	14-Nov-19
Organic Grain-Free Beef	1.15	40.00	0.47	35.00	16.00	38.18	14-Nov-19
Organic Grain-Free Beef & Liver	1.15	40.00	0.47	35.00	16.00	32.55	14-Nov-19
Organic Grain-Free Liver	1.15	40.00	0.47	35.00	16.00	30.91	14-Nov-19
Premium Turkey	1.15	40.00	0.47	35.00	16.00	32.55	14-Nov-19
Premium Turkey & Vegetable	1.15	40.00	0.47	35.00	16.00	34.00	14-Nov-19
Organic 95% Chicken Grain-Free Dinner	1.61	44.00	0.64	43.00	3.95	36.36	14-Nov-19
Organic 95% Chicken & Liver Grain-Free Dinner	1.61	44.00	0.64	43.00	3.95	36.55	14-Nov-19

	Phos	Prot	Sod	Fat	Carb	Cals	Obtained
Organic 95% Turkey Grain-Free Dinner	1.61	44.00	0.64	43.00	3.95	35.64	14-Nov-19
Organic 95% Turkey & Liver Grain-Free Dinner	1.61	44.00	0.64	43.00	3.95	35.64	14-Nov-19

NOW FRESH

	Phos	Prot	Sod	Fat	Carb	Cals	Obtained
Pork Pâté	1.00	39.00	0.32	19.00	35.00	31.59	31-Oct-19
Chicken Pâté	1.10	39.00	0.42	27.00	27.00	33.02	31-Oct-19
Wild Salmon Stew	1.10	40.00	0.30	23.00	39.00	30.72	31-Oct-19
Wild Salmon Pâté	1.10	40.00	0.35	23.00	29.00	30.04	31-Oct-19
Turkey Stew	1.10	40.00	0.40	24.00	26.00	30.21	31-Oct-19
Minced Chicken	1.30	49.00	0.79	29.00	13.00	27.57	31-Oct-19
Cod Pâté	1.40	43.00	0.50	24.00	25.00	31.94	31-Oct-19

NULO

	Phos	Prot	Sod	Fat	Carb	Cals	Obtained
FreeStyle Shredded Turkey & Halibut in Gravy	1.10	56.07	1.20	24.00	9.99	26.00	26-Nov-19
MedalSeries Shredded Turkey & Halibut in Gravy	1.10	56.07	1.20	24.00	9.99	26.00	26-Nov-19
FreeStyle Shredded Beef & Rainbow Trout in Gravy	1.17	58.56	1.17	19.96	10.37	24.67	26-Nov-19
MedalSeries Shredded Beef & Rainbow Trout in Gravy	1.17	58.56	1.17	19.96	10.37	24.67	26-Nov-19
MedalSeries Minced Turkey & Duck in Gravy	1.20	55.91	1.15	23.10	10.76	25.67	26-Nov-19
FreeStyle Minced Turkey & Duck in Gravy	1.20	55.91	1.15	23.10	10.76	25.67	26-Nov-19
MedalSeries Minced Beef & Mackerel in Gravy	1.21	57.99	1.16	19.53	11.24	24.67	26-Nov-19
FreeStyle Minced Beef & Mackerel in Gravy	1.21	57.99	1.16	19.53	11.24	24.67	26-Nov-19
MedalSeries Limited Ingredient Diet 95% Turkey & Turkey Liver in Broth	1.24	52.70	0.44	32.98	7.01	37.27	26-Nov-19

	Phos	Prot	Sod	Fat	Carb	Cals	Obtained
MedalSeries Salmon & Turkey in Gravy	1.36	55.62	1.41	22.29	10.71	25.00	26-Nov-19
FreeStyle Minced Salmon & Turkey in Gravy	1.36	55.62	1.41	22.29	10.71	25.00	26-Nov-19
FreeStyle Grain-Free Beef & Lamb	1.41	47.57	0.44	40.08	3.37	33.82	26-Nov-19
MedalSeries Grain-Free Beef & Lamb	1.41	47.57	0.44	40.08	3.37	33.82	26-Nov-19
FreeStyle Shredded Chicken & Duck in Gravy	1.41	55.61	1.17	22.63	10.78	25.33	26-Nov-19
MedalSeries Shredded Chicken & Duck in Gravy	1.41	55.61	1.17	22.63	10.78	25.33	26-Nov-19
FreeStyle Grain-Free Trout & Salmon	1.45	49.62	0.46	39.69	1.15	36.55	26-Nov-19
MedalSeries Grain-Free Trout & Salmon	1.45	49.62	0.46	39.69	1.15	36.55	26-Nov-19
FreeStyle Grain-Free Salmon & Mackerel	1.54	51.22	0.67	31.97	6.69	34.18	26-Nov-19
MedalSeries Grain-Free Salmon & Mackerel	1.54	51.22	0.67	31.97	6.69	34.18	26-Nov-19
FreeStyle Grain-Free Duck & Tuna	1.55	51.13	0.47	32.56	6.18	34.73	26-Nov-19
MedalSeries Grain-Free Duck & Tuna	1.55	51.13	0.47	32.56	6.18	34.73	26-Nov-19
FreeStyle Grain-Free Chicken & Herring	1.58	49.43	0.49	35.55	4.79	36.73	26-Nov-19
MedalSeries Grain-Free Chicken & Herring	1.58	49.43	0.49	35.55	4.79	36.73	26-Nov-19
FreeStyle Grain-Free Turkey & Chicken	1.78	49.44	0.41	37.73	1.34	35.09	26-Nov-19
MedalSeries Grain-Free Turkey & Chicken	1.78	49.44	0.41	37.73	1.34	35.09	26-Nov-19
MedalSeries Limited Ingredient Diet 95% Salmon in Broth	2.00	47.66	0.24	28.07	11.05	37.09	26-Nov-19
MedalSeries Limited Ingredient Diet 95% Chicken & Chicken Liver in Broth	2.12	47.60	0.37	38.77	0.00	39.45	26-Nov-19

NUTRISCA*

	Phos	Prot	Sod	Fat	Carb	Cals	Obtained
Truly Shredded Chicken & Chicken Liver Entrée In Savory Broth	0.89	58.90	0.35	24.40	8.90	27.41	21-Jan-20
Truly Flaked Tuna & Crab Entrée In Savory Broth	1.07	64.20	1.23	16.00	8.80	20.74	21-Jan-20
Truly Flaked Salmon Entrée In Savory Broth	1.12	54.10	0.51	24.80	12.70	22.96	21-Jan-20
Truly Flaked Tuna & Salmon Entrée In Savory Broth	1.14	60.60	0.47	14.40	16.30	22.22	21-Jan-20

NUTRISOURCE

	Phos	Prot	Sod	Fat	Carb	Cals	Obtained
Grain-Free High Plains Select	1.13	40.83	0.33	27.08	na	31.82	28-Jan-20
Grain-Free Ocean Select	1.17	57.17	0.54	28.88	na	31.82	28-Jan-20
Grain-Free Lamb & Lamb Liver Select	1.21	45.00	0.38	33.50	na	33.64	28-Jan-20
Grain-Free Pork & Pork Liver Select	1.25	49.92	0.67	25.00	na	30.91	28-Jan-20
Chicken, Turkey & Lamb	1.29	45.75	0.46	39.58	na	22.73	28-Jan-20
Grain-Free Chicken, Turkey & Lamb Select	1.29	45.75	0.46	39.58	na	35.64	28-Jan-20
Grain-Free Great Northwest Select[1][8]	1.29	55.83	0.46	44.04	na	37.27	28-Jan-20
Chicken & Rice	1.36	44.55	0.45	37.73	na	35.09	28-Jan-20
Chicken, Turkey, Lamb & Fish	1.36	46.82	0.45	37.73	na	na	28-Jan-20
Grain-Free Country Select	1.58	55.42	0.38	31.83	na	35.27	28-Jan-20
Grain-Free Meadow & Stream Select	1.67	50.67	0.71	31.08	na	32.00	28-Jan-20
Grain-Free Turkey & Turkey Liver Select	1.71	45.00	0.46	40.58	na	35.82	28-Jan-20

---

[8]This food contains over 100%, so something is incorrect. I have asked NutriSource to claarify but had not heard back at the time of this book's publication.

O

ONLY NATURAL PET*

	Phos	Prot	Sod	Fat	Carb	Cals	Obtained
Chicken & Egg Dinner	1.05	40.91	0.73	22.73	29.14	30.94	29-Jan-20
Chicken & Chicken Liver Dinner	1.05	40.91	0.73	22.73	29.09	31.89	29-Jan-20
Seafood Dinner	1.09	40.91	0.55	22.73	33.41	28.11	29-Jan-20
Turkey & Liver Dinner	1.18	40.91	0.86	22.73	31.91	34.15	29-Jan-20
Turkey & Chicken Dinner	1.23	40.91	0.86	22.73	30.55	34.34	29-Jan-20
Rabbit & Pork Dinner	1.41	40.91	0.45	22.73	20.86	34.72	29-Jan-20
Duck & Beef Dinner	1.41	40.91	0.68	22.73	21.59	34.53	29-Jan-20

OPEN FARM

	Phos	Prot	Sod	Fat	Carb	Cals	Obtained
Herring & Mackerel Rustic Blend	0.90	44.99	0.64	26.31	15.38	22.73	17-Jan-20
Wild-Caught Salmon Rustic Blend	0.90	47.18	0.64	26.31	13.19	24.55	17-Jan-20
Harvest Chicken Rustic Blend	1.53	44.99	0.50	38.98	7.11	28.36	17-Jan-20
Homestead Turkey Rustic Blend	1.53	44.99	0.53	34.39	4.19	36.36	17-Jan-20
Grass-Fed Beef Rustic Blend	1.53	44.99	0.53	34.39	4.19	30.73	17-Jan-20
Chicken & Salmon Rustic Blend	1.53	47.18	0.53	34.39	2.01	27.45	17-Jan-20

ORGANIX

	Phos	Prot	Sod	Fat	Carb	Cals	Obtained
Organic Turkey & Organic Spinach	0.64	36.36	0.49	31.05	23.01	36.00	29-Oct-19
Organic Turkey, Brown Rice & Chicken	0.66	34.61	0.40	28.47	21.30	35.45	29-Oct-19
Grain-Free Organic Shredded Chicken	0.93	44.20	0.74	29.70	14.42	31.64	29-Oct-19
Grain-Free Organic Chicken Pâté	0.94	45.10	0.85	39.20	5.90	35.27	29-Oct-19
Grain-Free Organic Shredded Chicken and Chicken Liver	1.01	41.80	0.70	33.80	12.94	31.82	29-Oct-19
Grain-Free Organic Turkey Pâté	1.03	41.60	0.76	42.40	7.86	34.91	29-Oct-19
Grain-Free Organic Chicken and Chicken Liver Pâté	1.05	47.50	0.84	36.60	5.31	33.27	29-Oct-19

P

PERFORMATRIN

	Phos	Prot	Sod	Fat	Carb	Cals	Obtained
Senior Chicken & Turkey	0.73	40.70	0.40	31.50	18.20	31.45	28-Nov-19
Ultra Grain-Free Senior Chicken Pâté	0.74	48.00	0.48	28.00	13.50	28.55	21-Jan-20
Ultra Grain-Free Tuna Bisque	0.91	63.00	1.03	14.00	9.10	26.36	21-Jan-20
Adult Grain-Free Beef	1.01	47.90	0.69	35.80	6.70	35.00	28-Nov-19
Ultra Grain-Free Trout Bisque	1.01	53.00	1.17	24.00	10.30	29.64	21-Jan-20
Ultra Grain-Free Beef Stew	1.03	49.40	0.91	23.70	13.70	32.00	28-Nov-19
Adult Grain-Free Beef & Liver	1.03	49.60	0.51	33.50	7.30	33.00	28-Nov-19
Healthy Weight Turkey	1.04	42.20	0.43	19.70	23.10	26.91	28-Nov-19
Indoor Chicken	1.09	43.20	0.46	24.00	15.80	29.27	28-Nov-19
Grain-Free Ultra Chicken Stew	1.16	57.10	0.81	20.10	9.10	26.36	28-Nov-19
Adult Grain-Free Turkey	1.17	49.40	0.50	37.10	3.60	34.00	28-Nov-19
Ultra Grain-Free Turkey, Salmon & Duck Pâté	1.21	44.90	0.42	40.30	4.20	39.45	28-Nov-19
Adult Grain-Free Chicken	1.21	45.40	0.58	41.10	3.70	38.00	28-Nov-19
Grain-Free Ultra Turkey Pâté	1.24	44.90	0.40	40.40	4.00	39.64	28-Nov-19
Ultra Grain-Free Turkey Stew	1.24	53.70	0.81	20.10	11.30	27.09	28-Nov-19
Kitten Grain-Free Chicken	1.38	45.80	0.49	39.60	4.50	39.82	28-Nov-19
Adult Grain-Free Chicken & Lamb	1.41	44.80	0.50	40.20	4.40	38.33	28-Nov-19
Indoor Salmon	1.42	42.20	0.64	22.40	10.70	27.82	28-Nov-19
Healthy Weight Ocean Whitefish	1.52	41.50	0.57	14.80	25.50	24.18	28-Nov-19
Ultra Grain-Free Salmon Bisque	1.54	41.50	0.92	36.90	8.30	37.27	28-Nov-19
Adult Grain-Free Salmon	1.58	50.10	0.93	34.50	3.80	32.67	28-Nov-19
Ultra Grain-Free Chicken Pâté	1.64	45.70	0.46	36.30	5.10	34.00	28-Nov-19
Adult Grain-Free Whitefish	1.66	54.30	0.73	28.90	3.30	30.55	28-Nov-19

PETGUARD

	Phos	Prot	Sod	Fat	Carb	Cals	Obtained
Organic Chicken & Vegetable	0.75	36.36	0.29	31.80	7.30	36.50	18-Dec-19
Weight Management Chicken & Stew Dinner	1.00	37.50	0.32	16.60	33.10	27.00	18-Dec-19

	Phos	Prot	Sod	Fat	Carb	Cals	Obtained
Weight Management Turkey & Barley Dinner	1.00	38.60	0.30	15.90	28.60	28.30	18-Dec-19
Premium Feast Dinner	1.00	45.40	0.37	22.70	17.70	31.00	18-Dec-19
Beef & Barley Dinner	1.10	43.00	0.27	22.70	19.50	31.00	18-Dec-19
Fish, Chicken & Liver Dinner	1.10	45.40	0.44	20.00	20.90	29.30	18-Dec-19
Chicken & Beef Dinner	1.10	45.50	0.32	29.50	11.30	34.10	18-Dec-19
Chicken & Wheat Germ Dinner	1.20	50.00	0.30	22.70	11.80	32.50	18-Dec-19
Savory Seafood Dinner	1.20	50.00	0.54	20.40	12.20	32.70	18-Dec-19

PETITE CUISINE

	Phos	Prot	Sod	Fat	Carb	Cals	Obtained
Sister Rose's Tuna, Pumpkin & Ocean Fish	1.10	74.70	1.68	19.50	na	23.21	29-Oct-19
Baby Bluebell's Chicken & Pumpkin	1.10	80.30	0.32	11.20	na	22.86	29-Oct-19
Sweet Ivy's Chicken & Sweet Potato Entrée in Broth	1.15	73.80	0.47	11.30	na	22.50	29-Oct-19
L'il Violet's Tuna, Pumpkin & Tilapia	1.26	70.70	1.15	15.90	na	22.86	29-Oct-19

PRESIDENT'S CHOICE

	Phos	Prot	Sod	Fat	Carb	Cals	Obtained
Extra Meaty Poached Trout	0.97	54.58	0.93	33.39	3.39	na	12-Dec-19
Extra Meaty Sliced Duck & Wild Rice	1.15	51.05	1.29	22.01	16.75	na	12-Dec-19
Extra Meaty Chicken	1.17	48.47	0.95	38.07	5.01	na	12-Dec-19
Extra Meaty Chicken & Liver	1.18	50.77	0.92	31.99	7.53	na	12-Dec-19
Extra Meaty Beef	1.29	50.86	0.86	34.46	5.88	na	12-Dec-19
Extra Meaty Turkey & Giblets	1.30	56.59	0.80	30.81	2.77	na	12-Dec-19
Extra Meaty Salmon	1.46	48.43	0.75	38.50	2.24	na	12-Dec-19
Extra Meaty Flaked Tuna	1.46	61.38	1.46	20.06	6.48	na	12-Dec-19
Extra Meaty Ocean Whitefish & Tuna	2.13	68.68	1.00	13.78	2.17	na	12-Dec-19
Extra Meaty Cod, Sole & Shrimp	2.44	65.38	0.77	11.92	5.56	na	12-Dec-19

PUREVITA

	Phos	Prot	Sod	Fat	Carb	Cals	Obtained
Grain-Free Beef Entrée	1.14	52.45	0.41	29.00	na	31.47	28-Jan-20
Grain-Free Whitefish Entrée	1.25	54.21	0.42	36.92	na	34.36	28-Jan-20
Grain-Free Chicken Entrée	1.27	53.64	0.45	43.36	na	35.24	28-Jan-20
Grain-Free Salmon Entrée	1.27	55.91	0.41	41.95	na	34.81	28-Jan-20
Grain-Free Turkey Entree	1.77	55.86	0.45	43.05	na	35.49	28-Jan-20

R

RAWZ

	Phos	Prot	Sod	Fat	Carb	Cals	Obtained
Shredded Chicken Breast & Egg Pouch	0.68	68.40	0.35	12.81	7.87	23.58	3-Dec-19
Shredded Chicken & Pumpkin	0.90	80.33	0.30	9.00	1.86	23.45	3-Dec-19
Shredded Chicken Breast & Cheese Pouch	0.90	80.33	0.30	9.00	11.80	23.98	3-Dec-19
Shredded Tuna & Salmon	0.91	66.80	0.61	15.50	8.08	24.00	3-Dec-19
Shredded Tuna & Chicken	0.91	66.80	0.61	15.50	8.08	23.45	3-Dec-19
Shredded Chicken & Chicken Liver	0.91	81.40	0.30	9.00	1.05	24.36	3-Dec-19
Shredded Chicken Breast, Pumpkin & New Zealand Green Mussels Pouch	0.92	66.44	0.35	12.54	10.33	23.17	3-Dec-19
Shredded Chicken & Duck	0.92	80.06	0.33	9.04	1.01	24.55	3-Dec-19
Shredded Salmon, Aku Tuna & Tuna Oil Pouch	0.97	61.36	0.74	22.41	7.54	26.02	3-Dec-19
Shredded Chicken Breast & Coconut Oil Pouch	0.97	61.36	0.74	22.41	7.82	26.83	3-Dec-19
Shredded Chicken	0.97	81.80	0.30	9.00	0.61	23.64	3-Dec-19
96% Turkey & Salmon Pâté	1.06	55.68	0.46	29.47	4.10	30.73	3-Dec-19
96% Beef & Beef Liver Pâté	1.13	51.64	0.65	24.76	11.38	32.00	3-Dec-19
96% Turkey & Turkey Liver Pâté	1.40	48.00	0.48	40.80	2.28	36.18	3-Dec-19
96% Salmon Pâté	1.43	44.57	0.47	40.31	2.33	36.00	3-Dec-19
96% Chicken & Chicken Liver Pâté	1.48	50.00	0.49	36.89	4.00	35.27	3-Dec-19
96% Duck & Duck Liver Pâté	1.55	49.58	0.48	32.80	6.05	32.91	3-Dec-19

	Phos	Prot	Sod	Fat	Carb	Cals	Obtained
96% Chicken & Herring Pâté	1.66	52.95	0.46	29.17	7.31	33.27	3-Dec-19
96% Rabbit & Pumpkin Pâté	1.75	48.92	0.42	29.46	9.42	30.18	3-Dec-19
96% Rabbit Pâté	1.83	47.24	0.46	30.60	8.70	31.27	3-Dec-19

RAYNE CLINICAL NUTRITION

	Phos	Prot	Sod	Fat	Carb	Cals	Obtained
Kangaroo-MAINT	0.94	51.66	0.42	19.39	22.99	29.64	27-Nov-19
Rabbit-MAINT	0.95	49.81	0.33	20.30	24.44	30.18	27-Nov-19
Growth/Sensitive-GI	1.00	52.01	0.45	23.65	18.67	33.82	27-Nov-19

REDBARN NATURALS

	Phos	Prot	Sod	Fat	Carb	Cals	Obtained
Beef Pâté for Urinary Support	0.73	42.92	0.39	30.55	20.40	31.64	31-Oct-19
Grain-Free Beef Stew	0.98	45.37	1.42	23.30	20.80	24.67	31-Oct-19
Lamb Pâté for Skin & Coat Health	1.20	43.31	0.28	41.20	7.70	37.27	31-Oct-19
Grain-Free Salmon Stew	1.23	50.12	1.50	31.18	6.87	27.67	31-Oct-19
Grain-Free Chicken Stew	1.24	42.93	1.44	33.94	12.20	26.00	31-Oct-19
Ocean Fish Pâté for Weight Control	1.27	51.82	0.38	25.00	12.80	30.18	31-Oct-19
Chicken Pâté for Indoor Cats	1.32	51.44	0.39	27.08	11.60	30.90	31-Oct-19
Grain-Free Tuna Pâté	1.33	52.51	0.43	36.00	2.50	35.45	31-Oct-19
Grain-Free Turkey Pâté	1.54	56.61	0.44	36.88	0.00	34.91	31-Oct-19

S

SHEBA*

	Phos	Prot	Sod	Fat	Carb	Cals	Obtained
Perfect Portions Premium Cuts in Gravy Roasted Chicken	1.61	45.74	1.30	26.74	13.30	na	7-Dec-16
Perfect Portions Premium Cuts in Gravy Tender Turkey	1.61	45.74	1.30	26.74	13.30	na	7-Dec-16
Perfect Portions Premium Cuts in Gravy Savory Salmon and Chicken	1.61	45.74	1.30	26.74	13.30	na	7-Dec-16
Perfect Portions Premium Cuts in Gravy Tender Trout	1.61	45.74	1.30	26.74	13.30	na	7-Dec-16

	Phos	Prot	Sod	Fat	Carb	Cals	Obtained
Perfect Portions Premium Cuts in Gravy Savory Mixed Grill	1.61	45.74	1.30	26.74	13.30	na	7-Dec-16
Perfect Portions Premium Cuts in Gravy Delicate Whitefish and Tuna	1.61	45.74	1.30	26.74	13.30	na	7-Dec-16

SOLID GOLD*

	Phos	Prot	Sod	Fat	Carb	Cals	Obtained
Flavorful Feast Grain-Free Pâté with Salmon & Beef	1.01	35.00	0.52	24.00	34.20	29.33	22-Jan-20
Five Oceans Shreds with Shrimp & Tuna in Gravy	1.08	68.00	0.32	15.00	9.00	19.83	22-Jan-20
Flavorful Feast Grain-Free Kitten Classic Pâté with Chicken	1.16	56.00	0.26	17.00	18.00	35.67	22-Jan-20
Five Oceans Shreds with Sardine & Tuna in Gravy	1.16	61.11	0.34	11.11	8.00	22.50	8-Nov-19
Five Oceans Shreds with Mackerel & Tuna in Gravy	1.18	61.11	0.39	11.11	9.00	22.17	8-Nov-19
Flavorful Feast Grain-Free Pâté Indoor Recipe with Chicken	1.20	56.00	0.23	17.00	18.00	34.00	22-Jan-20
Flavorful Feast Grain-Free Sardine & Tuna Classic Paté in Gravy	1.25	50.00	0.25	20.00	16.00	30.67	22-Jan-20
Five Oceans Shreds with Sea Bream & Tuna in Gravy	1.26	61.11	0.47	11.11	11.00	21.33	8-Nov-19
Triple Layer Grain-Free with Salmon & Pumpkin	1.30	50.00	0.54	18.00	22.00	32.00	22-Jan-20
Purrfect Pairings Grain-Free Savory Mousse with Chicken Liver & Goat Milk	1.30	50.00	2.50	18.18	na	27.64	8-Nov-19
Tropical Blendz Grain-Free Pâté with Chicken & Coconut Oil	1.34	46.00	0.35	18.00	28.00	37.00	22-Jan-20
Tropical Blendz Grain-Free Pâté with Turkey & Coconut Oil	1.34	46.00	0.36	18.00	28.00	37.33	22-Jan-20
Purrfect Pairings Grain-Free Savory Mousse With Tuna & Goat Milk	1.34	54.55	2.80	18.18	na	29.09	8-Nov-19

	Phos	Prot	Sod	Fat	Carb	Cals	Obtained
Tropical Blendz Grain-Free Pâté with Chicken Liver & Coconut Oil	1.38	46.00	0.32	18.00	28.00	34.33	22-Jan-20
Triple Layer Grain-Free with Turkey & Pumpkin	1.40	50.00	0.54	23.00	14.00	30.18	22-Jan-20
Purrfect Pairings Grain-Free Savory Mousse with Chicken & Goat Milk	1.40	50.00	2.50	22.73	na	31.27	8-Nov-19
Holistic Delights Grain-Free Creamy Bisque with Chicken Liver & Coconut Milk Pouch	1.40	56.00	0.20	19.00	10.00	23.33	22-Jan-20
Five Oceans Shreds with Blended Tuna in Gravy	1.40	68.00	0.30	10.00	10.00	26.67	22-Jan-20
Tropical Blendz Grain-Free Pâté with Salmon & Coconut Oil	1.41	46.00	0.34	18.00	28.00	35.33	22-Jan-20
Holistic Delights Grain-Free Creamy Bisque With Tuna & Coconut Milk Pouch	1.41	55.56	1.06	18.00	na	25.67	8-Nov-19
Holistic Delights Grain-Free Creamy Bisque with Chicken & Coconut Milk Pouch	1.43	55.56	1.75	22.22	na	27.33	8-Nov-19
Holistic Delights Grain-Free Creamy Bisque with Turkey & Coconut Milk Pouch	1.46	56.00	0.36	19.00	13.00	25.67	22-Jan-20
Purrfect Pairings Grain-Free Savory Mousse with Salmon & Goat Milk	1.50	63.64	2.40	9.09	na	28.36	8-Nov-19
Triple Layer Grain-Free with Beef & Pumpkin	1.50	64.00	0.53	9.00	17.00	31.64	22-Jan-20
Holistic Delights Grain-Free Creamy Bisque with Salmon & Coconut Milk Pouch	1.54	55.56	0.93	22.22	na	29.33	8-Nov-19
Holistic Delights Grain-Free Creamy Bisque with Beef & Coconut Milk Pouch	1.61	55.56	1.05	22.22	na	26.33	22-Jan-20
Wholesome Selects Grain-Free Turkey & Pumpkin Chunks in Gravy	1.68	53.00	0.67	22.92	20.68	29.00	22-Jan-20
Triple Layer Grain-Free with Chicken & Pumpkin	1.74	59.00	0.34	23.00	8.00	31.27	22-Jan-20

	Phos	Prot	Sod	Fat	Carb	Cals	Obtained
Wholesome Selects Grain-Free Chicken, Duck & Pumpkin Chunks in Gravy	1.80	48.00	0.54	22.55	16.60	28.00	22-Jan-20
Wholesome Selects Grain-Free Chicken & Liver Chunks in Gravy	1.94	50.00	0.21	22.70	17.00	28.00	22-Jan-20

SOULISTIC

	Phos	Prot	Sod	Fat	Carb	Cals	Obtained
Harvest Sunrise Chicken & Pumpkin in Gravy	0.59	56.47	0.16	12.30	27.81	21.27	27-Jan-20
Chicken Dinner Pâté	0.71	47.70	0.61	40.00	7.70	30.91	27-Jan-20
Chicken & Turkey Dinner Pâté	0.71	48.10	0.61	39.40	7.80	30.73	27-Jan-20
Moist & Tender Tuna & Duck in Gravy Pouch	0.72	62.61	0.64	16.11	14.61	20.73	27-Jan-20
Good Karma Chicken in Gravy Pouch	0.73	69.17	0.13	11.65	15.87	23.09	27-Jan-20
Golden Fortune Chicken & Tuna in Pumpkin Soup	0.78	62.78	0.32	12.22	19.44	20.00	27-Jan-20
Moist & Tender Tuna & Beef Dinner in Gravy Pouch	0.78	62.91	0.64	13.41	16.98	20.00	27-Jan-20
Sweet Salutations Chicken & Tuna Dinner in Gravy	0.79	59.63	0.22	13.68	22.68	21.82	27-Jan-20
Moist & Tender Tuna & Turkey Dinner in Gravy Pouch	0.79	62.68	0.61	15.26	15.74	21.82	27-Jan-20
Moist & Tender Tuna & Chicken Dinner in Gravy Pouch	0.79	67.81	0.65	15.17	10.84	20.36	27-Jan-20
Seaside Serenity Salmon & Tuna Dinner in Gravy	0.79	68.02	0.48	13.37	14.55	23.09	27-Jan-20
Moist & Tender Chicken Dinner in Gravy Canned	0.82	50.72	0.58	30.43	10.77	27.82	27-Jan-20
Triple Harmony Chicken, Salmon & Tuna Dinner in Gravy Pouch	0.82	60.93	0.39	9.84	24.86	20.00	27-Jan-20
Pure Bliss Tuna Whole Meat Dinner in Gravy	0.82	64.23	0.23	10.20	21.58	21.45	27-Jan-20
Autumn Bounty Chicken Dinner in Pumpkin Soup Pouch	0.82	78.32	0.13	7.61	9.73	19.45	27-Jan-20
Aromatic Chicken Dinner in Gelée	0.82	79.81	0.11	13.29	1.08	17.82	27-Jan-20

	Phos	Prot	Sod	Fat	Carb	Cals	Obtained
Moist & Tender Tuna & Lamb Dinner in Gravy Pouch	0.83	62.85	0.60	13.99	17.46	21.82	27-Jan-20
Nautical Nirvana Tuna & Skipjack Dinner in Gravy	0.83	64.86	0.37	14.68	16.33	25.27	27-Jan-20
Chicken & Lamb Pâté Pouch	0.85	53.90	0.44	31.30	9.70	23.00	27-Jan-20
Moist & Tender Turkey Dinner in Gravy Canned	0.85	54.73	0.50	30.35	7.56	27.09	27-Jan-20
Good Karma Chicken Dinner in Gravy Canned	0.85	65.60	0.42	12.00	18.75	22.55	27-Jan-20
Aqua Grill Tilapia & Tuna Dinner in Gravy	0.87	59.60	0.51	12.72	23.06	19.45	27-Jan-20
Midnight Delight Mackerel & Tuna Dinner in Gravy Pouch	0.91	59.95	0.22	13.71	21.73	22.55	27-Jan-20
Double Happiness Tuna & Crab Surimi Dinner in Gelée	0.92	69.64	0.62	22.05	2.15	24.18	27-Jan-20
Island Illusion Salmon & Tuna Dinner in Pumpkin Soup Pouch	0.93	65.06	0.55	14.20	15.62	18.55	27-Jan-20
Polynesian Picnic Chicken & Tilapia Dinner in Gelée	0.94	74.44	0.55	11.88	6.81	17.45	27-Jan-20
Shrimply Divine Tuna & Shrimp Dinner in Gelée	0.97	73.81	0.44	19.89	0.00	21.27	27-Jan-20
Luna Tuna Runa Dinner in Pumpkin Soup Pouch	0.97	79.09	0.28	10.29	5.37	19.09	27-Jan-20
Chicken & Salmon Pâté Pouch	0.99	61.10	0.29	22.90	9.50	21.33	27-Jan-20
Tri-Fusion Tuna with Grilled Salmon, Beef & Duck Dinner in Gravy	1.00	63.83	0.48	12.44	19.45	22.73	27-Jan-20
Chicken & Pumpkin Pâté Pouch	1.01	59.10	0.30	21.40	11.90	19.33	27-Jan-20
Chicken & Tuna Pâté	1.01	60.50	0.80	28.10	4.60	26.36	27-Jan-20
Upstream Dream Salmon & Tuna Dinner in Gelée	1.01	72.81	0.76	15.73	5.28	20.55	27-Jan-20
Moist & Tender Salmon Dinner in Gravy Canned	1.03	50.48	0.67	32.45	8.41	28.36	27-Jan-20
Tuna & Salmon Pâté	1.10	63.20	0.59	26.40	4.30	30.00	27-Jan-20
Moist & Tender Lamb Dinner in Gravy Canned	1.26	56.68	0.59	25.67	7.11	23.45	27-Jan-20
Duck & Tuna Pâté Pouch	1.39	64.80	0.54	19.60	7.70	18.33	27-Jan-20
Tuna and Beef Pâté	1.39	68.60	0.64	19.80	3.50	25.82	29-Jan-20

	Phos	Prot	Sod	Fat	Carb	Cals	Obtained
Duck & Tuna Pâté	1.74	62.50	0.85	23.10	5.20	24.00	27-Jan-20
Moist & Tender Duck Dinner in Gravy Canned	1.91	52.76	0.68	22.61	9.85	23.27	27-Jan-20
Moist & Tender Beef Dinner in Gravy Canned	1.95	56.84	0.79	20.00	9.05	21.64	27-Jan-20

STELLA AND CHEWY'S*

	Phos	Prot	Sod	Fat	Carb	Cals	Obtained
Marvelous Morsels Grain-Free Cage-Free Chicken	0.83	42.90	1.05	14.30	2.57	27.09	3-Dec-19
Marvelous Morsels Chicken & Salmon	0.89	41.20	1.08	13.70	2.97	27.27	3-Dec-19
Marvelous Morsels Grain-Free Cage-Free Turkey	0.98	39.10	0.42	17.40	3.72	27.45	3-Dec-19
Purrfect Pâté Grain-Free Cage-Free Chicken	1.63	39.00	0.86	19.50	5.77	32.55	3-Dec-19
Purrfect Pâté Grain-Free Chicken & Salmon	1.68	41.70	0.96	20.80	5.68	32.73	3-Dec-19
Purrfect Pâté Grain-Free Turkey	2.27	39.90	0.93	20.00	4.37	34.00	3-Dec-19

T

TASTE OF THE WILD

	Phos	Prot	Sod	Fat	Carb	Cals	Obtained
Rocky Mountain with Salmon and Roasted Venison in Gravy	1.20	48.30	1.20	22.90	17.80	27.50	23-Sep-19
Canyon River with Trout and Salmon in Gravy	1.20	48.30	1.20	30.00	10.70	26.93	23-Sep-19

TENDER AND TRUE*

	Phos	Prot	Sod	Fat	Carb	Cals	Obtained
Antibiotic-Free Turkey & Brown Rice	1.00	30.00	0.36	18.40	39.00	33.64	11-Nov-19
Ocean Whitefish & Potato	1.17	30.00	0.41	18.60	38.00	28.18	11-Nov-19
Organic Turkey & Liver	1.20	30.00	0.32	19.50	33.00	33.64	11-Nov-19
Organic Chicken & Liver	1.27	30.00	0.25	19.50	33.00	30.91	11-Nov-19

	Phos	Prot	Sod	Fat	Carb	Cals	Obtained
Antibiotic-Free Chicken & Brown Rice	1.30	30.00	0.29	18.40	39.00	33.64	11-Nov-19
Salmon & Sweet Potato	1.33	28.33	na	11.67	na	34.00	11-Nov-19

TIKI CAT*

	Phos	Prot	Sod	Fat	Carb	Cals	Obtained
Grain-Free After Dark Chicken	0.90	75.00	na	18.75	0.00	20.36	30-Jan-20
Grain-Free Succulent Chicken with Egg in Chicken Consommé (Koolina Luau)	1.00	72.73	na	18.18	0.00	25.00	30-Jan-20
Grain-Free Ahi Tuna with Crab in Tuna Consommé (Hana Grill)	1.00	75.00	na	16.67	0.00	26.79	30-Jan-20
Grain-Free Velvet Mousse Chicken with Egg	1.01	54.55	na	36.36	na	28.21	30-Jan-20
Grain-Free Ahi Tuna & Mackerel in Tuna Consommé (Papeekeo Luau)	1.04	79.17	na	16.67	0.00	25.71	30-Jan-20
Grain-Free Ahi Tuna & Chicken in Chicken Consommé (Hookena Luau)	1.04	83.33	na	12.50	0.00	29.64	30-Jan-20
Grain-Free Aloha Friends Tuna & Pumpkin	1.05	75.00	na	18.75	0.00	17.33	30-Jan-20
Grain-Free Velvet Mousse Chicken	1.06	59.09	na	36.36	na	28.21	30-Jan-20
Grain-Free Succulent Chicken in Chicken Consommé (Puka Puka Luau)	1.07	81.82	na	13.64	0.00	24.64	30-Jan-20
Grain-Free Velvet Mousse Chicken and Wild Salmon	1.10	61.90	na	33.33	na	28.93	30-Jan-20
Grain-Free Velvet Mousse Tuna & Chicken	1.11	68.18	na	27.27	na	26.79	30-Jan-20
Grain-Free Wild Salmon in Salmon Consommé (Hanalei Luau)	1.12	65.22	na	21.74	0.00	19.64	30-Jan-20
Grain-Free Aloha Friends Tuna, Tilapia & Pumpkin	1.13	77.78	na	16.67	0.00	18.67	30-Jan-20

	Phos	Prot	Sod	Fat	Carb	Cals	Obtained
Grain-Free Ahi Tuna with Prawns in Tuna Consommé (Manana Grill)	1.14	76.00	na	16.00	0.00	25.36	30-Jan-20
Grain-Free After Dark Chicken & Beef	1.15	66.67	na	16.67	0.00	24.29	30-Jan-20
Grain-Free Wild Salmon & Chicken in Chicken Consommé (Napili Luau)	1.16	73.91	na	17.39	0.00	25.36	30-Jan-20
Grain-Free Aloha Friends Tuna, Whitefish & Pumpkin	1.18	70.00	na	15.00	0.00	18.67	30-Jan-20
Grain-Free Ahi Tuna (Hawaiian Grill)	1.18	73.91	na	17.39	0.00	26.43	30-Jan-20
Grain-Free After Dark Chicken & Lamb	1.20	44.44	na	22.22	0.00	23.21	30-Jan-20
Grain-Free Velvet Mousse Wild Salmon	1.21	66.67	na	23.81	na	28.57	30-Jan-20
Grain-Free Aloha Friends Tuna, Calamari & Pumpkin	1.21	72.22	na	16.67	0.00	17.67	30-Jan-20
Grain-Free Ahi Tuna in Crab Surimi Consommé (Lanai Grill)	1.22	77.27	na	18.18	0.00	26.79	30-Jan-20
Grain-Free Seabass in Seabass Consommé (Oahu Luau)	1.26	63.16	na	21.05	0.00	26.07	30-Jan-20
Grain-Free Velvet Mousse Tuna & Mackerel	1.26	68.18	na	22.73	na	29.29	30-Jan-20
Grain-Free After Dark Chicken & Pork	1.29	60.00	na	26.67	0.00	23.57	30-Jan-20
Grain-Free After Dark Chicken & Duck	1.30	50.00	na	31.25	0.00	22.86	30-Jan-20
Grain-Free Tilapia in Tilapia Consommé (Kapi'olani Luau)	1.30	72.22	na	22.22	0.00	26.79	30-Jan-20
Grain-Free Aloha Friends Tuna, Shrimp & Pumpkin	1.36	70.59	na	17.65	0.00	18.00	30-Jan-20
Grain-Free Aloha Friends Chicken, Egg & Pumpkin Pouch	1.42	50.00	na	33.33	0.00	24.40	30-Jan-20
Grain-Free After Dark Chicken & Quail Egg	1.47	61.54	na	30.77	0.00	22.14	30-Jan-20
Grain-Free Aloha Friends Chicken, Beef & Pumpkin Pouch	1.74	52.17	na	34.78	0.00	25.60	30-Jan-20

	Phos	Prot	Sod	Fat	Carb	Cals	Obtained
Grain-Free Aloha Friends Chicken & Pumpkin Pouch	1.76	52.38	na	33.33	0.00	25.60	30-Jan-20
Grain-Free Aloha Friends Chicken, Lamb & Pumpkin Pouch	1.76	52.38	na	33.33	0.00	26.80	30-Jan-20
Grain-Free Aloha Friends Chicken, Duck & Pumpkin Pouch	1.82	54.55	na	31.82	0.00	24.40	30-Jan-20
Grain-Free Mackerel & Sardine in Calamari Consommé (Makaha Luau)	2.22	66.67	na	16.67	0.00	19.64	30-Jan-20
Grain-Free Sardine Cutlets (Tahitian Grill)	2.50	73.68	na	15.79	0.00	21.43	30-Jan-20
Grain-Free Sardine Cutlets in Lobster Consomme (Bora Bora Luau)	2.85	72.22	na	16.67	0.00	20.71	30-Jan-20

TRADER JOE'S

	Phos	Prot	Sod	Fat	Carb	Cals	Obtained
Chicken/Turkey & Rice	1.07	44.11	0.57	33.38	17.80	33.09	28-Nov-16
Turkey & Giblets	1.16	44.50	0.58	34.20	13.30	32.73	28-Nov-16
Ocean Fish, Salmon & Rice	1.16	45.82	0.72	31.99	14.66	32.00	28-Nov-16

TRULUXE

	Phos	Prot	Sod	Fat	Carb	Cals	Obtained
Steak Frites	0.57	61.90	0.22	27.80	7.50	20.67	26-Jan-20
On The Cat Wok	0.74	69.10	0.12	22.80	4.90	16.50	26-Jan-20
Meow Me A River	0.77	82.60	0.35	10.70	1.30	18.00	26-Jan-20
Peking Ducken	0.79	72.30	0.23	13.90	10.60	18.67	26-Jan-20
Mediterranean Harvest	0.88	69.20	0.74	9.20	14.20	20.50	26-Jan-20
Pretty In Pink	0.90	80.60	0.69	13.40	0.00	17.67	26-Jan-20
Glam 'N Punk	0.93	54.00	0.49	38.40	1.00	34.67	26-Jan-20
Kawa Booty	0.99	69.60	1.06	15.80	6.40	18.67	26-Jan-20
Quick 'N Quirky	1.02	78.60	0.36	13.80	0.50	17.17	26-Jan-20
Honor Roll	1.03	71.30	0.33	18.30	3.40	18.33	26-Jan-20

V

VERUS

	Phos	Prot	Sod	Fat	Carb	Cals	Obtained
Grain-Free Beef Pâté	0.85	43.00	0.58	28.10	0.00	33.82	27-Jan-20
Grain-Free Turkey Pâté	0.92	40.20	0.77	29.70	14.27	34.55	27-Jan-20
Chicken and Liver	1.16	49.40	0.76	38.00	0.20	30.91	27-Jan-20
Ocean Fish	1.40	51.80	0.93	33.20	0.10	30.00	27-Jan-20
Turkey, Chicken & Ocean Fish	1.57	46.10	0.87	37.30	0.40	32.18	27-Jan-20
Grain-Free Tuna Pâté	1.60	60.80	0.76	26.10	0.20	26.73	27-Jan-20
Grain-Free Chicken Pâté	1.80	49.80	0.61	38.70	0.30	32.55	27-Jan-20
Grain-Free Salmon Pâté	1.86	49.40	0.76	36.30	0.30	33.27	27-Jan-20

VICTOR

	Phos	Prot	Sod	Fat	Carb	Cals	Obtained
Grain-Free Shredded Chicken Dinner in Gravy	1.42	48.16	1.58	27.15	13.13	25.64	23-Nov-19
Turkey & Salmon Pâté	1.46	42.98	0.37	36.11	9.76	33.45	23-Nov-19

W

WELLNESS

	Phos	Prot	Sod	Fat	Carb	Cals	Obtained
Healthy Indulgence Morsels Chicken & Chicken Liver Pouch	0.55	37.87	1.54	30.91	23.01	20.67	1-Feb-20
Healthy Indulgence Morsels Chicken & Salmon Pouch	0.56	39.86	1.53	27.18	21.04	20.67	1-Feb-20
Healthy Indulgence Morsels Salmon & Tuna Pouch	0.60	42.70	1.61	25.32	20.23	20.67	1-Feb-20
Healthy Indulgence Morsels Chicken & Turkey Pouch	0.61	37.12	1.43	31.95	18.22	20.67	1-Feb-20
Healthy Indulgence Morsels Tuna Pouch	0.61	39.87	1.35	28.41	22.73	20.67	1-Feb-20
Healthy Indulgence Morsels Turkey & Duck Pouch	0.62	38.35	1.19	30.15	23.25	20.67	1-Feb-20

	Phos	Prot	Sod	Fat	Carb	Cals	Obtained
Healthy Indulgence Shreds with Chicken & Turkey Pouch	0.81	32.26	0.76	31.09	25.50	19.00	1-Feb-20
Core Tiny Tasters Tuna Pouch	0.88	48.75	1.17	34.63	7.56	36.00	1-Feb-20
Core Signature Selects Flaked Skipjack Tuna with Wild Salmon in Broth	0.90	55.96	0.61	22.02	15.75	25.09	1-Feb-20
Core Tiny Tasters Chicken Pouch	0.91	46.08	0.91	42.60	2.05	40.00	1-Feb-20
Core Tiny Tasters Chicken & Beef Pouch	0.92	43.64	0.87	38.77	8.74	37.14	1-Feb-20
Healthy Indulgence Gravies Chicken & Turkey Pouch	0.93	34.21	0.78	29.50	24.33	19.00	1-Feb-20
Core Signature Selects Shredded Chicken & Chicken Liver in Gravy	0.93	44.53	0.48	15.95	32.89	23.77	1-Feb-20
Core Signature Selects Flaked Skipjack Tuna with Shrimp Entrée in Broth	0.93	56.54	0.67	20.09	17.01	24.53	1-Feb-20
Core Signature Selects Chunky Chicken & Turkey in Sauce	0.96	39.37	0.53	18.96	34.09	25.28	1-Feb-20
Core Signature Selects Shredded Chicken & Turkey in Gravy	0.96	43.94	0.48	16.36	32.82	24.15	1-Feb-20
Core Tiny Tasters Chicken & Turkey Pouch	0.97	44.85	0.89	39.68	5.91	38.29	1-Feb-20
Core Tiny Tasters Tuna & Salmon Pouch	0.97	66.21	1.54	17.47	6.05	29.71	1-Feb-20
Core Signature Selects Shredded Chicken & Beef in Gravy	0.99	45.53	0.48	15.58	31.79	23.96	1-Feb-20
Core Signature Selects Chunky Beef & Chicken in Sauce	1.01	40.63	0.53	14.57	36.74	23.58	1-Feb-20
Core Grain-Free 95% Beef & Chicken	1.02	49.41	0.39	39.80	1.38	37.64	1-Feb-20
Core Signature Selects Chunky Chicken & Wild Salmon in Sauce	1.05	34.53	0.53	25.80	32.04	24.72	1-Feb-20
Complete Health Chicken Pâté	1.07	42.07	0.30	21.14	26.96	33.82	1-Feb-20
Healthy Indulgence Shreds with Skipjack Tuna & Shrimp Pouch	1.16	40.09	0.68	30.40	18.81	19.00	1-Feb-20
Core Tiny Tasters Duck Pouch	1.19	46.63	0.86	39.12	3.82	36.57	1-Feb-20
Core Hearty Cuts Shredded Whitefish & Salmon	1.22	50.89	1.45	18.73	18.68	23.64	1-Feb-20

145

	Phos	Prot	Sod	Fat	Carb	Cals	Obtained
Core Grain-Free 95% Turkey	1.25	46.85	0.40	42.00	0.32	39.45	1-Feb-20
Core Hearty Cuts Shredded Chicken & Turkey	1.27	46.92	1.19	25.18	16.78	28.00	1-Feb-20
Core Hearty Cuts Shredded Indoor Chicken & Turkey	1.28	44.37	1.14	21.90	19.04	26.18	1-Feb-20
Core Grain-Free Turkey & Duck Pâté	1.30	49.87	0.41	35.34	6.12	39.09	1-Feb-20
Healthy Indulgence Gravies Tuna & Mackerel Pouch	1.32	41.72	1.05	30.38	18.38	19.00	1-Feb-20
Core Hearty Cuts Shredded Chicken & Tuna	1.33	49.76	1.19	22.18	16.97	26.91	1-Feb-20
Core Grain-Free Beef, Venison & Lamb Pâté	1.34	55.24	0.65	30.19	4.02	33.64	1-Feb-20
Complete Health Gravies Turkey Dinner	1.50	51.06	1.61	23.72	13.36	23.64	1-Feb-20
Core Grain-Free 95% Chicken	1.61	46.14	0.40	36.87	6.14	35.82	1-Feb-20
Core Grain-Free 95% Chicken & Salmon	1.63	49.31	0.64	39.31	0.30	36.00	1-Feb-20
Core Grain-Free Salmon, Whitefish & Herring Pâté	1.68	50.51	0.86	22.47	12.53	28.55	1-Feb-20
Complete Health Gravies Salmon Dinner	1.68	51.10	1.73	21.72	13.90	22.91	1-Feb-20
Complete Health Morsels Turkey Dinner	1.70	48.62	1.60	27.44	11.15	27.27	1-Feb-20
Complete Health Beef & Salmon Pâté	1.79	46.45	1.22	36.50	4.60	34.00	1-Feb-20
Complete Health Gravies Tuna Dinner	1.79	55.56	1.63	16.29	13.81	21.45	1-Feb-20
Complete Health Minced Tuna Dinner	1.84	55.07	1.74	19.52	11.03	24.73	1-Feb-20
Complete Health Salmon & Trout Pâté	1.85	42.03	1.21	40.85	4.91	37.27	1-Feb-20
Complete Health Turkey Pâté	1.85	48.57	1.14	35.05	4.80	32.73	1-Feb-20
Complete Health Morsels Tuna Entrée	1.87	55.69	1.78	20.16	9.75	24.73	1-Feb-20
Complete Health Gravies Chicken Dinner	1.89	50.26	1.58	21.47	15.03	23.27	1-Feb-20

	Phos	Prot	Sod	Fat	Carb	Cals	Obtained
Complete Health Beef & Chicken Pâté	1.89	50.88	1.16	33.65	3.00	31.27	1-Feb-20
Core Grain-Free Chicken, Turkey & Chicken Liver Pâté	1.91	47.53	0.87	30.80	9.77	38.73	1-Feb-20
Complete Health Morsels Chicken Entrée	1.91	47.90	1.63	27.10	11.76	26.00	1-Feb-20
Complete Health Minced Salmon Entrée	1.91	48.90	2.10	26.41	9.10	25.00	1-Feb-20
Complete Health Morsels Turkey & Salmon Entrée	1.92	49.59	1.63	26.09	10.60	26.33	1-Feb-20
Complete Health Turkey & Salmon Pâté	1.92	50.15	1.28	31.12	5.69	30.36	1-Feb-20
Complete Health Sliced Salmon Entrée	1.93	50.07	2.13	24.36	10.83	24.18	1-Feb-20
Complete Health Morsels Salmon Dinner	1.94	50.12	2.13	24.63	10.40	23.67	1-Feb-20
Complete Health Kitten Pâté	1.94	50.50	1.11	34.02	2.35	32.33	1-Feb-20
Complete Health Minced Turkey Entrée	1.95	48.86	1.57	24.93	12.30	25.64	1-Feb-20
Complete Health Minced Chicken Dinner	1.97	46.50	1.58	27.26	12.86	26.73	1-Feb-20
Complete Health Sliced Chicken Entrée	1.97	46.59	1.59	27.40	12.60	24.00	1-Feb-20
Complete Health Minced Turkey & Salmon Entrée	1.97	48.85	1.63	25.02	12.13	25.82	1-Feb-20
Complete Health Sliced Turkey & Salmon Dinner	2.00	48.61	1.66	25.48	11.59	25.27	1-Feb-20
Complete Health Sliced Turkey Entrée	2.06	48.94	1.62	25.26	11.30	23.67	1-Feb-20
Core Indoor Chicken & Chicken Liver Pâté	2.12	52.42	1.12	20.48	12.10	26.91	1-Feb-20
Complete Health Chicken & Herring Pâté	2.21	53.51	1.23	28.26	4.29	29.09	1-Feb-20
Complete Health Chicken & Lobster Pâté	2.32	49.31	1.16	33.02	3.83	32.36	1-Feb-20
Core Kitten Chicken & Turkey Pâté[9]	4.72	49.30	1.89	31.69	4.75	36.18	1-Feb-20

[9] *The phosphorus content is extremely high, but Wellness has told me it is accurate*

147

WERUVA

	Phos	Prot	Sod	Fat	Carb	Cals	Obtained
What a Crock Pouch	0.71	42.70	0.55	40.80	12.40	33.67	26-Jan-20
Goody Stew Shoes	0.71	43.20	0.59	39.80	13.00	31.27	26-Jan-20
Simmer Down Pouch	0.71	44.00	0.59	38.00	13.90	32.33	26-Jan-20
Stew's Clues	0.71	44.60	0.59	37.30	14.10	31.82	26-Jan-20
Grandma's Chicken Soup	0.77	61.10	0.55	12.30	23.70	19.27	26-Jan-20
Mideast Feast	0.81	69.80	0.44	15.10	8.00	21.45	26-Jan-20
Press Your Lunch! Chicken Pâté	0.82	58.80	0.31	27.30	7.90	18.73	26-Jan-20
Funky Chunky	0.82	60.30	0.31	13.90	22.80	17.45	26-Jan-20
Paw Lickin' Chicken & Beef	0.82	77.00	0.24	15.70	3.90	19.09	26-Jan-20
Nine Liver	0.84	70.50	0.22	16.10	10.30	19.82	26-Jan-20
Stir the Pot Pouch	0.90	45.20	0.61	32.10	15.30	28.67	26-Jan-20
Stewy Lewis	0.92	45.80	0.62	31.30	15.50	28.18	26-Jan-20
Jeopurrdy Licious Chicken Breast Pâté Pouch	0.97	50.50	0.27	37.70	6.10	31.27	26-Jan-20
Family Food Chicken Breast Pâté with Tuna Pouch	0.97	59.50	0.40	36.40	0.00	23.82	26-Jan-20
Green Eggs & Chicken	0.97	67.50	0.27	17.50	11.00	21.27	26-Jan-20
Jolly Good Fares Chicken & Salmon Pâté	0.99	61.10	0.29	22.90	9.50	21.27	26-Jan-20
Meows n' Holler PurrAmid Chicken & Shrimp Pâté	1.00	62.60	0.46	20.80	9.10	20.73	26-Jan-20
Who wants to be a Meowionaire? Chicken & Pumpkin Pâté	1.01	59.10	0.30	21.40	11.90	19.33	26-Jan-20
Tic Tac Whoa! Tuna & Salmon Pâté	1.02	75.20	0.56	7.90	9.00	14.18	26-Jan-20
Meow Luau	1.04	74.90	0.29	15.90	3.60	20.91	26-Jan-20
Marbella Paella	1.05	73.40	0.42	18.00	1.00	20.55	26-Jan-20
Meal of Fortune Chicken Breast Pâté with Chicken Liver Pouch	1.06	59.90	0.34	24.10	9.70	20.00	26-Jan-20
Name 'Dat Tuna Tuna Pâté Pouch	1.09	71.70	0.18	14.60	7.30	15.64	26-Jan-20
Asian Fusion	1.22	73.40	1.00	18.00	1.00	21.82	26-Jan-20
Love Connection Chicken & Salmon Pâté Pouch	1.24	55.40	0.23	32.10	5.30	27.09	26-Jan-20
Mack & Jack	1.26	83.50	0.61	9.40	0.10	22.00	26-Jan-20

	Phos	Prot	Sod	Fat	Carb	Cals	Obtained
Too Hot to Handle Pouch	1.28	42.80	0.61	38.40	12.90	32.67	26-Jan-20
Stewbacca	1.30	43.20	0.65	37.20	13.50	30.91	26-Jan-20
Kettle Call Pouch	1.34	40.70	0.71	42.50	9.30	31.67	26-Jan-20
Taco Stewsday	1.35	41.20	0.72	41.80	9.40	31.09	26-Jan-20
Polynesian BBQ	1.57	81.30	0.51	15.70	7.40	20.91	26-Jan-20
Let's Make a Meal Lamb & Mackerel Pâté Pouch	1.59	54.80	0.29	30.80	5.30	27.82	26-Jan-20
Meal or No Deal! Chicken & Beef Pâté	1.75	62.90	0.55	22.50	4.60	16.91	26-Jan-20
The Slice is Right Wild Caught Salmon Pâté Pouch	1.79	61.60	0.27	17.90	11.50	16.73	26-Jan-20
Stewlander	1.88	43.30	0.71	34.30	14.20	29.27	26-Jan-20
Stick a Spark in It Pouch	1.89	42.90	0.68	35.30	13.50	31.00	26-Jan-20
The Newly Feds Beef & Salmon Pâté Pouch	2.03	66.40	0.43	16.80	5.40	18.73	26-Jan-20
Outback Grill	2.15	67.90	0.36	16.80	0.60	18.91	26-Jan-20

WHOLE EARTH FARMS

	Phos	Prot	Sod	Fat	Carb	Cals	Obtained
Grain-Free Real Salmon Morsels in Gravy	0.80	43.80	0.99	28.50	14.53	24.00	25-Oct-19
Grain-Free Real Salmon Pâté	1.05	45.20	0.32	30.80	11.77	33.20	25-Oct-19
Grain-Free Real Turkey Pâté	1.05	46.80	0.36	28.50	14.15	37.20	25-Oct-19
Grain-Free Real Chicken Pâté	1.13	47.20	0.30	25.90	12.29	33.60	25-Oct-19
Grain-Free Real Tuna & Whitefish Pâté	1.27	52.40	0.39	21.10	13.10	33.00	25-Oct-19
Grain-Free Chicken & Turkey Morsels in Gravy	1.61	49.60	2.32	21.30	15.04	28.73	25-Oct-19
Grain-Free Real Duck Pâté	1.66	40.80	0.30	41.30	5.27	35.20	25-Oct-19
Grain-Free Real Chicken & Turkey Pâté	1.67	44.84	0.73	27.55	16.54	31.80	25-Oct-19
Grain-Free Real Beef Pâté	1.71	54.50	2.07	27.10	5.54	26.20	25-Oct-19
Grain-Free Healthy Kitten Pâté	1.90	48.76	0.70	27.37	12.97	31.20	25-Oct-19

WYSONG

	Phos	Prot	Sod	Fat	Carb	Cals	Obtained
Epigen Duck	0.60	45.50	0.50	36.20	6.90	37.67	16-Oct-19
Epigen Turkey	0.60	45.10	0.50	35.70	7.80	39.15	16-Oct-19
Epigen Chicken	0.70	45.50	0.50	35.70	7.20	37.98	16-Oct-19
Epigen Rabbit	0.70	46.00	0.50	38.70	4.00	43.57	16-Oct-19
Epigen Salmon	0.70	44.30	0.50	31.40	8.80	36.43	16-Oct-19
Uretic with Organic Chicken	0.70	41.60	0.60	24.30	11.10	31.64	16-Oct-19
Epigen Beef	0.80	46.00	0.50	38.30	4.50	41.94	16-Oct-19

Z

ZIWIPEAK

	Phos	Prot	Sod	Fat	Carb	Cals	Obtained
New Zealand Rabbit & Lamb	1.34	54.00	0.39	21.00	15.00	31.11	1-Feb-20
New Zealand Venison	1.35	54.00	0.39	23.00	13.00	34.02	1-Feb-20
New Zealand Beef	1.43	45.00	0.38	29.00	16.00	35.40	1-Feb-20
New Zealand Mackerel & Lamb	1.43	55.00	0.38	22.00	16.00	34.02	1-Feb-20
New Zealand Free Range Chicken	1.46	46.00	0.31	31.00	13.00	37.54	1-Feb-20
New Zealand Lamb	1.49	43.00	0.37	31.00	16.00	37.54	1-Feb-20
New Zealand Mackerel	1.77	64.00	1.23	14.00	10.00	30.50	1-Feb-20
New Zealand Hoki	1.91	55.00	0.29	19.00	13.00	29.73	1-Feb-20

DRY FOODS IN BRAND ORDER

Please see pages 3 and 15 for information on how to use these tables. All data are on a dry matter analysis basis, except calories, which are provided per kg (2.2lbs) on an ME as fed basis.

Foods marked * show minimum values for protein and fat and in some cases phosphorus — the actual values could be much higher. Page 13 explains more about this.

"na" means the information was not available.

A

ACANA

	Phos	Prot	Sod	Fat	Carb	Cals	Obtained
Meadowland	0.89	39.00	0.33	22.00	27.00	4060	29-Oct-19
Wild Atlantic	0.89	39.00	0.66	22.00	25.00	4020	29-Oct-19
Grasslands	1.40	39.00	0.44	22.00	24.00	3980	29-Oct-19
Appalachian Ranch	1.40	39.00	0.39	22.00	24.00	3980	29-Oct-19

ADIRONDACK*

	Phos	Prot	Sod	Fat	Carb	Cals	Obtained
Kitten	0.87	34.44	0.30	20.00	na	3643	09-Jan-17
Lean /Senior	0.97	31.11	0.27	11.11	na	3269	09-Jan-17
Adult	0.98	33.33	0.26	15.56	na	3858	09-Jan-17

ANNAMAET

	Phos	Prot	Sod	Fat	Carb	Cals	Obtained
Original Chicken Meal & Brown Rice	0.87	33.00	0.36	15.00	31.50	4022	26-Nov-19
No 29 Sustain Grain-Free	1.01	37.00	0.43	16.00	26.50	3618	26-Nov-19
Grain-Free Chicken Meal & Whitefish Meal	1.05	44.00	0.41	20.00	15.50	4149	26-Nov-19

ARTEMIS

	Phos	Prot	Sod	Fat	Carb	Cals	Obtained
Fresh Mix Feline Formula	0.98	35.80	0.40	23.00	31.30	3922	23-Nov-16

	Phos	Prot	Sod	Fat	Carb	Cals	Obtained
OSOPure Grain-Free Salmon and Garbanzo Bean	1.50	40.40	0.39	21.90	25.60	3861	09-Dec-16

AUTHORITY

	Phos	Prot	Sod	Fat	Carb	Cals	Obtained
Adult Chicken & Rice	0.99	36.10	0.20	18.60	37.70	4163	13-Dec-16

AVODERM

	Phos	Prot	Sod	Fat	Carb	Cals	Obtained
Grain-Free Tuna with Lobster & Crab Meal	0.97	34.70	0.51	18.30	39.00	3595	24-Jul-19
Kitten Chicken & Herring Meal	0.98	39.13	0.35	23.91	23.00	4027	24-Jul-19
Adult Chicken & Herring Meal	1.02	34.78	0.33	21.74	28.50	3753	24-Jul-19
Adult Chicken & Herring Indoor Hairball Care	1.02	34.78	0.33	17.39	29.00	3564	24-Jul-19
Salmon & Brown Rice	1.09	36.96	0.33	19.57	27.00	3793	24-Jul-19
Adult Grain-Free Turkey Meal	1.20	33.70	0.43	18.48	30.00	3685	24-Jul-19
Adult Grain-Free Ocean Fish & Chicken Meal	1.20	33.70	0.54	17.39	31.00	3635	24-Jul-19
Grain-Free Duck with Turkey Meal	1.21	35.80	0.39	17.70	39.00	3563	24-Jul-19
Grain-Free Salmon with Tuna Meal	1.34	37.80	0.53	19.60	35.00	3595	24-Jul-19

AZMIRA*

	Phos	Prot	Sod	Fat	Carb	Cals	Obtained
Classic Cat	1.32	33.08	0.33	11.38	na	3425	16-Jan-20

B

BLACKWOOD*

	Phos	Prot	Sod	Fat	Carb	Cals	Obtained
Indoor Chicken Meal & Brown Rice	0.83	33.33	0.29	13.33	43.93	3824	27-Nov-19
Adult Chicken Meal & Brown Rice	0.86	33.33	0.28	18.89	37.46	3913	27-Nov-19

	Phos	Prot	Sod	Fat	Carb	Cals	Obtained
Kitten Chicken Meal & Brown Rice	0.87	36.67	0.30	23.33	29.20	4204	27-Nov-19
Special Diet Grain-Free Duck Meal, Salmon Meal & Field Pea	0.87	42.22	0.30	20.00	29.18	3763	27-Nov-19
Lean/Senior Chicken Meal & Brown Rice	0.89	33.33	0.32	12.22	47.04	3594	27-Nov-19
Special Diet Grain-Free Chicken Meal & Field Pea	0.98	44.44	0.31	20.00	27.30	3823	27-Nov-19

C

CANIDAE

	Phos	Prot	Sod	Fat	Carb	Cals	Obtained
All Life Stages Indoor Adult with Chicken, Turkey, Lamb & Fish Meals	1.20	33.15	0.33	15.76	39.00	4198	23-Jul-19
Grain-Free PURE Stream with Real Trout	1.30	34.78	0.33	17.39	35.00	3670	07-Dec-16
Grain-Free PURE Sea with Real Salmon	1.30	34.78	0.33	18.48	34.00	3750	07-Dec-16
Grain-Free PURE Elements with Real Chicken	1.30	38.04	0.33	19.57	29.00	3750	07-Dec-16
Grain-Free PURE Ocean Indoor Cat with Fresh Tuna	1.30	39.13	0.33	13.04	33.00	3400	07-Dec-16
All Life Stages with Chicken Meal & Rice	1.36	34.78	0.33	21.74	34.00	4400	23-Jul-19
All Life Stages with Chicken, Turkey, Lamb & Fish Meals	1.36	34.78	0.33	21.74	34.00	4585	23-Jul-19

CATERED BOWL*

	Phos	Prot	Sod	Fat	Carb	Cals	Obtained
Antibiotic-free Chicken & Brown Rice	1.02	33.33	0.27	17.06	37.00	3500	11-Nov-19
Antibiotic-free Turkey & Brown Rice	1.04	33.33	0.34	17.06	37.00	3750	11-Nov-19
Salmon & Sweet Potato	1.11	28.33	na	11.67	na	4700	11-Nov-19
Ocean Whitefish & Potato	1.22	33.33	0.38	17.06	35.00	3750	11-Nov-19

	Phos	Prot	Sod	Fat	Carb	Cals	Obtained
Organic Chicken & Liver	1.33	33.33	0.23	18.89	30.00	3500	11-Nov-19
Organic Turkey & Liver	1.33	33.33	0.29	18.00	30.00	3650	11-Nov-19

CHICKEN SOUP FOR THE SOUL

	Phos	Prot	Sod	Fat	Carb	Cals	Obtained
Grain-Free Chicken & Legumes	0.99	35.70	0.35	17.19	35.11	3585	28-Oct-19
Grain-Free Salmon & Legumes	1.04	35.75	0.30	17.19	35.42	3596	28-Oct-19
Classic Adult Chicken & Brown Rice	1.21	37.76	0.50	20.28	30.15	3732	28-Oct-19
Classic Indoor Chicken & Brown Rice	1.22	36.05	0.49	14.89	35.33	3425	28-Oct-19
Classic Weight & Mature Care Chicken & Brown Rice	1.26	37.81	0.49	9.38	37.15	3113	28-Oct-19
Classic Kitten Chicken, Brown Rice & Pea	1.48	40.06	0.37	22.42	24.72	3797	28-Oct-19

COUNTRY VET

	Phos	Prot	Sod	Fat	Carb	Cals	Obtained
Choice 30/11 Kitten & Adult	1.23	33.34	0.27	12.23	37.03	3280	17-Jan-20
Premium 30/15 Kitten & Adult	1.31	33.34	0.26	16.67	33.52	3570	17-Jan-20
Naturals 34/15 Grain-Free	1.33	37.78	0.29	16.67	30.47	3588	17-Jan-20

D

DAD'S*

	Phos	Prot	Sod	Fat	Carb	Cals	Obtained
Special Mix	1.13	37.17	0.74	10.75	49.34	3350	25-Nov-19
Original	1.25	36.24	0.41	11.51	47.76	3370	25-Nov-19
Gourmet Blend Natural	1.35	37.33	0.74	11.49	47.93	3380	25-Nov-19

DAVE'S*

	Phos	Prot	Sod	Fat	Carb	Cals	Obtained
Naturally Healthy Adult	1.25	41.81	0.32	20.80	na	3777	30-Dec-19

DIAMOND

	Phos	Prot	Sod	Fat	Carb	Cals	Obtained
Maintenance	0.77	34.30	0.36	16.70	42.00	3742	12-Nov-19
Care Urinary Support	0.90	32.90	0.49	16.30	43.90	3728	12-Nov-19
Care Weight Management	1.40	35.80	0.51	10.30	34.50	3080	12-Nov-19
Naturals Chicken & Rice Indoor	1.60	36.40	0.58	15.80	30.90	3350	12-Nov-19
Naturals Chicken & Rice Kitten	1.60	38.90	0.47	24.60	24.50	4052	12-Nov-19
Naturals Chicken & Rice Active Cat	2.00	46.40	0.66	22.40	17.20	4000	12-Nov-19

DR. ELSEY'S

	Phos	Prot	Sod	Fat	Carb	Cals	Obtained
Clean Protein Chicken Recipe	1.08	62.60	0.58	19.46	4.69	4008	22-Sep-19
Clean Protein with Salmon	1.20	58.35	0.65	19.02	9.06	3976	22-Sep-19

DR. POL'S

	Phos	Prot	Sod	Fat	Carb	Cals	Obtained
Grain-Free 34/15 Cat & Kitten	1.04	37.78	0.29	16.67	34.59	3715	17-Jan-20

DR. TIM'S

	Phos	Prot	Sod	Fat	Carb	Cals	Obtained
Chase	1.24	38.00	0.74	22.00	20.00	4140	29-Oct-19

E

EARTHBORN HOLISTIC

	Phos	Prot	Sod	Fat	Carb	Cals	Obtained
Feline Vantage	1.20	39.10	0.30	15.20	39.10	3770	15-Jan-20
Grain-Free Primitive Feline	1.50	47.80	0.30	21.70	20.10	3925	15-Jan-20
Grain-Free Wild Sea Catch	1.60	47.80	0.40	21.70	19.00	3895	15-Jan-20

EVANGER'S

	Phos	Prot	Sod	Fat	Carb	Cals	Obtained
Evanger's Grain-Free Meat Lover's Medley with Rabbit	1.20	35.60	0.20	15.10	31.00	na	16-Sep-16
Grain-Free Catch of the Day	1.30	35.60	0.20	18.60	29.50	3758	16-Sep-16

EXCLUSIVE*

	Phos	Prot	Sod	Fat	Carb	Cals	Obtained
Chicken & Brown Rice Weight Management/Hairball Care	1.10	32.50	0.66	10.08	31.94	3320	12-Nov-19
Chicken & Brown Rice	1.10	32.50	0.67	21.30	25.56	3860	12-Nov-19

F

FARMINA

	Phos	Prot	Sod	Fat	Carb	Cals	Obtained
Natural and Delicious Low Ancestral Grain Chicken & Pomegranate Neutered	1.06	40.43	0.74	10.64	34.26	3877	11-Dec-16
Natural and Delicious Low Ancestral Grain Chicken & Pomegranate	1.17	38.30	0.53	21.28	29.79	4383	11-Dec-16
Natural and Delicious Low Ancestral Grain Codfish & Orange	1.22	38.30	0.85	21.28	29.89	4476	11-Dec-16
Natural and Delicious Low Ancestral Grain Lamb & Blueberry	1.28	38.30	0.64	21.28	29.79	4240	11-Dec-16
Natural and Delicious Grain-Free Lamb & Blueberry	1.38	44.68	0.64	21.28	22.66	4417	11-Dec-16
Natural and Delicious Grain-Free Kitten Chicken & Pomegranate	1.38	46.81	0.64	21.28	20.96	4344	11-Dec-16
Natural and Delicious Grain-Free Adult Chicken & Pomegranate	1.38	46.81	0.64	21.28	20.96	4448	11-Dec-16
Natural and Delicious Grain-Free Boar & Apple	1.38	46.81	0.64	21.28	20.74	4396	11-Dec-16
Natural and Delicious Grain-Free Fish & Orange	1.38	46.81	0.85	21.28	20.96	4456	11-Dec-16

	Phos	Prot	Sod	Fat	Carb	Cals	Obtained
Natural and Delicious Grain-Free Chicken & Pomegranate Neutered	1.38	48.94	0.64	11.70	24.47	3904	11-Dec-16

FELINE MEDLEY

	Phos	Prot	Sod	Fat	Carb	Cals	Obtained
Chicken, Turkey & Fish	0.91	31.60	0.26	16.30	40.77	na	19-Nov-19

FIRSTMATE

	Phos	Prot	Sod	Fat	Carb	Cals	Obtained
Grain-Free Chicken Meal with Blueberries	1.00	40.00	0.40	18.00	29.00	3530	25-Nov-19
Cat/Kitten	1.20	36.00	0.80	21.00	29.00	3660	25-Nov-19
Indoor	1.30	39.00	0.80	13.00	33.00	3295	25-Nov-19
Grain-Free Pacific Ocean Fish Meal with Blueberries	1.30	47.00	1.70	20.00	22.00	3700	25-Nov-19

FROMM

	Phos	Prot	Sod	Fat	Carb	Cals	Obtained
Chicken À La Veg	0.90	35.04	0.41	20.90	34.99	3871	31-Jan-20
Beef Liváttini Veg	0.93	38.80	0.39	21.22	29.24	3802	31-Jan-20
Duck À La Veg	1.05	37.16	0.43	21.66	32.95	3757	31-Jan-20
Gold Kitten	1.09	37.16	0.43	21.66	32.76	4410	31-Jan-20
Hasen Duckenpfeffer	1.10	37.32	0.41	19.37	21.16	3708	31-Jan-20
Gold Mature	1.13	33.28	0.40	13.77	43.79	4017	31-Jan-20
Salmon À La Veg	1.13	35.18	0.47	17.20	39.20	3679	31-Jan-20
Game Bird Recipe	1.16	38.60	0.44	20.09	30.81	3654	31-Jan-20
Salmon Tunachovy	1.18	38.70	0.45	17.18	33.57	3621	31-Jan-20
Gold Adult	1.19	34.96	0.44	19.68	36.93	4318	31-Jan-20
Surf & Turf	1.24	41.99	0.48	21.79	23.80	3696	31-Jan-20
Chicken au Frommage	1.27	38.10	0.52	21.02	na	3752	31-Jan-20

FUSSIE CAT*

	Phos	Prot	Sod	Fat	Carb	Cals	Obtained
Market Fresh Salmon	0.89	38.89	0.22	16.67	29.00	3550	17-Jan-20

	Phos	Prot	Sod	Fat	Carb	Cals	Obtained
Market Fresh Chicken & Turkey	0.89	40.00	0.39	17.78	27.00	3598	17-Jan-20
Market Fresh Salmon & Chicken	0.89	40.00	0.36	17.78	27.00	3604	17-Jan-20
Quail & Duck Meal	1.44	36.67	na	16.67	na	3598	17-Jan-20
Guinea Fowl & Turkey Meal	1.67	38.89	na	16.67	na	3598	17-Jan-20

G

GATHER

	Phos	Prot	Sod	Fat	Carb	Cals	Obtained
Free Acres Organic Free Run Chicken	0.90	33.00	0.49	18.00	37.00	3664	31-Oct-19

GO! SOLUTIONS

	Phos	Prot	Sod	Fat	Carb	Cals	Obtained
Skin + Coat Care Grain-Free Salmon	1.00	34.00	0.32	16.00	39.00	4122	31-Oct-19
Sensitivities Limited Ingredient Grain-Free Pollock	1.00	34.00	0.38	17.00	41.00	4232	31-Oct-19
Sensitivities Limited Ingredient Duck	1.00	35.00	0.45	18.00	36.00	4222	31-Oct-19
Skin + Coat Care Chicken	1.00	36.00	0.28	22.00	33.00	4604	31-Oct-19
Carnivore 74% Grain-Free Salmon & Cod	1.10	46.00	0.45	18.00	25.00	4239	31-Oct-19
Carnivore 70% Grain-Free Lamb & Wild Boar	1.20	47.00	0.47	16.00	26.00	4147	31-Oct-19
Sensitivity + Shine Grain-Free Freshwater Trout & Salmon	1.30	50.00	0.65	21.00	20.00	4444	31-Oct-19
84% Carnivore Grain-Free Chicken, Turkey & Duck	1.50	51.00	0.49	21.00	17.00	4298	31-Oct-19

GRANDMA MAE'S*

	Phos	Prot	Sod	Fat	Carb	Cals	Obtained
Country Naturals Grain-Free Salmon	0.89	34.44	0.24	21.11	na	3820	23-Nov-19
Country Naturals Grain-Free Chicken Meal & Brown Rice	0.89	37.78	0.29	22.22	na	3900	23-Nov-19

	Phos	Prot	Sod	Fat	Carb	Cals	Obtained
Country Naturals Grain-Free Chicken & Herring	0.89	38.89	0.26	18.89	na	3700	23-Nov-19
Country Naturals Grain-Free Indoor & Weight Control	1.00	33.33	0.21	8.89	na	2950	23-Nov-19

H

HALO

	Phos	Prot	Sod	Fat	Carb	Cals	Obtained
Holistic Grain-Free Chicken & Chicken Liver Senior	0.90	33.50	0.60	14.20	40.40	3520	30-Jan-20
Holistic Grain-Free Wild Salmon & Whitefish Senior	0.90	34.00	0.70	13.70	39.40	3470	30-Jan-20
Holistic Sensitive Stomach Seafood Medley	0.90	34.80	0.50	18.60	36.70	3760	30-Jan-20
Holistic Chicken & Chicken Liver Adult	0.90	34.80	0.51	21.60	30.50	3780	30-Jan-20
Holistic Wild Salmon & Whitefish Adult	0.90	35.00	0.60	16.80	36.30	3730	30-Jan-20
Holistic Sensitive Stomach Turkey & Turkey Liver	0.90	35.20	0.50	21.30	32.30	3770	30-Jan-20
Holistic Healthy Weight Grain-Free Wild Salmon & Whitefish Indoor	0.90	36.80	0.60	17.20	33.60	3550	30-Jan-20
Holistic Grain-Free Wild Salmon & Whitefish Kitten	0.90	38.50	0.40	20.90	29.70	3870	30-Jan-20
Holistic Healthy Weight Grain-Free Game Bird Medley Indoor	1.00	34.00	0.70	18.20	35.70	3630	30-Jan-20
Holistic Healthy Weight Grain-Free Chicken & Chicken Liver Indoor	1.00	35.20	0.70	17.10	36.30	3610	30-Jan-20
Holistic Grain-Free Chicken & Chicken Liver Kitten	1.00	36.00	0.40	22.90	29.40	3870	30-Jan-20

HEALTH EXTENSION

	Phos	Prot	Sod	Fat	Carb	Cals	Obtained
Chicken & Brown Rice	1.24	38.00	0.26	20.00	31.00	3719	07-Dec-16

	Phos	Prot	Sod	Fat	Carb	Cals	Obtained
Grain-Free Turkey & Salmon Recipe	1.24	39.00	0.23	20.00	33.00	3744	07-Dec-16

HILL'S

	Phos	Prot	Sod	Fat	Carb	Cals	Obtained
Science Diet Adult Urinary Hairball Control	0.62	34.20	0.35	18.80	32.20	3681	01-Feb-20
Science Diet Adult Oral Care	0.66	33.50	0.39	21.10	30.60	3762	01-Feb-20
Science Diet Adult 7+ Youthful Vitality Chicken & Rice Recipe	0.67	35.40	0.39	16.50	41.00	3870	01-Feb-20
Science Diet Adult 7+ Chicken	0.68	32.10	0.35	21.30	38.70	4006	01-Feb-20
Science Diet Adult 11+ Indoor	0.68	34.70	0.33	20.90	29.90	3790	01-Feb-20
Science Diet Adult 11+ Chicken	0.69	32.70	0.33	22.50	37.00	4089	01-Feb-20
Healthy Advantage Adult Oral+ Feline Nutrition	0.69	33.40	0.41	22.30	30.10	4120	01-Feb-20
Science Diet Adult 7+ Indoor	0.69	34.10	0.35	17.00	33.80	3593	01-Feb-20
Healthy Advantage Adult	0.69	34.20	0.48	22.70	35.70	4117	01-Feb-20
Science Diet Adult 7+ Hairball Control	0.70	33.90	0.35	19.10	31.40	3674	01-Feb-20
Science Diet Adult Chicken	0.70	35.00	0.45	21.40	35.20	4021	01-Feb-20
Science Diet Adult Multiple Benefit	0.72	34.60	0.41	13.00	37.00	3325	01-Feb-20
Science Diet Adult Indoor	0.76	36.10	0.55	16.10	31.70	3515	01-Feb-20
Science Diet Adult Perfect Weight	0.76	40.20	0.35	12.00	33.20	3409	01-Feb-20
Science Diet Adult Light	0.78	38.00	0.53	9.10	39.50	3179	01-Feb-20
Science Diet Adult Hairball Control	0.79	33.90	0.45	19.30	31.00	3673	01-Feb-20
Science Diet Adult Sensitive Stomach & Skin	0.79	35.00	0.45	22.00	36.30	4104	01-Feb-20
Science Diet Adult Hairball Control Light	0.79	40.00	0.44	9.60	35.10	3172	01-Feb-20
Science Diet Adult Sensitive Stomach & Skin Grain-Free	0.80	35.00	0.45	21.90	35.20	4068	01-Feb-20
Healthy Advantage Kitten	1.05	37.30	0.43	24.80	28.30	4139	01-Feb-20
Science Diet Kitten Chicken	1.06	37.80	0.56	23.50	30.00	4152	01-Feb-20
Science Diet Kitten Indoor	1.18	38.40	0.54	20.70	31.50	3997	01-Feb-20

HOLISTIC SELECT

	Phos	Prot	Sod	Fat	Carb	Cals	Obtained
Grain-Free Indoor Health/Weight Control (Turkey, Chicken & Herring Meal)	1.37	36.80	0.33	14.84	35.03	3547	01-Feb-20
Grain-Free Adult & Kitten Health Chicken Meal	1.37	38.80	0.41	20.98	28.63	3851	01-Feb-20
Grain-Free Adult Anchovy & Sardine & Salmon Meal	1.47	38.12	0.46	21.68	28.04	3921	01-Feb-20

HORIZON

	Phos	Prot	Sod	Fat	Carb	Cals	Obtained
Complete All Life Stages	1.24	33.52	0.46	18.05	31.36	3680	25-Nov-19
Legacy Cat & Kitten Grain-Free	1.89	42.51	0.40	19.38	20.44	3870	25-Nov-19

I

I AND LOVE AND YOU

	Phos	Prot	Sod	Fat	Carb	Cals	Obtained
Nude Food Surf n' Chick	1.46	49.95	na	23.33	na	3817	08-Nov-19
Nude Food Poultry & Plenty	1.47	49.90	na	21.85	na	3732	08-Nov-19
Naked Essentials Salmon & Trout	1.50	42.87	0.50	17.37	na	3421	08-Nov-19
Naked Essentials Chicken & Duck	1.63	42.21	0.54	17.33	na	3502	08-Nov-19
Lovingly Simple Salmon & Sweet Potato	1.65	42.13	0.87	15.70	na	3538	08-Nov-19

INFINIA

	Phos	Prot	Sod	Fat	Carb	Cals	Obtained
Holistic Chicken & Pea	0.93	36.70	0.45	18.90	23.87	3765	14-Nov-19

INSTINCT

	Phos	Prot	Sod	Fat	Carb	Cals	Obtained
Ultimate Protein Duck	1.00	52.00	0.56	18.89	18.89	4510	08-Nov-19
Limited Ingredient Diet Rabbit	1.10	38.00	0.55	20.88	24.18	3890	08-Nov-19

	Phos	Prot	Sod	Fat	Carb	Cals	Obtained
Limited Ingredient Diet Salmon	1.30	41.00	0.88	18.70	28.57	4400	08-Nov-19
Ultimate Protein Chicken	1.40	52.00	0.67	18.89	13.33	4470	08-Nov-19
Raw Boost Indoor Health Chicken	1.50	41.00	0.66	14.29	26.37	3861	08-Nov-19
Raw Boost Healthy Weight Chicken	1.50	41.00	0.77	13.19	25.27	3709	08-Nov-19
Raw Boost Indoor Health Rabbit	1.90	43.00	0.55	15.93	26.37	3913	08-Nov-19
Raw Boost Grain-Free Real Salmon	2.00	46.00	0.88	20.30	17.58	4488	08-Nov-19
Original Grain-Free Salmon Meal	2.00	47.00	0.66	19.78	17.58	4470	08-Nov-19
Limited Ingredient Diet Turkey	2.20	39.00	0.55	18.13	26.37	4070	08-Nov-19
Raw Boost Duck	2.20	44.00	0.77	25.82	12.09	4387	08-Nov-19
Original Grain-Free Duck	2.20	44.00	0.77	25.82	13.19	4397	08-Nov-19
Kitten Chicken	2.20	47.00	0.66	24.73	13.19	4456	08-Nov-19
Original Grain-Free Rabbit Meal	2.30	45.00	0.66	24.73	13.19	4346	08-Nov-19
Original Grain-Free Chicken Meal	2.60	45.00	0.66	23.08	15.38	4300	08-Nov-19
Raw Boost Grain-Free Real Chicken	2.60	45.00	0.66	24.18	14.29	4327	08-Nov-19

L

LIFE'S ABUNDANCE

	Phos	Prot	Sod	Fat	Carb	Cals	Obtained
All Life Stages	0.86	35.48	0.46	22.58	31.20	4023	27-Nov-19
All Life Stages Grain-Free	1.08	40.86	0.63	20.43	30.10	3961	27-Nov-19

LONE STAR

	Phos	Prot	Sod	Fat	Carb	Cals	Obtained
Meow for More	1.10	34.16	0.49	11.44	na	3370	01-Feb-20

LOTUS

	Phos	Prot	Sod	Fat	Carb	Cals	Obtained
Grain-Free Oven-Baked Sardines & Herring	0.80	38.00	0.53	15.78	33.43	3457	28-Jan-20
Grain-Free Oven-Baked Low Fat Chicken	1.00	34.61	0.37	11.06	40.33	3206	28-Jan-20

	Phos	Prot	Sod	Fat	Carb	Cals	Obtained
Oven-Baked Chicken Adult	1.22	39.17	0.41	21.39	26.27	3697	28-Jan-20
Grain-Free Oven-Baked Duck Adult	1.32	38.60	0.59	17.22	31.69	3531	28-Jan-20

LOVIBLES

	Phos	Prot	Sod	Fat	Carb	Cals	Obtained
Kitten	1.09	36.10	0.48	16.60	33.00	4185	22-Jan-20
Seafood	1.10	34.80	0.48	14.50	35.80	4060	22-Jan-20
Chicken	1.18	35.00	0.50	14.50	34.70	4021	22-Jan-20

M

MERRICK

	Phos	Prot	Sod	Fat	Carb	Cals	Obtained
Limited Ingredient Grain-Free Turkey	1.24	39.20	0.78	15.60	34.62	3588	18-Nov-16
Limited Ingredient Grain-Free Chicken	1.46	41.02	0.64	16.16	29.65	3588	18-Nov-16
Purrfect Bistro Grain-Free Healthy Kitten Recipe Kitten	1.50	43.63	0.38	20.06	22.52	3755	26-Jun-19
Purrfect Bistro Grain-Free Healthy Weight Recipe Adult	1.54	46.60	0.55	15.50	28.64	3215	26-Jun-19
Purrfect Bistro Grain-Free Healthy Senior Recipe Senior	1.63	44.44	0.62	16.56	29.13	3431	26-Jun-19
Purrfect Bistro Grain-Free Real Salmon & Sweet Potato	1.68	46.81	0.57	18.38	26.43	3748	26-Jun-19
Purrfect Bistro Grain-Free Real Chicken & Sweet Potato	1.80	47.51	0.54	17.39	25.66	3731	26-Jun-19

N

NATURAL BALANCE

	Phos	Prot	Sod	Fat	Carb	Cals	Obtained
Original Ultra Whole Body Health Chicken & Salmon	1.71	38.84	0.59	18.61	31.13	na	07-Oct-19

NATURAL PLANET

	Phos	Prot	Sod	Fat	Carb	Cals	Obtained
Organic Chicken & Pea All Life Stages	0.81	34.02	0.66	15.75	na	3980	28-Jan-20

NATURE'S HARVEST*

	Phos	Prot	Sod	Fat	Carb	Cals	Obtained
Adult Grain-Free Chicken	1.06	38.89	na	22.22	23.33	4260	02-Dec-19
Senior/Weight Management	1.11	32.22	na	13.33	40.00	3870	02-Dec-19
Adult/Kitten Grain-Free	1.11	35.56	na	21.11	28.89	3690	02-Dec-19
Grain-Free Cod	1.11	40.00	0.44	22.22	na	na	03-Feb-20

NATURE'S LOGIC

	Phos	Prot	Sod	Fat	Carb	Cals	Obtained
Chicken Meal Feast	1.08	40.90	0.36	22.40	28.62	3964	20-Feb-20
Turkey Meal Feast	1.33	41.50	0.32	15.60	27.50	3957	20-Feb-20
Rabbit Meal Feast	1.38	41.60	0.36	16.00	23.90	4041	20-Feb-20
Sardine Meal Feast	1.88	42.20	0.60	15.50	25.80	3504	20-Feb-20

NEWMAN'S OWN

	Phos	Prot	Sod	Fat	Carb	Cals	Obtained
Adult Cat	1.00	35.00	0.30	18.00	32.00	na	14-Nov-19

NOW FRESH

	Phos	Prot	Sod	Fat	Carb	Cals	Obtained
Grain-Free Senior/Weight Management	0.50	34.00	0.31	15.00	39.00	3571	31-Oct-19
Grain-Free Fish	0.60	34.00	0.33	22.00	35.00	3988	31-Oct-19
Grain-Free Adult	0.68	35.73	0.35	21.59	34.00	3862	31-Oct-19
Grain-Free Kitten	0.90	38.00	0.31	24.00	30.00	3947	31-Oct-19

NULO

	Phos	Prot	Sod	Fat	Carb	Cals	Obtained
MedalSeries Adult Hairball Management Chicken & Cod	0.86	43.78	0.42	17.57	23.26	3534	26-Nov-19

	Phos	Prot	Sod	Fat	Carb	Cals	Obtained
Freestyle Freeze-Dried Raw Cat & Kitten Turkey & Duck	0.96	46.90	0.36	43.62	1.02	5214	26-Nov-19
MedalSeries Grain-Free Limited Ingredient Diet Cat & Kitten Chicken	1.02	41.57	0.65	19.73	27.85	3799	26-Nov-19
MedalSeries Grain-Free Limited Ingredient Diet Cat & Kitten Turkey	1.06	41.57	0.28	19.73	25.60	3726	26-Nov-19
Freestyle Grain-Free Indoor Adult Duck & Lentils	1.16	43.78	0.45	19.73	23.21	3724	26-Nov-19
MedalSeries Grain-Free Adult Salmon & Lentils	1.19	43.51	0.36	21.89	22.65	3881	26-Nov-19
MedalSeries Grain-Free Indoor Adult Duck & Cod	1.19	43.78	0.39	16.49	26.34	3493	26-Nov-19
MedalSeries Grain-Free Cat & Kitten Turkey & Cod	1.21	44.86	0.37	21.89	21.54	3953	26-Nov-19
MedalSeries Grain-Free Indoor Adult Turkey & Chicken	1.22	41.71	0.35	18.41	27.13	3632	26-Nov-19
MedalSeries Grain-Free Indoor Adult Trout & Duck	1.22	41.89	0.35	15.75	28.50	3428	26-Nov-19
MedalSeries Grain-FreeSenior Cat Turkey, Alaska Pollock & Red Lentils	1.22	42.31	0.35	15.66	28.61	3454	26-Nov-19
MedalSeries Grain-Free Cat & Kitten Cod & Duck	1.22	43.10	0.36	17.84	27.22	3685	26-Nov-19
MedalSeries Grain-Free Adult Chicken & Peas	1.23	43.51	0.37	21.89	22.71	3868	26-Nov-19
Freestyle Grain-Free Cat and Kitten Chicken & Cod	1.25	44.23	0.33	22.25	21.44	3868	26-Nov-19
Freestyle Grain-Free Adult Trim Salmon & Lentils	1.25	45.86	0.37	13.76	23.89	3538	26-Nov-19
MedalSeries Grain-Free Adult Weight Management Salmon & Sweet Potato	1.29	43.51	0.41	14.05	28.79	3446	26-Nov-19
MedalSeries Grain-Free Limited Ingredient Diet Cat & Kitten Cod	1.30	39.19	0.37	17.57	31.10	3657	26-Nov-19
Freestyle Freeze-Dried Raw Cat & Kitten Chicken & Salmon	1.31	60.62	0.45	30.10	0.78	4437	26-Nov-19

165

	Phos	Prot	Sod	Fat	Carb	Cals	Obtained
Freestyle Adult Hairball Management Turkey & Cod	1.33	44.98	0.40	17.57	21.75	3534	26-Nov-19
Freestyle Grain-Free Cat and Kitten Turkey & Duck	1.45	43.78	0.45	19.73	23.36	3696	26-Nov-19
Freestyle Grain-Free Senior Cat Grain-Free Alaska Pollock, Duck & Sweet Potato	1.73	42.75	0.35	15.41	27.48	3454	26-Nov-19

NUTRISCA*

	Phos	Prot	Sod	Fat	Carb	Cals	Obtained
Grain-Free Chicken Recipe	1.02	42.80	0.46	16.60	24.60	3645	21-Jan-20
Grain-Free Salmon Recipe	1.52	40.30	0.93	15.70	30.20	3560	21-Jan-20

NUTRISOURCE

	Phos	Prot	Sod	Fat	Carb	Cals	Obtained
Senior/Weight Management	0.90	28.92	0.63	9.06	na	3250	28-Jan-20
Cat & Kitten Chicken Meal, Salmon & Liver	0.90	33.70	0.60	19.70	na	4170	28-Jan-20
Cat & Kitten Chicken & Rice	1.06	32.40	0.59	19.25	na	4098	28-Jan-20
Grain-Free Country Select Entrée	1.10	36.00	0.30	16.00	na	4036	28-Jan-20
Grain-Free Ocean Select Entrée	1.40	36.70	1.50	16.00	na	4004	28-Jan-20

O

ONLY NATURAL PET

	Phos	Prot	Sod	Fat	Carb	Cals	Obtained
Feline Powerfood Kitten Power Dinner	1.53	50.89	0.52	23.44	na	3750	29-Jan-20
Feline Powerfood High Protein Grain-Free Rabbit	1.76	42.22	0.54	22.22	na	3650	29-Jan-20
Feline Powerfood High Protein Grain-Free Poultry	1.92	52.22	0.43	20.00	18.89	3630	29-Jan-20
Feline Powerfood High Protein Grain-Free Fish & Fowl	2.00	50.00	0.44	21.11	17.78	3665	29-Jan-20

OPEN FARM

	Phos	Prot	Sod	Fat	Carb	Cals	Obtained
Homestead Turkey & Chicken	1.22	44.57	0.37	21.74	21.74	3840	17-Jan-20
Catch-of-the-Season Whitefish	1.28	44.57	0.37	21.74	21.74	3840	17-Jan-20
Wild Caught Salmon	1.30	44.57	0.37	21.74	21.74	3840	17-Jan-20
Pasture Raised Lamb	1.33	44.57	0.37	21.74	21.74	3840	17-Jan-20

ORIJEN

	Phos	Prot	Sod	Fat	Carb	Cals	Obtained
Cat & Kitten	1.10	44.00	0.44	22.00	21.00	4060	23-Sep-19
Six Fish	1.40	44.00	0.78	22.00	20.00	4060	23-Sep-19
Regional Red	1.50	44.00	0.56	22.00	19.00	4060	23-Sep-19
Tundra	1.56	44.00	0.44	22.00	20.00	4120	23-Sep-19
Fit & Trim	1.70	48.90	0.42	16.70	17.80	3710	23-Sep-19

ORGANIX

	Phos	Prot	Sod	Fat	Carb	Cals	Obtained
Organic Chicken & Sweet Potato	0.80	36.90	0.23	15.40	39.90	3739	29-Oct-19
Grain-Free Organic Chicken & Brown Rice	0.83	32.60	0.24	15.60	41.10	3726	29-Oct-19
Grain-Free Organic Healthy Kitten	1.14	37.50	0.31	16.30	37.57	3590	17-Nov-16

P

PERFORMATRIN

	Phos	Prot	Sod	Fat	Carb	Cals	Obtained
Ultra Grain-Free Senior	0.69	33.00	0.28	17.00	30.80	4021	21-Jan-20
Ultra Limited Potato & Turkey	0.84	36.30	0.37	19.00	30.10	3835	28-Nov-19
Ultra Limited Green Pea & Duck	0.88	33.20	0.44	13.20	37.30	3630	28-Nov-19
Ultra Limited Sweet Potato & Chicken	0.89	33.30	0.34	13.40	37.80	3630	28-Nov-19
Adult Grain-Free Chicken & Potato	0.91	35.70	0.37	20.10	28.80	4095	16-Jan-20
Ultra Limited Potato & Salmon	0.95	36.30	0.27	19.00	30.50	3835	28-Nov-19
Ultra Grain-Free Ocean	0.95	42.00	0.53	20.00	20.60	4186	21-Jan-20

	Phos	Prot	Sod	Fat	Carb	Cals	Obtained
Senior	0.96	35.20	0.35	18.40	35.20	3920	28-Nov-19
Hairball	1.03	36.30	0.52	21.00	21.10	3830	28-Nov-19
Ultra Healthy Weight with Salmon	1.05	37.20	0.49	13.20	30.70	3380	28-Nov-19
Ultra Chicken & Brown Rice	1.07	36.10	0.45	22.00	29.30	3865	28-Nov-19
Adult	1.09	35.90	0.53	20.10	30.20	4110	28-Nov-19
Healthy Weight	1.09	36.20	0.46	14.30	24.40	3360	28-Nov-19
Indoor	1.09	36.80	0.51	16.70	29.70	3740	28-Nov-19
Kitten	1.13	38.60	0.57	23.30	25.80	4230	28-Nov-19
Ultra Lamb & Brown Rice Adult	1.14	35.90	0.49	21.10	29.00	3865	28-Nov-19
Ultra Original Grain-Free Kitten	1.39	44.60	0.37	20.20	20.20	3915	16-Jan-20
Ultra Grain-Free	1.39	44.60	0.37	20.20	20.20	3915	28-Nov-19

PETGUARD

	Phos	Prot	Sod	Fat	Carb	Cals	Obtained
LifeSpan Cat & Kitten	0.88	35.55	0.40	15.55	47.70	3485	18-Dec-19

PETKIND*

	Phos	Prot	Sod	Fat	Carb	Cals	Obtained
Green Tripe & High Seas	1.38	37.78	1.01	17.78	25.50	3705	17-Jan-20

PRO PAC

	Phos	Prot	Sod	Fat	Carb	Cals	Obtained
Ultimates Deep Sea Select	1.10	34.80	0.40	16.30	39.10	3705	11-Nov-19
Ultimates Savanna Pride	1.10	37.00	0.30	16.30	39.10	3730	11-Nov-19

PUREVITA

	Phos	Prot	Sod	Fat	Carb	Cals	Obtained
Grain-Free Salmon & Green Pea Entrée	1.10	31.40	0.90	18.30	na	4068	28-Jan-20
Grain-Free Chicken & Peas Entrée	1.10	32.70	0.70	18.80	na	3992	28-Jan-20
Grain-Free Duck & Red Lentils Entrée	1.30	35.00	0.40	14.50	na	3880	28-Jan-20

R

RACHAEL RAY NUTRISH*

	Phos	Prot	Sod	Fat	Carb	Cals	Obtained
Real Chicken & Brown Rice	1.00	37.36	0.50	15.38	na	3635	06-Jan-20
Indoor Chicken with Lentils & Salmon	1.01	37.36	0.48	13.19	na	3499	06-Jan-20
PEAK Rustic Woodlands Indoor with Chicken, Turkey, & Duck	1.42	43.96	0.58	15.38	na	3551	06-Jan-20
PEAK Woodland Catch with Chicken, Trout & Salmon	1.54	43.96	0.88	19.78	na	3756	06-Jan-20

RANCHER'S CHOICE

	Phos	Prot	Sod	Fat	Carb	Cals	Obtained
31.5/11 Cat & Kitten	1.31	35.00	0.29	12.23	36.93	3325	17-Jan-20

RAWZ

	Phos	Prot	Sod	Fat	Carb	Cals	Obtained
Meal Free Salmon, Dehydrated Chicken & Whitefish	1.08	45.30	0.41	16.46	28.56	3710	03-Dec-19
Meal Free Dehydrated Chicken, Turkey & Chicken	1.33	48.12	0.36	14.48	25.69	3710	03-Dec-19

RAYNE CLINICAL NUTRITION

	Phos	Prot	Sod	Fat	Carb	Cals	Obtained
Growth/Sensitive-GI	1.01	36.93	0.54	14.60	36.30	3500	27-Nov-19
Rabbit Maintenance	1.04	38.72	0.64	14.62	35.41	3530	27-Nov-19

RED FLANNEL

	Phos	Prot	Sod	Fat	Carb	Cals	Obtained
Cat Formula	1.10	37.00	0.40	18.00	44.00	3776	12-Nov-19

REGAL*

	Phos	Prot	Sod	Fat	Carb	Cals	Obtained
Kitten Bites	0.81	37.28	0.30	23.44	na	3993	05-Jan-17

169

	Phos	Prot	Sod	Fat	Carb	Cals	Obtained
Lean Cat Bites	0.96	31.49	0.30	9.10	na	3276	05-Jan-17
Cat Bites	0.99	33.86	0.34	19.96	na	3813	05-Jan-17

S

SOLID GOLD*

	Phos	Prot	Sod	Fat	Carb	Cals	Obtained
Winged Tiger with Quail & Pumpkin	0.83	33.33	0.30	11.11	41.11	3560	08-Nov-19
Fit as a Fiddle with Alaskan Pollock	0.90	33.33	na	11.11	na	3110	08-Nov-19
Let's Stay In with Salmon, Lentil & Apple	1.00	36.00	0.38	16.00	25.00	na	23-Jan-20
Katz-N-Flocken with Lamb & Brown Rice & Pearled Barley	1.00	37.78	0.32	13.33	37.78	3525	08-Nov-19
Touch of Heaven with Chicken & Sweet Potato	1.00	40.00	0.30	20.00	27.78	3810	08-Nov-19
Indigo Moon with Peas, Chicken & Egg	1.00	42.00	0.30	20.00	17.00	3860	22-Jan-20
Indigo Moon with Alaskan Pollock & Egg	1.00	42.00	0.30	20.00	17.00	na	23-Jan-20
Let's Stay In with Chicken, Lentil & Apple	1.02	36.00	0.38	16.00	25.00	na	22-Jan-20

STAR PRO

	Phos	Prot	Sod	Fat	Carb	Cals	Obtained
Premium Feline Formula	0.91	33.41	0.33	17.03	33.33	3705	01-Feb-20

STELLA AND CHEWY'S*

	Phos	Prot	Sod	Fat	Carb	Cals	Obtained
Raw Blend Cage-Free Recipe	1.04	44.30	0.25	17.60	35.10	3818	21-Jan-20
Raw-Coated Cage-Free Chicken	1.06	43.20	0.25	18.20	31.00	3837	21-Jan-20
Raw-Coated Cage-Free Salmon	1.17	39.80	0.25	15.90	36.40	3687	21-Jan-20

SUMMIT

	Phos	Prot	Sod	Fat	Carb	Cals	Obtained
Summit	1.40	31.00	0.37	18.00	40.00	3499	31-Oct-19

SUPREME SOURCE*

	Phos	Prot	Sod	Fat	Carb	Cals	Obtained
Chicken Meal & Turkey Meal	1.00	38.89	0.33	16.67	33.33	3650	03-Dec-19
Grain-Free Whitefish Meal & Salmon Meal	1.00	38.89	0.33	16.67	33.33	3660	03-Dec-19

T

TASTE OF THE WILD

	Phos	Prot	Sod	Fat	Carb	Cals	Obtained
Prey Limited Ingredient Turkey	1.09	36.80	0.44	14.20	37.50	3689	18-Oct-19
Canyon River with Trout & Smoked Salmon	1.20	36.00	0.38	17.50	36.40	3741	23-Sep-19
Rocky Mountain with Roasted Venison & Smoked Salmon	1.31	47.00	0.44	19.70	21.50	3745	23-Sep-19
Prey Limited Ingredient Angus Beef	1.42	33.60	0.42	14.20	41.30	3650	18-Oct-19
Lowland Creek with Roasted Quail and Roasted Duck	1.86	40.30	0.55	17.50	29.10	3558	18-Oct-19

TENDER AND TRUE*

	Phos	Prot	Sod	Fat	Carb	Cals	Obtained
Antibiotic-free Chicken & Brown Rice	1.02	33.33	0.27	17.06	37.00	3500	11-Nov-19
Antibiotic-free Turkey & Brown Rice	1.04	33.33	0.34	17.06	37.00	3750	11-Nov-19
Salmon & Sweet Potato	1.11	28.33	na	11.67	na	4700	11-Nov-19
Ocean Whitefish & Potato	1.22	33.33	0.38	17.06	35.00	3750	11-Nov-19
Organic Chicken & Liver	1.33	33.33	0.23	18.89	30.00	3500	11-Nov-19
Organic Turkey & Liver	1.33	33.33	0.29	18.00	30.00	3650	11-Nov-19

TRADER JOE'S*

	Phos	Prot	Sod	Fat	Carb	Cals	Obtained
Premium Chicken	0.83	33.33	0.27	20.00	na	3832	28-Nov-16

V

VERUS

	Phos	Prot	Sod	Fat	Carb	Cals	Obtained
Feline Life Advantage	1.03	34.10	0.26	20.66	29.21	4785	27-Jan-20

VICTOR

	Phos	Prot	Sod	Fat	Carb	Cals	Obtained
Mers Classic	1.78	35.34	0.35	18.29	38.39	3596	23-Nov-19

W

WELLNESS

	Phos	Prot	Sod	Fat	Carb	Cals	Obtained
Complete Health Indoor Chicken & Chicken Meal	0.96	35.11	0.33	13.70	41.08	3532	01-Feb-20
Complete Health Chicken, Chicken Meal & Rice	1.07	42.07	0.30	21.14	26.96	3952	01-Feb-20
Complete Health Grain-Free Adult Chicken & Chicken Meal	1.10	47.12	0.29	19.67	21.83	3907	01-Feb-20
Complete Health Grain-Free Kitten Chicken & Chicken Meal	1.10	47.12	0.29	19.67	21.83	3907	01-Feb-20
Complete Health Healthy Weight Chicken, Chicken Meal & Turkey Meal	1.12	33.97	0.24	13.48	43.58	3520	01-Feb-20
Complete Health Senior Chicken & Chicken Meal	1.14	43.10	0.32	16.14	29.40	3738	01-Feb-20
Natural Hairball Control Chicken Meal & Rice	1.27	41.63	0.28	18.29	27.72	3614	01-Feb-20
Complete Health Grain-Free Indoor Chicken & Chicken Meal	1.27	41.91	0.30	13.91	29.91	3451	01-Feb-20

	Phos	Prot	Sod	Fat	Carb	Cals	Obtained
Complete Health Grain-Free Indoor Healthy Weight Chicken & Turkey	1.27	41.91	0.30	13.91	29.91	3451	01-Feb-20
Complete Health Grain-Free Senior Chicken & Chicken Meal	1.40	46.66	0.43	14.75	26.12	3392	01-Feb-20
RawRev indoor with 100% Raw Freeze-Dried Turkey Liver	1.41	42.55	0.29	15.49	31.47	3627	01-Feb-20
CORE Indoor Cat Chicken & Turkey	1.41	43.26	0.29	14.95	29.35	3561	01-Feb-20
Complete Health Grain-Free Salmon & Salmon Meal	1.42	42.17	0.61	17.42	26.18	3672	01-Feb-20
CORE Grain-Free Indoor Salmon & Herring	1.43	43.04	0.41	11.32	30.39	3277	01-Feb-20
Complete Health Grain-Free Indoor Salmon & Herring	1.52	38.21	0.53	12.55	31.77	3432	01-Feb-20
CORE Grain-Free Adult Turkey, Turkey Meal & Duck	1.66	44.29	0.28	20.74	21.14	3902	01-Feb-20
CORE Grain-Free Original Turkey & Chicken	1.68	51.36	0.51	21.30	14.17	3977	01-Feb-20
CORE Grain-Free Kitten Turkey & Chicken	1.68	51.36	0.51	21.30	14.17	3977	01-Feb-20
RawRev Original with 100% Raw Freeze-Dried Turkey Liver	1.68	52.66	0.51	21.36	12.76	3871	01-Feb-20
Complete Health Salmon & Salmon Meal	1.72	42.07	0.61	19.84	26.03	3873	01-Feb-20

WHOLE EARTH FARMS

	Phos	Prot	Sod	Fat	Carb	Cals	Obtained
Grain-Free Real Salmon	0.97	40.50	1.06	30.84	15.60	3458	25-Oct-19
Grain-Free Real Turkey & Duck	1.45	39.87	0.70	16.80	30.27	3515	25-Oct-19
Grain-Free Real Chicken	1.46	41.02	0.83	16.16	29.65	3459	25-Oct-19
Grain-Free Healthy Kitten	1.95	42.50	1.30	17.20	28.03	3500	25-Oct-19

WYSONG

	Phos	Prot	Sod	Fat	Carb	Cals	Obtained
Vegan (I do not recommend vegan food for cats)	0.80	29.50	0.20	11.40	40.80	3312	16-Oct-19

	Phos	Prot	Sod	Fat	Carb	Cals	Obtained
Uretic	0.90	46.20	0.80	18.00	20.50	3528	16-Oct-19
Anergen	1.30	30.30	0.20	13.50	37.20	3301	16-Oct-19
Geriatrx	1.30	36.90	0.40	16.30	27.30	3528	16-Oct-19
Vitality	1.40	38.70	0.40	17.20	23.80	3552	16-Oct-19
Nurture	1.40	40.40	0.40	15.90	23.30	3584	16-Oct-19
Fundamentals	1.40	42.10	0.40	15.80	24.60	3480	16-Oct-19
Nurture with Quail	1.40	43.70	0.40	17.10	22.30	3608	16-Oct-19

Y

YOUNG AGAIN

	Phos	Prot	Sod	Fat	Carb	Cals	Obtained
ZERO Mature TruCarnivore 54/24	0.50	57.90	0.31	28.80	0.00	4510	01-Feb-20
LID (Limited Ingredient) ZERO Mature TruCarnivore 54/25	0.52	59.50	0.38	27.40	0.00	4446	01-Feb-20
Mature Health CalPhosMag 54/22	0.65	57.60	0.31	28.60	6.00	4657	01-Feb-20
ZERO Cat & Kitten Trucarnivore 54/26	0.81	57.60	0.25	28.60	0.00	4482	01-Feb-20
Original Cat & Kitten 50/22	0.91	56.50	0.21	26.80	6.00	4465	01-Feb-20
Li'l Bites Kitten 50/22	0.91	56.50	0.21	26.80	6.00	4465	01-Feb-20

Z

ZIWIPEAK

	Phos	Prot	Sod	Fat	Carb	Cals	Obtained
New Zealand Air-Dried Venison	1.43	54.00	0.77	32.00	7.00	4700	01-Feb-20
New Zealand Free Range Chicken	1.50	48.00	0.68	39.00	1.00	5500	01-Feb-20
New Zealand Air-Dried Lamb	1.56	43.00	0.77	41.00	3.00	5600	01-Feb-20
New Zealand Air-Dried Mackerel & Lamb	1.67	51.00	0.77	33.00	4.00	4800	01-Feb-20
New Zealand Air-Dried Beef	1.88	47.80	0.86	38.00	2.20	5500	01-Feb-20

RAW FOOD DATA IN ORDER OF BRAND AND PHOSPHORUS CONTENT

I do not recommend raw foods for CKD cats (my reasons for this can be found at http://www.felinecrf.org/which_foods.htm#raw_food), but I know some people do feed raw so I am including these data.

Please see pages 3 and 15 for information on how to use these tables. All data are on a dry matter analysis basis, except calories, which are as fed per ounce for the fresh foods and per kg (2.2lbs) on an ME as fed basis for the dehydrated foods.

Foods marked * show minimum values for protein and fat and in some cases phosphorus — the actual values could be much higher. Page 13 explains more about this.

"na" means the information was not available.

	Phos	Prot	Sod	Fat	Carb	Cals	Obtained
ANSWERS*							
Detailed Beef	0.95	59.09	0.91	36.36	na	25.00	28-Jan-20
Detailed Pork	0.95	59.09	0.91	36.36	na	25.00	28-Jan-20
Detailed Chicken	1.36	59.09	0.91	36.36	na	25.00	28-Jan-20
Detailed Turkey	1.36	59.09	0.91	36.36	na	25.00	28-Jan-20
AUNT JENI'S*							
Beef	0.87	65.38	0.31	23.08	11.54	33.75	27-Nov-19
Fish	1.66	66.66	0.62	14.29	19.05	24.00	27-Nov-19
Chicken	1.89	48.28	0.31	34.48	17.24	40.63	27-Nov-19
Turkey	2.42	60.00	0.32	20.00	20.00	31.88	27-Nov-19
BALANCED BLENDS							
Species Balanced Raw Turkey	1.50	62.37	0.53	30.37	na	38.70	01-Dec-19
Species Balanced Raw Chicken	1.57	62.16	0.54	29.89	na	37.90	01-Dec-19
Species Balanced Raw Beef Heart & Offal	1.64	59.90	0.53	30.59	na	33.40	01-Dec-19
COUNTRYPET NATURALS*							
Lamb & Chicken	1.30	41.20	0.40	29.40	7.40	48.00	20-Jan-20
Turducken	1.40	42.90	0.40	31.40	2.90	48.00	21-Jan-20

	Phos	Prot	Sod	Fat	Carb	Cals	Obtained
EZCOMPLETE							
with Turkey Breast	0.80	85.00	0.32	11.00	0.00	na	02-Dec-19
FRESH IS BEST							
Feline Chicken Recipe Dehydrated	0.94	53.50	0.32	25.83	10.38	4432	30-Oct-19
Feline Turkey Recipe Dehydrated	1.04	61.67	0.44	23.39	4.42	4301	30-Oct-19
Feline Beef Recipe Dehydrated	1.14	59.96	0.37	23.51	5.38	4285	30-Oct-19
INSTINCT							
Frozen Bites Cage-Free Chicken	1.67	40.00	0.80	27.00	7.00	49.00	08-Nov-19
Signature Bites Cage-Free Chicken	1.82	42.00	0.61	27.00	7.88	49.00	08-Nov-19
Signature Medallions Cage-Free Chicken	1.82	42.00	0.61	27.00	7.88	49.00	08-Nov-19
Signature Bites Rabbit	2.06	44.00	0.59	26.00	7.94	51.00	08-Nov-19
Signature Medallions Real Rabbit	2.06	44.00	0.59	26.00	7.94	51.00	08-Nov-19
LOTUS							
Free-Range Chicken	0.52	57.17	0.08	19.95	9.74	35.49	28-Jan-20
Pasture Raised Venison	1.00	62.77	0.46	17.25	10.20	27.47	28-Jan-20
Vegetarian-Fed Pork	1.20	57.97	0.50	15.83	11.99	29.46	28-Jan-20
Free Range Turkey	1.33	56.97	0.59	18.74	14.21	29.63	28-Jan-20
Pasture Raised Lamb	1.56	50.61	0.37	25.59	13.64	35.44	28-Jan-20
Grass-Fed Beef	1.85	51.10	0.42	25.22	12.26	35.49	28-Jan-20
PETS4LIFE							
Rabbit	0.71	47.00	0.08	14.00	5.00	41.90	26-Nov-19
Wild Salmon	0.75	62.00	0.29	27.00	5.00	47.40	26-Nov-19
Chicken	0.88	58.00	0.66	27.00	4.00	47.30	26-Nov-19
Turkey	1.24	67.00	0.25	15.00	4.00	40.00	26-Nov-19
Duck	1.59	64.00	0.52	16.00	2.00	47.00	26-Nov-19

	Phos	Prot	Sod	Fat	Carb	Cals	Obtained
PRIMAL*							
Frozen Turkey	1.07	55.56	0.52	33.33	1.48	45.00	29-Jan-20
Frozen Beef & Salmon	1.13	48.39	0.29	32.26	7.74	53.00	29-Jan-20
Frozen Pork	1.26	65.22	0.26	26.09	4.35	38.00	29-Jan-20
Frozen Venison	1.37	53.33	0.27	23.33	7.67	45.00	29-Jan-20
Frozen Duck	1.81	40.54	0.30	40.54	7.57	71.00	29-Jan-20
Frozen Chicken & Salmon	1.81	48.15	0.33	37.04	1.85	47.00	29-Jan-20
Frozen Quail	1.87	53.33	0.17	26.67	1.67	44.00	29-Jan-20
Frozen Rabbit	2.29	61.29	0.26	16.13	6.45	39.00	29-Jan-20
QUEST*							
Prey Model Beef Diet	0.42	50.00	0.40	34.62	0.69	36	29-Jan-20
Prey Model Pork Diet	1.10	50.00	0.48	39.29	0.70	36	29-Jan-20
Prey Model Emu Diet	1.30	49.12	0.51	38.60	1.16	42	29-Jan-20
THE HONEST KITCHEN							
Prowl Grain-Free Chicken	1.01	41.10	0.22	29.50	na	5070	26-Nov-19
Grace Grain-Free Turkey	1.24	40.30	0.30	36.10	na	5470	26-Nov-19
SOJOS							
Complete Turkey Recipe Freeze-Dried	0.55	37.10	0.25	13.10	36.90	3531	17-Jan-20
STEVE'S REAL FOOD*							
Chicken Freeze-Dried	1.30	52.01	0.30	34.79	3.37	4900	29-Jan-20
Turducken Freeze-Dried	1.43	57.85	0.50	33.48	3.80	4930	29-Jan-20
Pork Freeze-Dried	2.20	53.34	0.37	38.83	2.45	5140	29-Jan-20
WYSONG							
Archetype Pollock	0.70	71.10	0.20	2.80	9.40	na	16-Oct-19
Archetype Rabbit	0.90	50.10	0.30	22.90	8.20	na	16-Oct-19
Archetype Quail	1.00	51.30	0.30	26.80	7.50	na	16-Oct-19
Archetype Chicken	1.20	45.50	0.40	37.60	3.20	na	16-Oct-19
Uncanny	1.30	31.90	1.10	14.90	37.20	na	16-Oct-19

INDEX

Made in the USA
Middletown, DE
25 September 2023

39318366R00104